2017.

University of Brighton

Queenwood Library
Darley Road
Eastbourne BN20 7UN
Telephone 01273 643822

Online renewal http://library.brighton.ac.uk

306.483/SLE

SOCIAL ISSUES IN SPORT

Also by Mike Sleap

MINI SPORT

Social Issues in Sport

Mike Sleap
Lecturer in Education
University of Hull

First published in Great Britain 1998 by
MACMILLAN PRESS LTD
Houndmills, Basingstoke, Hampshire RG21 6XS and London
Companies and representatives throughout the world

A catalogue record for this book is available from the British Library.

ISBN 0–333–69150–4

 First published in the United States of America 1998 by
ST. MARTIN'S PRESS, INC.,
Scholarly and Reference Division,
175 Fifth Avenue, New York, N.Y. 10010

ISBN 0–312–17602–3

Library of Congress Cataloging-in-Publication Data
Sleap, Mike.
Social issues in sport / Mike Sleap.
p. cm.
Includes bibliographical references and indexes.
ISBN 0–312–17602–3
1. Sports—Sociological aspects.   I. Title.
GV706.5.S59 1997
306.4'83—dc21   97–8879
                                                                CIP

© Mike Sleap 1998

All rights reserved. No reproduction, copy or transmission of this publication may be made without written permission.

No paragraph of this publication may be reproduced, copied or transmitted save with written permission or in accordance with the provisions of the Copyright, Designs and Patents Act 1988, or under the terms of any licence permitting limited copying issued by the Copyright Licensing Agency, 90 Tottenham Court Road, London W1P 9HE.

Any person who does any unauthorised act in relation to this publication may be liable to criminal prosecution and civil claims for damages.

The author has asserted his right to be identified as the author of this work in accordance with the Copyright, Designs and Patents Act 1988.

This book is printed on paper suitable for recycling and made from fully managed and sustained forest sources.

10 9 8 7 6 5 4 3 2 1
07 06 05 04 03 02 01 00 99 98

Printed and bound in Great Britain by
Antony Rowe Ltd, Chippenham, Wiltshire

Contents

List of Figures vi

List of Tables vii

Acknowledgements ix

Introduction xiii

1. Clarifying the Nature of Sport 1
2. Participation Patterns in Sport 16
3. Explanations of Sporting Behaviour 28
4. Sport and Health 43
5. Women and Sport 59
6. Social Class Issues in Sport 90
7. Racial Issues in Sport 107
8. Drug Abuse in Sport 129
9. Football Hooliganism 160
10. Commercialism and Sport 183

Author Index 207

Subject Index 210

List of Figures

1.1	The interrelationship between play, sport and work	10
2.1	Participation in sports and physical activities by age, 1993	23
3.1	The theory of planned behaviour	32
3.2	Interactional model of sport behaviour	33
3.3	A conceptual model of the recreational activity adoption process	34
3.4	Eccles' expectancy value model of activity choice	36
4.1	Comparison of former Harvard University athletes and their classmates in incidence of first heart attack	49
4.2	Sports participation in relation to health rating and absence from work	50
4.3	Sports participation and cholesterol levels	52
4.4	Sports participation and health score	54
5.1	Boys' and girls' participation in sport out of school	60
5.2	Men's and women's participation in activities requiring physical effort	65
5.3	Comparison of men's and women's sporting improvement	69
5.4	Appropriate and inappropriate sports	74
6.1	Sports participation by socio-economic group and sex	96
8.1	Sanctions for testing positive for anabolic steroids (first offence)	151
9.1	Psychological model of crowd behaviour	171
9.2	Value-oriented approach to football hooliganism	175

List of Tables

1.1	The production and consumption of sport	11
2.1	Participation of young people in specific sports outside of lessons	19
2.2	Rank order of most popular sports played in the four weeks prior to interview	21
2.3	Sports participation rates, 1977–93	22
2.4	Activity levels of men and women	24
2.5	Most popular sports and recreations	25
4.1	Health benefits of exercise	44
4.2	Energy expenditure in different sports	47
4.3	Level of participation and belief about being in good health	51
5.1	Rank order of sports played by girls out of PE lessons at least ten times in previous year	61
5.2	Most popular sports of men and women	62
5.3	Comparison of women's four-week and twelve-month involvement in selected sports	62
5.4	Activity levels for men and women	63
5.5	Sports and recreations played by men and women	64
5.6	Morphological differences between men and women	66
5.7	Physiological differences between men and women	67
5.8	Myths and facts about women's participation in sport	68
5.9	Percentages of male and female Olympic athletes and coaches, 1976–88	79
5.10	Television coverage of the 1991 World Athletic Championships and the 1992 Summer Olympic Games	81
6.1	Participation in specific activities according to socio-economic group	98
6.2	The constraints affecting leisure participation	101
7.1	Popular sporting misconceptions about ethnic minority groups	111
8.1	Effects of use and potential harm of drugs in sport	137
8.2	Different sports: different drugs	141
8.3	Doping control in sport: testing procedures	146
9.1	Social class membership of football hooligans	167
9.2	Situational conditions and triggers most likely to provoke football hooliganism	172

List of Tables

10.1	Factors influencing attendance at sporting events	188
10.2	Work practices in sport	195
10.3	Publicity achieved through sponsorship of motor sport	197
10.4	Tobacco-sponsored sport on BBC TV	201

Acknowledgements

I would like to express my thanks to the following friends and colleagues who have offered comments and suggestions during the preparation of this book: Mike Atsalakis, Sue Chedzoy, Michelle Cornes, Pauline Dorrell, Richard English, Alastair Loadman, Mick Mawer, Robert Protherough, Paul Robinson, Michele Verroken Peter Warburton and Maurice Whitehead.

For particular permission to use tables and figures in the text, the author and publishers would like to record their thanks to:

Fig. 2.1 Reprinted from English Sports Council, *Young People and Sport* (1995), p. 84.
Table 2.3 Reprinted from English Sports Council and Health Education Authority, *Allied Dunbar National Fitness Survey* (1992), p. 48.
Table 2.4 Reprinted from English Sports Council and Health Education Authority, *Allied Dunbar National Fitness Survey* (1992), p. 62.
Table 4.2 Adapted from English Sports Council and Health Education Authority, *Allied Dunbar National Fitness Survey* (1992), p. 13.
Fig. 5.1 Reprinted from English Sports Council, *Young People and Sport* (1995), p. 19.
Table 5.1 Adapted from English Sports Council, *Young People and Sport* (1995), p. 87/89.
Table 5.4 Adapted from English Sports Council and Health Education Authority, *Allied Dunbar National Fitness Survey* (1992), p. 48.
Table 5.5 Reprinted from English Sports Council and Health Education Authority, *Allied Dunbar National Fitness Survey* (1992), p. 62.
All with kind permission from the English Sports Council, 2 Tavistock Place, London WC1H 9RA.

Table 8.1 Adapted from United Kingdom Sports Council, *Doping in Sport* (1995).
Table 8.3 Adapted from United Kingdom Sports Council, *Testing Procedures – A Guide for Competitors and Officials* (1994).
Fig. 8.1 Reprinted from United Kingdom Sports Council, *Doping Control in the UK: A Survey of the Experiences and Views of Elite Competitors 1995* (1995), p. 4.
All with kind permission from the United Kingdom Sports Council, Walkden House, 3–10 Melton Street, London NW1 2EB.

Acknowledgements

Fig. 3.3   Reprinted from *Leisure Studies*, 1, Brandenburg J. et al., 'A Conceptual Model of How People Adopt Recreational Activities,' 263–76 (1982).

Fig. 4.2; Table 4.3   Reprinted from *Leisure Studies*, 8, Gratton, C. & Tice, A. 'Sports Participation and Health,' 77–92 (1989).

Table 5.10   Reprinted from *Women's Studies International Forum*, 17, Alexander, S. 'Gender Bias in British Television Coverage of Major Athletic Championships,' 647–54 (1994).

All with kind permission from Elsevier Science Ltd, The Boulevard, Langford Lane, Kidlington OX5 1GB, UK.

Table 4.1   Adapted from Health Education Authority, *Health Update 5: Physical Activity* (1995), p. 7.

Table 10.4   Adapted from Health Education Authority, *Tobacco and the BBC* (1992), pp. 8/9.

Both with kind permission from the Health Education Authority, Hamilton House, Mabledon Place, London, WC1H 9TX.

Fig. 3.1   Reprinted with permission from I. Ajzen, *Attitudes, Personality, and Behavior* (1988), Open University Press.

Fig. 3.2   Reprinted by permission from M.R. Weiss, S.D. Glenn, 1992, 'Psychological Development and Females' Sport Participation: An Interactional Perspective,' *Quest*, 44 (2): 149.

Fig. 4.1   Reprinted with permission from R.S. Paffenbarger, A.L. Wing & R.T. Hyde, 'Physical Activity as an Index of Heart Attack Risk in College Alumni,' *American Journal of Epidemiology*, 108 (1978), 161–75.

Fig. 5.3   Reprinted with permission from S. Chatterjee & M. Laudato, Gender and Performance in Athletics,' *Social Biology*, 42 (1995), 124–32.

Table 5.6   Reprinted by permission from C.L. Wells, 1991, *Women, Sport & Performance*, 2nd ed. (Champaign, IL: Human Kinetics Publishers), 17.

Table 5.7   Reprinted by permission from C.L. Wells, 1991, *Women, Sport & Performance*, 2nd ed. (Champaign, IL: Human Kinetics Publishers), 34.

Table 5.9   Reprinted with permission from J. Hargreaves, 1994, *Sporting Females* (London: Routledge), 201.

Table 7.1   Reprinted with permission from T. Bayliss, 'PE and Racism: Making Changes,' *Multicultural Teaching*, 7 (1989), 19–22.

Table 9.1   Reprinted with permission from E. Dunning, P. Murphy & J. Williams, 1988, *The Roots of Football Hooliganism* (London: Routledge), 190.

Fig. 9.1 Reprinted with permission from J.M. Brindley, 1982, 'Disruptive Crowd Behaviour – A Psychological Perspective,' *The Police Journal*, 55, 28–38 (Barry Rose Law Periodicals).

Table 10.1 Adapted by permission from B.D. McPherson, J.E. Curtis, & J.W. Loy, 1989, *The Social Significance of Sport* (Champaign, IL: Human Kinetics Publishers), 121.

Introduction

IS THIS BOOK FOR YOU?

- Are you interested in the problem of drug abuse in sport?
- Would you like to know more about why companies sponsor sport?
- Are some sports really more appropriate for men rather than women?

If you are at all interested in *sport* then this book will be of interest to you. If you are studying sport at school, college or university then it is a must. It provides essential information for anyone studying A-Level, B Tech, GNVQ or First Degree courses. If your course is called sport and society, sociology of sport, social aspects, social issues in sport, or something similar, then this book will have topics that can help you – and it is written in plain English with mainly British sources. You do not have to puzzle over American terms such as 'jocks' or struggle to understand the franchising irregularities of an American Football team!

THIS BOOK IS UNIQUE

Social Issues in Sport is a general textbook which aims to introduce students to a sociological study of sport. It covers a wide range of social topics that are usually included in examination syllabuses. It is the first book of its kind to draw mainly from British sources for its material. There are a number of North American sociology of sport books available, but they do not provide a true reflection of sport in Britain.

THE PURPOSE OF THE BOOK

Sport is one of the most significant aspects of modern life. It is a multibillion pound industry, generating massive television viewing audiences and attracting millions of participants worldwide. Some people may only have a passing interest in sport, while others, like professional athletes, spend all their waking hours engrossed in a specific activity. The proliferation of sport has led to all kinds of study of sport. While young children may learn about a sporting topic at primary school, a researcher at university may use the most advanced technology to measure the performance of an athlete.

This book is concerned with the way in which sport affects society and how society affects sport. It has three main aims:

- First, it aims to *describe the nature and extent* of sporting issues prevalent in society nowadays. For example, in the case of drugs and sport, the book describes the background and development of drug involvement in sport, examines drug testing procedures and discusses the many controversial issues surrounding the use of performance-enhancing drugs.
- Second, the book aims to *analyse research studies* relating to each sporting issue. This is the first book to assemble research material on social issues that is drawn mainly from Britain. However, data from other countries are presented where applicable: for example, if no pertinent British research is available. The findings of research studies are presented as clearly as possible, often in the form of tables and graphs, and a critical approach is taken to help you evaluate the conclusions drawn by authors about their research.
- Third, the book aims to *offer explanations in respect of the sporting issues examined*. One of the main roles of the social scientist is to find explanations for social behaviour, although this is no easy task because human behaviour is so complex. This book presents various theories and models which have been put forward to explain sporting issues. For example, many theories are outlined which help us to understand the reasons for football hooliganism or gender differences in sport.

WHAT WILL YOU LEARN?

As a result of studying this book you will:

- have a sharper awareness of various social issues relating to sport
- understand the scope and nature of social issues that exist in sport
- learn about research studies that have examined social issues in sport
- be introduced to the main theories relating to social issues in sport.

WHAT IS THE VALUE OF STUDYING SOCIAL ISSUES IN SPORT?

A greater knowledge of social issues can help to improve sport in a number of ways:

- We now have a clearer idea of the sporting behaviour of the British population. If you can understand *why* people do or do not participate in sport, it may help you to promote sport more effectively in the future.
- It is easy to ignore the fact that in our civilised, postindustrial society there is a lack of equity in many areas of sport. If more people understood the problems faced by women, the working class and ethnic minorities, there would be an improved chance of progress towards equity.
- As sport evolves, different problems emerge. In recent times the enjoyment of sport has been spoiled by crowd violence, financial disputes and drug abuse problems. A more informed sporting profession can adopt a knowledgeable and prudent stance to help minimise disruptions to sporting occasions.

BRIEF SKETCH OF ISSUES IN THIS BOOK

Chapter 1: Clarifying the Nature of Sport

This chapter looks at the various ways in which sport has been defined and aims to help you understand the nature of sport in contemporary society. The characteristics of sport are examined in order to provide a foundation for the ensuing chapters.

Chapter 2: Participation Patterns in Sport

Who participates in sport? Which sports have most participants? Which sports are increasing or decreasing in popularity? This chapter will attempt to answer these questions and others by undertaking a critical review of major participation surveys conducted in recent years.

Chapter 3: Explanations of Sporting Behaviour

What motivates one individual to play squash every week while another would never consider going near a squash court? This chapter offers an insight into the many theories that have been put forward to explain sporting behaviour.

Chapter 4: Sport and Health

Nowadays there is great interest in the relationship between exercise and health. Although there has been extensive research to examine the effect of physical activity on health, there has been little that has focused specifically on the role played by sport. This chapter looks initially at the relationship between physical activity and health, before research evidence is analysed with regard to the potential health benefits of involvement in sport.

Chapter 5: Women and Sport

Despite claims of equality of opportunity in sport, there is still a lack of equity in respect of male and female involvement in sport. Initially, this chapter considers the historical background to gender issues before addressing current female involvement in sport. A large part of the chapter explores sociological, psychological and physical factors which lead to gender differences in sport, before the chapter concludes with a review of the present situation.

Chapter 6: Social Class Issues in Sport

This chapter examines the notion of social inequality in sport. Survey findings are analysed to assess the extent of social inequality in terms of participation in recreational and élite sport. Consideration is also given to claims that sport can be an avenue for upward social mobility.

Chapter 7: Racial Issues in Sport

Sport is sometimes heralded as a way of promoting integration among different racial groups. Attention is focused on racial problems that exist in school sport, after which the issues of racial stereotyping, racial discrimination and racial integration are explored. Finally, prospects for the future are examined.

Chapter 8: Drug Abuse in Sport

Copious publicity has been given to the problem of drug abuse in sport. After an introductory explanation of the types of drugs used in sport, the problems, principles and procedures of doping control are described. The remainder of the chapter contains a discussion of the main issues surrounding usage of performance-enhancing drugs in sport.

Chapter 9: Football Hooliganism

Football hooliganism has caused widespread social unrest in Britain and has even led to the exclusion of British football clubs from European competition. The main section of this chapter focuses on theories that seek to explain crowd violence, with particular reference to football hooliganism. This is followed by an investigation of strategies adopted to prevent violence and an evaluation of their effectiveness.

Chapter 10: Commercialism and Sport

From a relatively modest starting point, sport has now become a multibillion pound industry. This relatively new area of study is concerned with the ways in which sport is affected by commercial factors. A major part of the chapter involves a discussion of the issue of sponsorship in sport, with specific consideration given to the part played by tobacco companies.

1 Clarifying the Nature of Sport

PERCEPTIONS OF SPORT

There are records of games being played in virtually all cultures and in all periods of history, but they were not necessarily viewed in the same way as the sports of today. The term 'sport' is a human construct, like 'art' or 'work', defined by the way in which it is used. Was the football game of Tsu Chu, reportedly played over 3000 years ago in China, perceived by its participants in the same way as football is seen in modern times? There are clearer records of the value that the Ancient Greeks attached to physical activities, revered in ritualised sporting spectacles such as the Olympic Games, but again it is uncertain how far these activities embodied functional skills rather than being seen as sports in the current sense. Indeed, Elias (1978) has suggested that sport, in its true meaning, has only developed since the industrial revolution of the nineteenth century, and must be distinguished from the chaotic and violent games of former times: for example, primitive football between competing villages, with no limits on the numbers involved, bear and bull baiting, cock fighting and badger hunting.

In Britain the earliest use of the word 'sport' in the fifteenth century referred widely to different forms of amusement, entertainment, dancing or practical joking. Shakespeare and other writers used the word in these senses and virtually never applied them to games. Military exercises like jousting, archery, fencing and quarterstaff fighting were too serious to be considered as sports. It was only in the seventeenth and eighteenth centuries that the word began to be applied to outdoor exercise, and then almost exclusively to the pastimes of killing wild animals, birds and fish. It is significant that *The Chronology of the Modern World* (Williams, 1994), which lists events for each year under a variety of headings, has no entry for sport until the St Leger horse race in 1776 and the Derby in 1779.

In the nineteenth century English public schools utilised sport as an essential element in character building, as part of the training of a gentleman – harking back to Ancient Greek civilisation. Team games, previously deplored as common, were sanctified and 'playing the game' became a term of approbation; the rowdiness of Regency bare-knuckle fighting became the noble art of self-defence. Out of this educational setting there arose the organisation and standardisation of sports on a national level, since it was necessary for school teams to have agreed rules when playing against one another. Thus, although sport has elements of games played throughout history, organised sport, as it is perceived today, has fairly recent origins.

Definitions of Sport

Despite its magnitude, and perhaps because of its magnitude, the true meaning of sport is difficult to pin down. It is an ambiguous term that has different meanings to different people. For example, sport can encompass activities such as international hockey matches, rounders on the beach, the Olympic Games, potholing, chess, aerobics, round-the-world yachting and thousands more.

It thus becomes necessary to appreciate the various ways in which sport has been classified and defined. It is important also to separate sport, where possible, from other terms such as recreation and exercise, so that the social issues in the following chapters can be understood more clearly. A number of writers have attempted to define sport and a selection is given here. Is it possible to identify any weaknesses in the following definitions? For example, do they establish the true meaning of sport in contemporary society or do they leave certain issues unresolved?

> Sport is an institutionalised system of competitive, delimited, codified and conventionally governed physical practices which have the avowed aim of selecting the best competitor. (Brohm, 1978, p. 69)

> Sports are institutionalised competitive activities that involve vigorous physical exertion or the use of relatively complex physical skills by individuals whose participation is motivated by a combination of intrinsic and extrinsic factors. (Coakley, 1994, p. 21)

> Sport is free, spontaneous physical activity engaged in during leisure time; its functions being recreation, amusement and development. (Council of Europe, 1971, pp. 5–6, 22)

> Sport is a physical activity that is fair, competitive, nondeviant, and that is guided by rules, organization, and/or tradition. (Curry and Jiobu, 1984, p. 8)

Sport is a human activity that involves specific administrative organisation and a historical background of rules which define the objective and limit the pattern of human behaviour; it involves competition and/or challenge and a definite outcome primarily determined by physical skill.

(Singer, 1976, p. 40)

Inevitably, there are problems with definitions of sport, a point acknowledged by Wertz (1985, p. 83):

There are many generalizations that attempt to characterize or define sport, but none of these seem to apply just to sport and nothing else.

Clarifying the Nature of Sport

The purpose of defining terms in this book is not to conduct a semantic exercise, but to identify the essence of a term, which may help to avoid error and confusion in the discussion of issues. When the word 'sport' is used in everyday conversation, everybody has his or her idea of what is meant by the term. However, a closer examination reveals a number of problems and inconsistencies:

- Beach volleyball was played in the 1996 Olympic Games at Atlanta and ballroom dancing has been proposed for inclusion in future Games. Are these activities to be considered as sports?
- An outdoor pursuit such as canoeing is generally accepted as a sport, but how might mountaineering and potholing be classified? The Collins dictionary (Hanks, 1988) describes potholing as a sport, while a mountaineer is only described as someone who climbs mountains.
- There is no surprise in seeing activities like football and rugby reported on the sports pages of newspapers, but why is it also possible to read about chess and bridge on the same pages?
- Does the fact that there are national aerobics competitions mean that the thousands of people attending aerobics classes every week are involved in a sport?
- Should the activities shown on the television programme *Transworld Sports* be considered as legitimate sports or are they closer to the circus world? Some skills such as tumbling and balancing are common to circuses and gymnastics.

CHARACTERISTICS OF SPORT

What is it about sport that makes it different from other human endeavours? Are there particular markers which enable us to label something as a sport? Osterhoudt (Wertz, 1985) has suggested that the defining properties of sport are play, competition and physicality, while Goldlust (1987, p. 1) considered that sport could be distinguished by:

- attributes of physical activity and physical skills
- elements of competition in achieving particular goals
- authoritative codification of a clearly defined, formalised body of rules to which participants feel morally bound.

At first glance, these interpretations would seem quite useful and yet they are not entirely satisfactory. The following characteristics feature significantly in attempts to delineate sport:

Play (Ludic Element)

Most people recognise that sport involves a fun or play element. In general, the play element seems to be greatest in recreative forms of sport and seems to be less evident in professional, élite competitions. However, there are many exceptions to this since many local league matches seem to be as serious as any professional contest and there can be few light-hearted, play moments in sport which surpass the backward, overhead flick kick used by Rene Higuita, the Colombian goalkeeper, in an international football match against England. It is also fascinating to ponder where games like fantasy football and fantasy cricket fit into all of this.

Physical Prowess

A major feature of sport is that it involves physical skill and ability. No matter whether it is recreational or élite sport, physical prowess is a fundamental aspect – an impromptu game of football in the park needs physical proficiency, albeit at a lower level than that required in a World Cup final. The situation is not straightforward, however. Some physical activities, such as modern dance and ballet, demand high levels of physical skill and yet they are acknowledged as performing arts rather than sports. Activities like chess and bridge require mental abilities, while physical prowess is not needed. Does this mean that they should not be classified as sports?

Physical Activity

It is clear that many sports require great physical effort and, at the highest levels, can involve incredible levels of strength, mobility and endurance. However, it is equally evident that this is not the case in all sports. While activities like snooker and darts require considerable skill, it is clear that speed of foot is not needed. There are also sporting activities in which the individual is transported by boat, horse or car. All of these examples require physical effort of some kind but, on the other hand, so do activities like gardening, hoovering and cleaning windows. It is thus very difficult to distinguish sports from other activities when considering the criterion of physical activity alone.

Physical Recreation

Physical recreation is another term that needs to be analysed in this discussion. It is not used so frequently as sport and possibly has quite a specific meaning for most people. Recreations, in general, tend to be recognised as activities undertaken in free time for relaxation and enjoyment. There are literally thousands of recreational activities and the difference between work and recreation can often be blurred. Watching a film may be an entertaining recreation for many people and yet it is an aspect of work for a film critic. The question might be asked: are all physical recreations sports? While it is clear that physical recreations like netball and hockey are sports, it is surely the case that walking the dog and swimming in the sea on holiday are physical recreations that could not be classified as sports.

Exercise

In its strictest sense, exercise is a planned and structured set of bodily movements, usually undertaken to improve or maintain physical fitness. Clearly, exercise also has a vital part to play in developing the physical fitness of sportsmen and sportswomen, while, in a non-sporting context, exercise contributes to the general health of the individual. In everyday conversation, exercise is often seen as part of functional activities like gardening, and people are also considered to be exercising when taking part in sports requiring physical effort. It should therefore be realised that sport and exercise are not the same thing. Exercising is not a sport in itself, although it can obviously help to prepare people to take part in sport more effectively. It should also be noted that activities such as aerobics and weight training should be seen as forms of exercise and not as sports.

Although terms like sport, exercise and physical recreation are used interchangeably in everyday conversation, they each have a particular meaning and in a discussion of social issues it is important to use terms carefully. For example, if an assessment is being made of participation trends in sport, an erroneous picture will be created if physical recreations, such as walking the dog, are included in the analysis. Equally, it is important to separate recreational bodybuilders from competitive athletes in a discussion of drug abuse in sport.

Competition

Competition is another major element of sport and it may be characterised in a number of ways. The most obvious form of competition is where individuals or teams play matches against one another or perhaps swim, walk, run or cycle against one another. However, sport may involve competition against the clock, achieving a particular distance, reaching a certain destination or surpassing some other standard or record. Looked at from another perspective, sport may involve competition with animate (for example, hunting) or inanimate objects of nature (for example, mountaineering). Competitive sport may thus involve trying to be first, attempts to defeat an opponent and efforts to achieve records by doing better than others in similar circumstances.

There are confusing elements to this, however. An impromptu game of football in the park involves teams competing against one another and thus would seem to qualify as sport rather than play. On the other hand, competitive swimming can clearly be considered as a sport and yet individuals who swim recreationally in a pool on a hot day will not be competing in any sense of the word.

Aesthetics

Aesthetic elements feature in an ice skating routine and a goalkeeper's dive in football. In fact, any activity that incorporates movement of the body could be said to exhibit an aesthetic element. It is somewhat harder to accept that physically passive activities like chess and bridge have an aesthetic dimension. Nevertheless, even chess games are reported to have contained 'elegant' gambits, a descriptive term that has an aesthetic feel to it. Do all sports therefore contain aesthetic characteristics?

Structure

An important feature of sports is that they are governed by rules. This was a significant consideration in the definition of game-playing provided by Suits (1978). Most sports have specified playing areas, fixed durations and rules of play which are determined by a sport's governing body. Usually, there are officials who check that the sport is played 'according to the rules'. Activities that do not have this kind of structure might be considered as forms of play rather than as sports. However, difficulties arise. How is an impromptu game of football in the park to be defined? The players may adhere to most of the rules of play of the formal game of football, but not have a referee, not use a specified playing area and not play for the normal duration of a football game.

Sport can also be said to be institutionalised. This means that, like the media and banking, sport has become a relatively permanent part of social life, with an organisation and structure which will continue long into the future. It also means that ways of playing a sport are broadly accepted throughout the country, and this would not have been the case in previous periods of history.

Goal Orientation

During participation in sport the objective may be to score points, to run a faster time, to achieve a greater distance or to score goals. Participants of different sports and of different standards may have different goals, but they will have specific criteria to determine whether success has been achieved. Professional sportsmen and sportswomen may see financial rewards as important, while a village cricketer may gauge success by scoring fifty runs against a rival team.

Most things in life have a meaningful purpose. For example, eating keeps us alive and child rearing brings on the next generation. On the surface, sport does not seem to have a meaningful purpose since the sporting outcome does not produce anything. However, for the participant, sport gives psychological, social and health benefits, while the spectator derives entertainment and diversion from vicarious involvement.

Unpredictability

A characteristic of sport often overlooked is that it can be very unpredictable. Despite massive scientific assistance now given to sport, the outcomes of sporting contests can still be uncertain. This is a feature that gives sport considerable appeal and fascination among players and spectators alike. The defeat of football league clubs to non-league opposition in the FA Cup and the loss of tennis seeds at Wimbledon provide drama, excitement and the tantalising prospect of further upsets.

Allied to this is the significant part often played by luck or chance. Where individuals or teams are evenly matched, a result may easily be determined by a 'stroke of fortune'. A cricketer may lose his or her wicket early by being caught and yet be dropped in the next innings and make a century. The fact that luck can play a part in sport often encourages players to adopt superstitious practices, such as the tying up of bootlaces in the same way for every match.

The characteristics described above illustrate the diverse nature of sport. Quirky superstitions can be as significant as multimillion pound sporting contests. Perhaps it is because sport contains so many fascinating characteristics that it is such a popular phenomenon in the world today.

UNDERSTANDING THE RELATIONSHIP BETWEEN PLAY, SPORT AND WORK

In a study of sport it is useful to examine the relationship between play, sport and work. The complexity of the issue can be illustrated by recognising that a professional sportsman or sportswoman can be described as *playing* a *sport* while at *work*! Children play for fun, fantasy and excitement. Play can be spontaneous and freely chosen or regulated and orderly. At times, play seems to have a developmental purpose when children act out adult roles, and yet, on other occasions, it defies any kind of explanation. Indeed, children are not the only ones to play. Adults play for fun, excitement, diversion and entertainment – they might play in the park with their children or play pranks on their workmates in the factory.

Play is evident in an impromptu game in the park, in a competitive local league match and in a professional, international tournament. Play can also be organised such that rules are created, not only to define ways of playing, but also to separate play from reality. At some point the play experience also becomes a sport experience. This may be viewed differently by different people at different times. In general, the greater the organisation and regulation, the more likely it is to be considered as a sporting occasion, rather than purely as a play situation. However, there can be frivolous, playful moments in a professional contest, while a game in the park can be a matter of intense seriousness. A perceptive analysis by Huizinga (1949, p. 13) underlined this idea when calling play:

> a free activity standing quite consciously outside 'ordinary' life as being 'not serious', but at the same time absorbing the player intensely and utterly.

Sport contains internal and external rewards. The exhilaration and pleasure gained from winning a rally in tennis is a reward felt within the individual; the cup, money and ranking points received from winning the tennis tournament are external rewards. It is sometimes thought that the greater the internal reward, the more it is likely to be a play experience; and the greater the external reward, the more it is seen as a work experience. This may hold true in general but there will always be exceptions. An individual earning a vast amount of money in a golf tournament may still experience immense inward satisfaction from playing attractive and successful golf.

Work may be viewed in two ways. One aspect of work is where an individual is paid for being employed in a job, while another is where an unpaid task or duty is undertaken, such as a domestic chore in the home. A major characteristic of work is that it is functional: in other words, it serves a purpose rather than something done simply to pass the time. Work is usually seen in contrast to play, although closer inspection reveals some intriguing problems with this division. For example, children often imitate work situations when at play and this is considered to be a valuable social learning process for them.

Sport can clearly be a form of work since professional sportsmen and sportswomen are employed and paid for their performances. The question then arises as to whether play and work are mutually exclusive. Can a professional sportsperson be at play while at work? This is a difficult issue since the professional sportsperson does not have freedom of choice about competing and yet freedom is considered a major characteristic of play. At the same time, every professional sportsperson would probably say that there is enjoyment and excitement in their sport, features that are considered significant attributes of play. It also seems quite natural to say that the professional *plays* tennis or *plays* rugby. Figure 1.1 illustrates the curious interrelationship between play, sport and work.

Figure 1.1 The interrelationship between play, sport and work

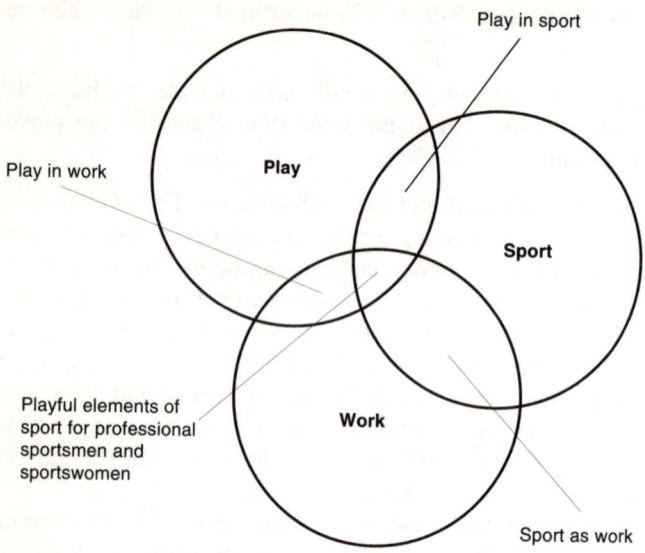

SPORT AS A PART OF CONTEMPORARY CULTURE

As far as the twentieth century is concerned, it is often assumed that sport has become more and more available to the general population. To a large extent this is true since increased affluence has led to the building of a wide range of sporting facilities and people have more free time that can be spent playing sport. It should not be forgotten, however, that long hours of work have persisted in some occupations like the service sector and the cost of playing sports regularly has remained beyond the means of some people.

A study of sport is concerned not only with people who physically take part in sport, but also with those who take an interest in and watch sport. In fact it is more complex than this since the world of sport has both producers and consumers: those who plan, organise and stage sporting events and those who attend, take part, listen to, watch or read about the events. Table 1.1 illustrates the variety of roles found in sport nowadays.

Sport is often seen as something that is unreal or separate from the main business of life. Clarke and Clarke (1982, p. 62) disputed this notion when they said:

it becomes impossible to treat sport as if it stands outside of all the other social relations within which we spend our life. Sport is not a 'privileged space' into which we can retreat from real life – rather it is systematically and intimately connected with society.

They support this by showing how sport is socially constructed, containing integral elements of society like local and national identity, competition and sexual division. In fact, a stark example of the reality of the sporting experience has been the prosecution of sportsmen for violent offences committed while on the field of play. Although there may be fantasy sporting games in the newspapers, sport has very real consequences for its participants whether played in the local park or in a national stadium.

Table 1.1 The production and consumption of sport

Producers	Consumers
Owners	Active participants
Promoters	Spectators at live events
Sponsors	Television spectators
Coaches	Radio listeners
Managers	Book, magazine, newspaper readers
Match/event officials	
Broadcasters	
Reporters	
Photographers	
Groundkeepers	
Trainers	
Physiotherapists	

Source: Adapted from Loy, McPherson and Kenyon, 1978, p. 18.

Viewed from a sociological perspective, sport exhibits values which are at the heart of capitalist society. Within sport there is an acceptance of rules, an obedience to authority, an emphasis on competitive struggle and a concern for individual effort. In addition, it is often seen as a way in which violent male youths can release their aggression within a socially acceptable context. Sport could therefore be conceived as a form of social control which maintains the capitalist status quo.

It is perhaps not surprising that sport contains the structures and processes of society. In the twentieth century, society is relatively well organised and it would be strange if people did not organise sport in the same way. Thus, it is not surprising to find that the values of society are replicated in sport. For example, dedication is admired as a positive attribute in the work sphere and it is also an important feature of sport. While society struggles to eradicate racial discrimination, football organisations attempt to curb racist attitudes in football.

The pervasive nature of sport in modern life was neatly summed up by Boyle (1963, pp. 3–4):

> Sport permeates any number of levels of contemporary society, and it touches upon and deeply influences such disparate elements as status, race relations, business life, automotive design, clothing styles, the concept of the hero, language, and ethical values.

It might be added that sport now has a significant influence on leisure, education, economics, mass communications and international diplomacy, while also impinging on art, law and even politics.

The Nature of Modern Sport

Like everything else in society, sport is always changing. For most of the twentieth century, sport has been dominated by the words of Baron Pierre de Coubertin (1908):

> The most important thing in the Olympic Games is not winning but taking part, just as the most important thing in life is not the triumph but the struggle.

In Britain, generations of children have probably been confused by a situation where their teachers have extolled the virtues of 'taking part' in sport while, at the same time, placing immense importance on winning leagues and cups for the school. At the highest level, the prizes for winning in sport have changed from prestige to fame and fortune. In the competitive, professional world of sport, 'taking part' is not usually enough to avoid being made redundant. Success is measured not by the 'struggle' but by the 'triumph'.

The ever increasing need for victory has arguably changed the nature of sport, leading to an emphasis on the measurable and quantifiable rather than the quality of performance. Is this in fact true or is it a romantic notion that, in years gone by, the important thing in sport really was the 'taking part'?

Levels of Sport

A sociological study of sport needs to recognise the different levels of sport in contemporary society. At one end of the spectrum *élite sport* is contested by high level, international sportsmen and sportswomen who are mostly professionals and can be worldwide superstars. At the other end are the millions of people who engage in recreational sport. In between there will be a great many people of varying standards with different aspirations. For example, some will be young, aspiring athletes moving towards élite levels, while there will be thousands who play at a reasonably good standard, but will never reach élite status. There is also a further group who, with increasing age, settle into club sport after perhaps having attained higher levels in their youth. If discussion of a particular issue is concerned with the characteristics of élite sportsmen and sportswomen, it would therefore be misleading if the thousands of recreational sports participants were also incorporated.

Sport For All
The 'Sport For All' movement stems from a Council of Europe (1966) 'declaration of principle' which asserted that institutions concerned with sport had a responsibility to help people understand the meaning of sport and encourage them to engage in it throughout their lives. The campaign was adopted in Britain during the 1970s and has continued ever since. It is considered a right of everyone to be able to take part in sport and is seen as a desirable social concept. It should also be recognised that this includes people with mental and physical disabilities, and the Sports Council has supported this all-embracing concept from its inception.

THE SOCIOLOGICAL STUDY OF SPORT

For almost one hundred years there has been substantial scientific enquiry into sport, encompassing the realms of human biology, biomechanics, exercise physiology and other sub-disciplines. In contrast, although sport has been a significant element of popular culture throughout the twentieth century, it has been largely neglected by sociologists until quite recently. It is only in the last twenty years that there has been a surge of books and journal articles with a social science perspective, ranging from GCSE textbooks to substantive theoretical works.

This book has not been written from any particular sociological position. Rather, it attempts to draw together research findings and to outline theoretical discussions of important sporting issues. Where writers have offered sociological perspectives, these have been reported. In the main, the sociological study of sport has been *functionalist*, in that sport has been seen to benefit individuals in one way or another and, consequently, to benefit society as a whole. Sport helps to shape individuals into existing ways of society, while curbing and controlling potentially disruptive sections of the population. Thus, sport functions to develop character, to offer opportunities for socialising and to provide fulfilment in leisure. More recently, a number of other sociological perspectives have emerged to shed new light on the place of sport in society. For example, the critical *feminist* approach adopted by Hargreaves (1994, p. 5) showed how women's sports can be 'a process of accommodation to existing structures of power and control, and to dominant ideologies'. Taking a different approach, Goldlust (1987, p. 10) embraced the *conflict* perspective when he explored how the media had helped dominant groups in society to structure, organise and give meaning to sport 'in accordance with their group interests and their particular ideological and moral precepts'.

Generally, the sociological study of sport has been related to perceived problems in society. Consequently, there have been investigations related to crowd violence at sporting events and the apparent underrepresentation of women in sport. More recently, there have been enquiries surrounding the abuse of drugs in sport and the way that commercialisation has become a menacing part of the sporting scene. The following chapters provide an overview of the main social issues that have stimulated an academic study of sport. An attempt has been made to locate British sources for the material in this book and a substantial number have been uncovered. Inevitably, however, there are many gaps and, in these cases, reference has been made to pertinent work from overseas.

REFERENCES

Boyle, R.H., *Sport: Mirror of American Life* (Boston: Little, Brown, 1963).
Brohm, J.-M., *Sport: A Prison of Measured Time* (London: Ink Links, 1978).
Clarke, A. and Clarke, J., 'Highlights and Action Replays: Ideology, Sport and the Media'. In J. Hargreaves (ed.), *Sport, Culture and Ideology* (London: Routledge and Kegan Paul, 1982), pp. 62–87.
Coakley, J.J., *Sport in Society* (St Louis: Mosby, 1994).
Council of Europe, *Minutes of Committee for Out-of-School Education and Cultural Development* (1966), 6–10 June.
Council of Europe, *Minutes*, 2 (1971).
Curry, T.J. and Jiobu, R.M., *Sports: A Social Perspective* (Englewood Cliffs: Prentice Hall, 1984).

de Coubertin, P., cited in a speech to officials of the Olympic Games at a banquet in London, 24 July 1908.
Elias, N., *The Civilizing Process* (Oxford: Blackwell, 1978).
Goldlust, J., *Playing For Keeps: Sport, The Media and Society* (Melbourne: Longman Cheshire, 1987).
Hanks, P. (ed.), *Collins Concise Dictionary of the English Language* (London: Collins, 1988).
Hargreaves, J., *Sporting Females* (London: Routledge, 1994).
Huizinga, J., *Homo Ludens: A Study of the Play-Element in Culture* (London: Routledge and Kegan Paul, 1949).
Loy, J.W., McPherson, B.D. and Kenyon, G., *Sport and Social Systems* (Reading: Addison-Wesley, 1978).
Singer, R.N., *Physical Education: Foundations* (New York: Holt, Rinehart and Winston, 1976).
Suits, B., *The Grasshopper: Games, Life and Utopia* (Toronto: University of Toronto Press, 1978).
Wertz, S.K., 'Is Sport Unique? A Question of Definability', *Journal of the Philosophy of Sport*, XXII (1985), pp. 83–93.
Williams, N., *The Chronology of the Modern World* (Oxford: Helican, 1994).

FURTHER READING

Davis, R.J., Bull, C.R., Roscoe, J.V. and Roscoe, D.A., *Physical Education and the Study of Sport* (London: Wolfe, 1992).

Although American, clarifications of sport can be found in the works by Coakley, Curry and Jiobu (cited above) and in:

McPherson, B.D., Curtis, J.E. and Loy, J.W., *The Social Significance of Sport* (Champaign: Human Kinetics, 1989).
Snyder, E.E. and Spreitzer, E., *Social Aspects of Sport* (Englewood Cliffs: Prentice Hall, 1983).

2 Participation Patterns in Sport

INTRODUCTION

The twentieth century has witnessed an expansion in sporting opportunities for the general population in Britain. The underlying reason for the development of sport has been the change in living conditions for the majority of people. The relative growth in affluence and the greater availability of free time have given the masses the chance to engage in sport. In addition, schools have introduced children to sport, raising awareness and developing skills to prepare them for future participation.

The many benefits of sports participation are widely acknowledged and, through the Sports Council, the government encourages the population to take part. The extensive media coverage of sport and the prevalence of playing fields, sports centres and other sporting facilities suggests that Britain is a sport-loving nation. However, the question that might be asked is: are the British public merely armchair sportsmen and sportswomen or actively engaged in sporting activities? After a brief historical sketch, this chapter examines surveys that provide information about the sports participation patterns of young people and adults.

SPORTS PARTICIPATION IN THE FIRST HALF OF THE TWENTIETH CENTURY

It is only in recent years that extensive surveys have been conducted in relation to sport and, therefore, estimates must be made of participation in the early and middle part of the twentieth century. However, it is quite clear that a relatively small proportion of the population actively participated in sport, due to a lack of money, time and facilities. Country pursuits like hunting, coursing, shooting and horse racing, many of which had been popular for centuries, continued during the twentieth century, but were mainly limited to a small number of affluent people and country dwellers. However, activities such as fishing and walking (rambling) probably involved much larger numbers of participants since they were inexpensive, had no social barriers and were accessible to most people who were interested.

Swimming as a recreation attracted a comparatively large number of people, although it would have been limited to an occasional summertime dip in the river or sea until swimming pools were built later in the century. Traditional team sports like football and cricket gained popularity in the early years of the twentieth century, especially after the 1918 Fisher Education Act, which allowed local education authorities to provide playing fields and other recreational facilities. Sports such as rugby, hockey and rowing were popular at public schools and universities, with many participants continuing to play these sports in clubs after having left school and college. Golf and tennis were popular throughout the twentieth century, although, apart from a few exceptions, they were the preserve of a wealthy minority who could afford the relatively high fees of private clubs.

Cycling has an interesting development. While it was urban, middle class men who first engaged in cycling, it also became possible for women to ride without too much censure in the early part of the century. The number of men and women involved in track and road racing was very small but, in mid-century, larger numbers escaped from towns into the countryside on bikes, with guide books, hotels and repair shops catering for a vibrant bicycle touring fraternity. Clubs developed for various other sporting pursuits as diverse as mountaineering, motor cycle racing, gymnastics and equestrian events, but the number of participants would have been small, involving a minute fraction of the general population.

RECENT SPORTS PARTICIPATION TRENDS

Sport For All

An apparent expansion in sports participation occurred during the second half of the twentieth century. Increasing numbers were able to afford the time and money to play sport and were not physically exhausted by the demands of work. Television raised awareness about different sports, while an improved transportation system provided access to a rapidly expanding variety of facilities. Perhaps the most significant factor, however, was a change in attitude whereby sport became acknowledged as the right of everyone, rather than the preserve of a few. By the 1960s this was endorsed by the concept of 'Sport For All', a campaign supported by British governments through the Sports Council, which attempted to offer sporting opportunities to the entire population.

Young People

Schools are now required to offer a variety of sporting experiences to children and teenagers as part of the National Curriculum and, after a decline in extra-curricular sports participation during the 1980s and 1990s (Education, Science and Arts Committee, 1991), the government indicated that it wished to reverse the trend through a wide-ranging package of proposals (Department of National Heritage, 1995). Little is known about the sporting habits of primary age children outside of school, although a study by Sleap and Warburton (1996), using a direct observation technique, offered an insight into the most popular physical activities of preadolescents in England. While there are a wide range of sports available nowadays, soccer was by far the most common sport, although it was mainly played by boys. Swimming, cycling, gymnastics and tennis were also popular, but overall it was concluded that young children engaged in a limited amount of sport in their free time outside of school.

The Sports Council recently reported the sports involvement of more than 4000 young people aged 6–16 years (Sports Council, 1995). Outside of school lessons, young people, on average, took part in ten sports at least once in the previous year, although frequent participation (at least ten times in a year) was limited to an average of four sports. Just over half had participated frequently in a team sport, half had swum regularly and just under half had taken part in an athletic or gymnastic activity. There was no significant difference between primary and secondary age children, but at secondary level, girls took part in fewer sports than boys.

Table 2.1 shows the popularity of particular sports played outside of lessons. A large number of young people took part in a wide range of sporting activities at least once in the previous year, with participation highest in swimming, cycling, football and tennis. However, the figures for frequent participation (at least ten times in the year) were significantly lower. The Sports Council's definition of 'frequent' could also be questioned since participation 'at least ten times a year' does not necessarily indicate a regular commitment to sport. Additionally, it could be argued that activities like swimming, cycling, walking, ten-pin bowling, aerobics, ice skating, putting/pitch and putt, and dance

Table 2.1 Participation of young people in specific sports outside of lessons

Sports listed in rank order for total participating at least once out-of-lessons	Percentages At least once	Percentages At least ten times	Rank orders At least once	Rank orders At least ten times
Swimming (diving, lifesaving)	82	50	1	2
Cycling, riding a bike	80	57	2	1
Football (inc. 5-a-side)	60	37	3	3
Walking (>1hr), hiking	59	23	4	4
Tennis	53	21	5	5
Cricket	40	17	6	6
Rounders	39	13	7	=8
Tenpin bowls, skittles	38	8	8	=16
Athletics – track or field	34	13	9	=8
Aerobics, keep fit (inc. skipping)	32	14	10	7
Badminton	31	11	11	12
Cross country, jogging, (road running)	30	10	=12	13
Ice skating	30	6	=12	23
Basketball	29	12	=14	11
Table tennis	29	9	=14	=14
Golf, putting, pitch and putt	29	8	=14	=16
Gymnastics (gym, trampolining, climbing frames)	29	13	=14	=8
Horse riding (pony trekking)	19	7	18	=18
Angling, fishing	18	7	19	=18
Rugby	17	7	=20	=18
Netball	17	7	=20	=18
Rowing, water-skiing, canoeing	16	4	22	=25
Climbing, abseiling, potholing	15	3	=23	=28
Dance classes	15	9	=23	=14
Baseball, softball	15	4	=23	=25

Source: Sports Council, 1995, p. 84.

classes were mostly social and recreational in nature, involving little or no competitive sporting element.

The Sports Council survey gives a flattering view of sports participation among young people. Much of the analysis relates to sport undertaken in PE lessons at school or participation at least once in the previous year. In addition, activities such as cycling will include a high proportion of non-sporting cycling activity and young people are known to overestimate their participation in self-report surveys of this nature.

In a survey of more than 900 adolescents, Williams (1988) found that quite a high proportion (52 per cent) of 14/15-year-olds claimed to participate in physical activity outside of school, but only half of these took part at least once a week. Using heart rate monitoring, Armstrong and colleagues (1990) established that adolescents were far less active than was popularly thought, with very few engaging in regular activity. Since heart rate monitoring encompasses all forms of physical activity (for example, climbing stairs), frequent involvement in sport was presumably quite limited. Relatively low levels of physical activity were also reported in a study of over 3000 adolescents in Northern Ireland (Riddoch, 1990), with a striking decline in activity among girls between the ages of 11 and 18 years. A conclusion must be that, outside of compulsory PE lessons in school, only a modest proportion of young people regularly participate in competitive forms of sport in Britain.

ADULT PARTICIPATION IN SPORT

A number of large scale studies of adult participation in physical activity have been conducted in recent years. However, it is difficult to compare results because of different objectives and varying methodologies. For example, definitions of physical activity sometimes include pursuits such as gardening as well as traditional team sports like rugby and netball. The following analysis attempts to extract information about the sports participation patterns of adults.

General Household Survey

The *General Household Survey* (Office of Population, Censuses and Surveys, 1993) regularly provides data on the leisure activities, including sport, of more than 17 000 people aged 16 years or over. In 1993, if walking was excluded, 47 per cent of adults claimed to have taken part in at least one sport during the four weeks prior to interview and this rose to 68 per cent in the twelve months before interview. Table 2.2 lists the most popular sports and physical activities.

Walking, swimming, cue sports, keep fit/yoga and cycling had the most participants, each attracting more than 10 per cent of the population. It is likely that most of these activities would have been of a

Table 2.2 Rank order of most popular sports played in the four weeks prior to interview

Men	Women
1. Walking	Walking
2. Snooker/pool/billiards	Keep fit/yoga
3. Swimming	Swimming
4. Cycling	Cycling
5. Soccer	Snooker/pool/billiards
6. Golf	Tenpin bowls/skittles
7. Weight lifting/training	Darts
8. Darts	Weight lifting/training
9. Running (excluding track)	Badminton
10. Keep fit/yoga	Running (excluding track)

Source: Office of Population, Censuses and Surveys, 1993, p. 141.

social or functional nature rather than having a competitive, sporting element. Additionally, the infrequent nature of active participation can be gauged by the fact that no activity attracted a greater average frequency than one occasion per month.

Although a change in questioning method[1] in 1987 gave an artificial boost to participation figures, there seems to have been a genuine increase in sports participation in Britain since 1977. Table 2.3 shows that keep fit/yoga, cycling, weight lifting/training, golf and tenpin bowls/skittles became more popular, while cue sports and darts lost participants.

In their analysis of *General Household Survey* data between 1977 and 1987, Gratton and Tice (undated) noted that, while there had been a modest increase in sports participation generally, indoor sport expanded 60 per cent in ten years. They also found that higher proportions of women, manual workers and the elderly were taking part in sport in the 1980s, compared to the 1970s. Gratton and Tice also reported that participation in sports and physical activities had increased far more than participation in other leisure pursuits. Although starting from a small base, the proportion of the population involved in sport has regularly expanded since 1977 (if walking is excluded), while most other pursuits have only shown a modest increase in popularity, and some, like dressmaking, needlework and knitting, experienced a decline.

---

[1] A prompt card with a list of sports was introduced. Prompt cards usually produce higher responses in surveys.

Table 2.3 Sports participation rates, 1977–93 (% participating four weeks prior to interview)

	1977	1987	1993
Swimming	6	13	15
Snooker/pool/billiards	6	15	12
Keep fit/yoga	1	9	12
Cycling	1	8	10
Darts	9	9	6
Weight lifting/training	–	–	5
Golf	2	4	5
Running (jogging, etc.)	–	5	5
Soccer	3	5	4
Tenpin bowls/skittles	–	–	4
Badminton	2	3	3
Tennis	1	2	2
Fishing	2	2	2
Bowls	–	–	2
Squash	2	3	2
Table tennis	2	2	2
Horse riding	–	1	1
Cricket	1	1	1

Note: Walking omitted and figures not available for some sports.
Source: Adapted from Office of Population, Censuses and Surveys, 1993, p. 150; Matheson, 1991, p. 8.

Age

It is generally assumed that sports participation decreases with age and this was confirmed in the *General Household Survey*. Figure 2.2 demonstrates a consistent decline in participation from 16 years to 70 years and over. It should be noted that the inclusion of walking can give an artificial boost to sports participation figures, especially with older age groups.

Analysis and discussion of sports participation by women and individuals from different social classes are given in Chapters 5 and 6. With its large sample and regular updating, the *General Household Survey* provides a useful insight into participation trends in sport. However, its limitations need to be acknowledged. First, it includes activities that might not be considered as sport, such as walking, keep fit/yoga and recreational swimming (for example, occasional dips on holiday), and thus an artificial level of sports participation may be portrayed.

The accuracy of responses must also be questioned. This is exemplified by the change from unprompted to prompted responses between

Figure 2.1 Participation in sports and physical activities by age, 1993

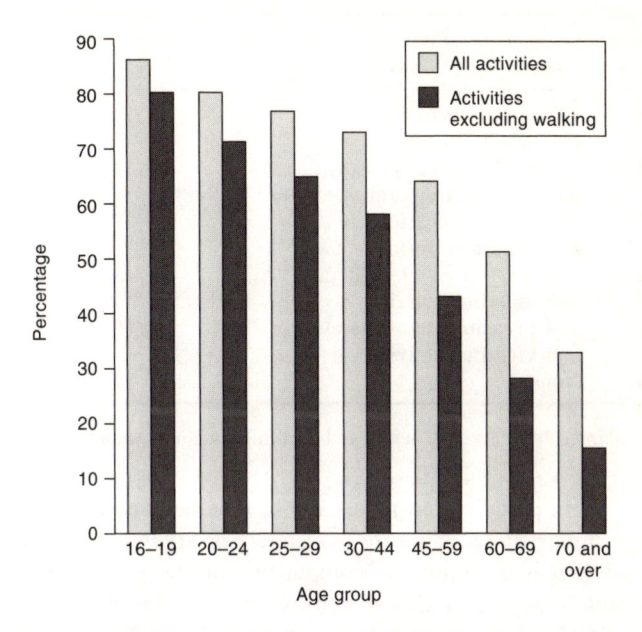

Source: Office of Population, Censuses and Surveys, 1993, p. 141.

1986 and 1987, when participation rates changed dramatically. It is also well known that accuracy of recall over a twelve-month period is suspect, and consequently the findings do not inspire confidence. This kind of survey tends to overestimate participation and therefore it is probable that the proportion of the adult population who are genuine sports participants is less than that depicted by the *General Household Survey*.

Allied Dunbar National Fitness Survey

The *Allied Dunbar National Fitness Survey* (Sports Council and Health Education Authority, 1992) assessed, by structured interview, the physical activity patterns of more than 4000 adults. Table 2.4 shows that, in terms of frequency and intensity, the sample exhibited relatively low activity levels, with only 49 per cent of men and 41 per cent of women achieving level 3, which might be considered as the minimum criterion for maintaining optimum health.

In addition, these activity levels include non-sporting activities such as walking and functional activities like gardening and occupational

Table 2.4 Activity levels of men and women

Frequency and intensity of activity 20 minute occasions in previous four weeks		Men %	Women %
Level 5:	12 or more occasions of vigorous activity	14	4
Level 4:	12 or more occasions of moderate and vigorous activity	12	10
Level 3:	12 or more occasions of moderate activity only	23	27
Level 2:	5–11 occasions of moderate and vigorous activity	18	25
Level 1:	1–4 occasions of moderate and vigorous activity	16	18
Level 0:	None	17	16

Source: Adapted from Sports Council and Health Education Authority, 1992, p. 48.

activity; sports participation levels would thus be even lower. Not surprisingly, among those who were moderately or vigorously active, sports participation was a significant component for the young, but less so for the middle aged and almost non-existent for the elderly.

Table 2.5 shows the most popular sports and recreations among men and women, illustrating the difficulty of gaining an accurate idea of genuine sports participation from this kind of survey. Despite their potential health value, activities such as swimming, exercises, social dancing, jogging/running and rambling could not be considered as competitive sports, and yet they constituted a substantial amount of the moderate and vigorous physical activity recorded.

Health and Lifestyle Survey

Among various health and lifestyle indicators, the *Health and Lifestyle Survey* studied, by means of interview, the exercise patterns of more than 9000 adults in England, Scotland and Wales (Cox *et al.*, 1987). A follow-up survey of more than 5000 of the original sample was conducted seven years later by the Health Promotion Research Trust (Cox *et al.*, 1993), in order to see if any changes had taken place. The findings revealed that:

> Except in the youngest men, overall the proportion of people of both sexes and all ages taking part in activities involving physical effort had risen compared to the same age groups seven years ago. (Cox *et al.*, 1993, p. 13)

Table 2.5 Most popular sports and recreations

Sport/recreation	Past four weeks Men %	Past four weeks Women %	Past year Men %	Past year Women %	Intensity category
Swimming	17	19	45	44	(Vig./mod.)
Exercises	18	18	24	24	(Mod./light)
Social dancing	12	18	21	31	(Mod./light)
Snooker	16	2	27	5	(Light)
Darts	10	3	17	6	(Light)
Jogging/running	9	2	17	6	(Vigorous)
Rambling	6	5	12	9	(Mod./light)
Football	10	1	20	3	(Vig./mod.)
Weight training	8	2	13	6	(Vig./mod.)
Keep fit	2	7	3	14	(Vig./mod.)
Golf	9	1	17	3	(Mod./light)
Badminton	3	3	10	9	(Vig./mod.)
Aerobics	1	5	1	10	(Vig./mod.)
Squash	4	1	11	3	(Vigorous)
Tennis	3	2	11	7	(Vig./mod.)
Table tennis	3	1	10	5	(Mod./light)
Ten-pin bowling	3	3	11	9	(Light)
Fishing	4	–	10	1	(Light)
Cricket	3	–	10	1	(Mod./light)
Bowls	2	1	7	3	(Light)
Cycling	16	12	30	22	(Vig./mod.)

Source: Sports Council and Health Education Authority, 1992, p. 62.

Involvement in cycling and swimming was found to have increased and more women were participating in keep fit and yoga. While offering an insight into activity patterns, it must be remembered that, like the *General Household Survey* and the *Allied Dunbar Survey*, the *Health and Lifestyle Survey* included physical activities in general and, although sport would have featured strongly, other activities such as walking and work activities would have inflated the figures.

The Liverpool Study

The University of Liverpool conducted a series of studies between 1986 and 1990 to investigate sports provision in six cities and to explore sport and health-related data among more than 4000 adults (Roberts and Brodie, 1992). The sample mainly consisted of sports centre users and is therefore not representative of the general population. Nevertheless, the findings provided useful information about the characteristics of participants and their sports careers.

This particular research focused on seven activities only: badminton, bowls, keep fit, martial arts, snooker, soccer and weight training. Younger players were far more prominent in martial arts, soccer and snooker, while the other four activities had older participants, with bowls not surprisingly showing the most elderly profile. An important feature of sports participants in the Liverpool study was that they exhibited continuity of sporting interest from youth to retirement. Although dropout from sport occurred to some extent in middle age, it was found that, if sport was still being played at the age of 30, it was unlikely to be disrupted for many years. A substantial dropout from sport occurs during teenage years and, if this could be reduced, lifetime sports involvement could well increase. Roberts and Brodie found that, although specific promotional campaigns could entice the long term inactive into sports centres, their participation in sport was invariably of a temporary nature.

Interestingly, the Liverpool study identified three distinct groups in the population:

- participants with continuous sports careers
- individuals who dropped out of sport when young and revived their participation temporarily from time to time
- non-participants who claimed that 'nothing would encourage them to resume sport' (Roberts and Brodie, 1992, p. 71).

CONCLUSIONS

The above surveys offer an insight into sports participation in Britain, although their accuracy is open to question because of imprecise definitions of sport and the self-report nature of the methodology. It is clear that participation has increased in recent years, although not to the extent that might have been expected, since regular involvement in active, competitive sport is still limited to a small percentage of the general population. There seems to be some shift in participation trends and yet this tends to be affected by the way in which sport is defined. For example, women now appear to be nearly as active as men if aerobics and other keep fit activities are taken into account and yet, if these activities are excluded, there would still be a considerable variation in sporting involvement between the sexes. Thus, in general, men participate more than women, the young take part more than the elderly and those in non-manual occupations are more active than those in manual jobs.

REFERENCES

Armstrong, N., Balding, J., Gentle, P. and Kirby, B., 'Patterns of Physical Activity among 11 to 16-year-old British Children', *British Medical Journal*, 301 (1990), pp. 203–5.
Cox, B.D. et al., *Health and Lifestyle Survey: Preliminary Report* (London: Health Promotion Research Trust, 1987).
Cox, B.D. et al., *Health and Lifestyle Survey: Seven Years On* (Aldershot: Dartmouth, 1993).
Department of National Heritage, *Sport: Raising the Game* (London: Department of National Heritage, 1995).
Education, Science and Arts Committee, *House of Commons Report: Sport in Schools* (London: HMSO, 1991).
Gratton, C. and Tice, A., *Sports Participation in Britain 1977–1987* (Cambridge: Health Promotion Research Trust, undated).
Matheson, J., *Participation in Sport: General Household Survey 1987* (London: HMSO, 1991).
Office of Population, Censuses and Surveys, *General Household Survey* (London: HMSO, 1993).
Riddoch, C., *The Fitness, Physical Activity, Attitudes and Lifestyles of Northern Ireland Post-primary School Children* (Belfast: DHSS, 1990).
Roberts, K. and Brodie, D.A., *Inner-city Sport: Who Plays, and What are the Benefits?* (Voorthuizen: Giordano Bruno Culemborg, 1992).
Sleap, M. and Warburton, P., 'Physical Activity Levels of 5–11-year-old Children in England: Cumulative Evidence from Three Direct Observation Studies', *International Journal of Sports Medicine*, 17 (1996), pp. 248–53.
Sports Council, *Young People and Sport* (London: Sports Council, 1995).
Sports Council and Health Education Authority, *Allied Dunbar National Fitness Survey* (London: Sports Council and Health Education Authority, 1992).
Williams, A., 'Physical Activity Patterns among Adolescents: Some Curriculum Implications', *Physical Education Review*, 11 (1988), pp. 28–39.

FURTHER READING

Analyse in more detail the reports from the *General Household Survey, Allied Dunbar National Fitness Survey, Health and Lifestyle Survey* and the Liverpool study (Roberts and Brodie, 1992).

3 Explanations of Sporting Behaviour

INTRODUCTION

Sporting behaviour, like all forms of behaviour, is a complex process which cannot be easily explained. Although certain participation patterns were noticeable in the previous chapter, they do not provide a full understanding of sporting behaviour. Why is it that one individual becomes addicted to playing tennis while a next door neighbour does not even own a tennis racket? Why do some people give up playing sport in youth, while others continue into old age? In addition to psychological and sociological approaches which attempt to explain sporting behaviour, there are now many multidimensional models which embrace a combination of perspectives. This chapter provides an introduction to work on this issue. A brief review is also presented of theories that examine why people withdraw from sport, and finally, consideration is given to new approaches to sports promotion.

PSYCHOLOGICAL APPROACHES

Psychological theories focus on characteristics of the individual person. Although practicalities, such as the financial cost of participation, need to be taken into consideration, the underlying motivation to take part in sport comes from the individual. Thus, sporting behaviour can be understood as a function of the needs of the individual, with life satisfaction dependent upon the selection of activities which fulfil his or her needs.

The strength of an individual's needs may influence the type of sport to which he or she might be attracted. Early studies (for example, Allen, 1982; Tinsley, Barrett and Kass, 1977) concluded that specific needs could be satisfied by particular leisure activities, including sports. Despite concerns regarding the methodology of these studies, this approach does have an attractive logic to it. If, for example, an individual has a strong need for independence, it seems plausible for him or her to be attracted to individual sports.

Perceptions of physical ability (sometimes called self-efficacy, self-confidence or competence) influence the initiation and maintenance of sport involvement. For example, in her competence motivation model, Harter (1978) proposed that individuals felt inherent pleasure from mastering physical tasks, and therefore a favourable perception of physical ability led to heightened motivation, increased effort and persistence, and a wide range of activity choices. Success and positive feedback in sport motivate the individual to continued participation, since self-confidence in sport is especially affected by the social expectations of others. Not surprisingly, it has been found that élite athletes have a strong self-concept, including positive views of their physical ability, physical appearance and general self-esteem (Barnett and Wright, 1994).

SOCIALISATION INTO SPORT

From birth onwards, individuals are influenced by the world around them, and therefore it is difficult to untangle the extent to which sporting behaviour is determined by inherited characteristics or by learned social influences. Socialisation involves learning and internalising skills, social norms, attitudes and values of life. An important contribution to understanding on this issue is social-cognitive theory (Bandura, 1986), which involves reciprocal interaction between behaviour, cognition and environment.

Childhood experiences may influence adult leisure behaviour and if sports are played in youth, the experiences may determine whether sports are played in later life. An individual who is introduced to a sport during youth will become knowledgeable about it, develop skills and become aware of clubs where the sport can be played. This socialisation process could provide a basis for participation in adulthood. Of course, if early experiences are negative, perhaps because of feelings of embarrassment, participation in later life may be less likely. Early research into the influence of socialisation upon leisure behaviour was inconclusive. Some studies (for example, Yoesting and Burkhead, 1973) indicated that childhood experiences affected adult leisure behaviour, while others (Kelly, 1977) found that some adult leisure behaviour was unrelated to upbringing.

A considerable amount of research has studied the socialisation process in relation to élite athletes, and a consistent, if unsurprising, finding is that:

individuals who receive positive reinforcement for sport participation are more likely to become and remain involved than those who receive neutral or negative messages. (McPherson, Curtis and Loy, 1989, p. 49)

In childhood the family is the most influential socialising agency, especially if parents and siblings take part in sport. Later, teachers, peer group and sports coaches can act as role models or provide social support for the continuance of competitive sport. Studies exploring the relationship between childhood socialisation and adult recreational sport are sparse, although evidence from the *Allied Dunbar National Fitness Survey* (Sports Council and Health Education Authority, 1992) seems to suggest that engagement in physical activity during childhood and youth influences physical activity patterns during adulthood.

Many suggestions have been floated as to why some individuals persist with sports participation while the majority opt out. These include differing childhood sporting experiences and critical lifestyle incidents such as marriage, parenthood and change of occupation. The Liverpool study of sports centre users interestingly revealed that:

> the characteristic that distinguished the early sport socialisation of the adults in our panel who persisted was the number of different sports that they had played regularly and in which they became proficient during childhood and youth. (Roberts and Brodie, 1992, pp. 41–2)

With a varied repertoire of sporting interests, individuals could change sports as they moved through different life stages and experienced critical life events. Those who were limited to one sport such as football, for example, rarely continued this type of organised, vigorous contact sport through middle age and beyond. A broad activity experience during youth would seem to provide a foundation from which satisfying sporting experiences can be maintained in adulthood. However, the findings of this study were based on a limited sample (mostly participants using sports centres) and more research is needed on this issue.

SOCIO-DEMOGRAPHIC VARIABLES

Researchers continually try to match human behaviour with socio-demographic variables. Age, occupation, marital status, parenthood, car ownership and place of residence are examples of variables often studied in relation to sporting behaviour. With sufficient background data, it becomes possible to establish a profile of variables that separate sports participants from non-participants. It is also possible to correlate variables with specific sports. For example, those involved in ocean racing might be expected to come almost exclusively from wealthy backgrounds.

Assessing the relative importance of variables is extremely difficult, however, because of great variance between individuals and change over time. Thus, getting married may affect sports participation for some but not others and yet this may change in later years. The equation becomes even more complex if variables are correlated with participation in specific sports and with different levels of sport involvement. There may be certain variables that are associated with competitive swimmers – for example, young, single and student – and yet recreational swimmers may exhibit a mix of quite different variables.

An early study by Boothby and colleagues (1981) used discriminant analysis to assess the influence of social variables on sports participation. While acknowledging the limitations of the method, the authors maintained that sporting levels could be predicted by reference to social, economic and demographic variables. This study was helpful, for example, in revealing how certain variables, such as age of children, could influence a parent's participation both positively and negatively. It also suggested that 'problems of physical opportunity are secondary to those of the psychosocial sort' (Boothby *et al.*, 1981, p. 52). For example, sporting opportunities may be scarce in a particular town and yet some people will be so enthusiastic that they travel to another town to play.

Matheson (1991) analysed data from the 1987 *General Household Survey* and confirmed associations that were not unexpected. Men were more likely than women to have participated in sports, participation in sport declined as age increased, there were age differences between participants in different sports and participation was higher among non-manual than manual workers. Roberts and Brodie (1992) examined the social variables of sports participants in the Liverpool study and also found that men played more sport than women and that participation decreased as age increased. However, as far as sports centre participation was concerned, they were surprised to find that:

> Males who lived in council houses were playing slightly more sport than owner-occupiers, and the unemployed were playing more than full-time employees. (Roberts and Brodie, 1992, p. 58)

It must be remembered that the sample was drawn from sports centre users and two of the seven sports studied were soccer and snooker,

Figure 3.1 The theory of planned behaviour

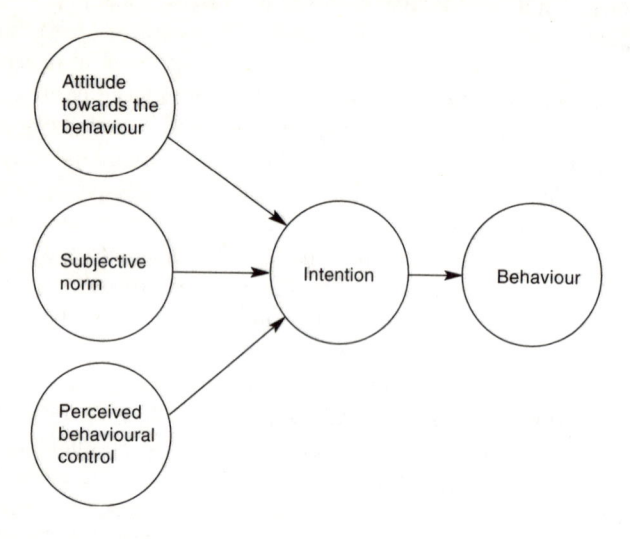

[Diagram: Three circles labeled "Attitude towards the behaviour", "Subjective norm", and "Perceived behavioural control" with arrows pointing to a circle labeled "Intention", which has an arrow pointing to a circle labeled "Behaviour".]

Source: Ajzen, 1988, p. 133.

which would presumably have affected the results. While useful in assessing sporting patterns and possibly predicting participation, it should be remembered that an analysis based on socio-demographic variables does not reveal causation in relation to sporting behaviour.

MULTIDIMENSIONAL APPROACHES

Theory of Planned Behaviour

The theory of planned behaviour (Ajzen, 1988) is a social-cognitive approach which aims to predict intention and behaviour. It has been used extensively in relation to leisure behaviour, although not specifically for sport (for example, Atsalakis and Sleap, 1996; Ajzen and Driver, 1991). Figure 3.1 illustrates how intention and behaviour can be predicted by an individual's attitude towards performing the behaviour, his or her perception of social pressure to perform or not perform the behaviour (subjective norm) and perception of how easy or difficult performance of the behaviour is likely to be (perceived behavioural control).

Figure 3.2 Interactional model of sport behaviour

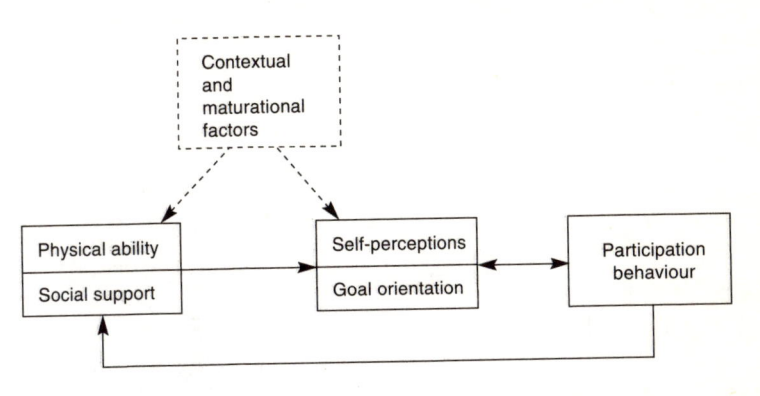

[Figure: Contextual and maturational factors influence Physical ability/Social support and Self-perceptions/Goal orientation, which lead to Participation behaviour, with reciprocal arrows.]

Source: Weiss and Glenn, 1992, p. 149.

The theory of planned behaviour is based on the notion that behaviour is dependent on beliefs held by an individual which are relevant to the behaviour. In turn, three types of belief can be distinguished:

- *behavioural beliefs* – influencing attitude toward behaviour
- *normative beliefs* – concerned with the expectations of others
- *control beliefs* – relating to ease or difficulty of performing behaviour.

Behaviour can thus be predicted by assessing the strength of beliefs with measurement instruments developed by Ajzen. This theory is clearly helpful for prediction purposes and, in the light of its success with leisure behaviour, has the potential to explain and predict sporting behaviour. However, its reliance on personal beliefs and cognitions means that other significant influences (for example, practical constraints) may be omitted.

Interactional Model of Sporting Behaviour

The multidimensional approach proposed by Weiss and Glenn is based on viewing 'the individual as an integrated whole rather than as a fragmented being' (Weiss and Glenn, 1992, p. 139). Their interactional model, illustrated in Figure 3.2, shows how sporting behaviour is influenced by biological, maturational, psychological and social factors. It suggests that the influences of physical ability and social support upon sports participation are mediated by psychological processes such as self-perceptions and goal orientations. A reciprocal relationship exists

Figure 3.3 A conceptual model of the recreational activity adoption process

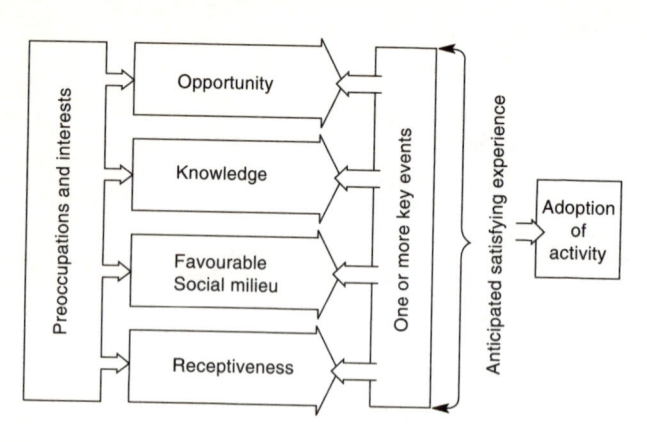

[Diagram: Preoccupations and interests → Opportunity, Knowledge, Favourable Social milieu, Receptiveness → One or more key events → Anticipated satisfying experience → Adoption of activity]

Source: Brandenburg *et al*., 1982, p. 269.

between these elements because sport experiences also influence perceptions of competence and goal perspectives. In turn, sport involvement will additionally have an effect on individual ability and the nature of social support. The interactional model of sport behaviour is clearly more sport specific than the theory of planned behaviour, and consequently, more attention is given to features such as physical ability in determining the sporting behaviour of the individual. While the theoretical basis of the interactional model appears attractive, its true value will not be known until it has been thoroughly tested.

The Recreational Activity Adoption Process

A valuable contribution to the understanding of sporting behaviour was made by a model of the recreational activity adoption process, as proposed by Brandenburg and colleagues (1982). Figure 3.3 shows the wide-ranging nature of this model, encompassing aspects such as practical opportunity as well as social-cognitive influences. Preoccupations and interests are mental ideas and feelings about activities and it is clearly logical to expect people to have an interest in a sport in which they might participate. However, there will be exceptions since individuals may have no thoughts about an activity and suddenly be given, and accept, an opportunity to take part. Also, the degree of interest in a sport may affect participation since a strong desire to take part will be needed if barriers like high costs exist.

The model shows that certain conditions need to be satisfied if an activity is to be adopted. First, opportunity needs to exist – swimming will not be possible if no pool is available – while awareness or knowledge of the activity is generally a prerequisite. A favourable social milieu, where friends or family support participation, is another important feature, as is receptiveness, a willingness to accept a new experience such as joining a sports club. However, even if these preliminary conditions exist, there is still a need for a key event to trigger adoption of an activity. For example, this may be encouragement from a friend to take part or responding to an advertisement for new members to join a sports club.

The model provides a useful insight into the adoption process, although the relative strength of each part of the model is clearly important. For example, an unfavourable social milieu may not prevent activity adoption if other parts of the model have a stronger influence – for example, many people adopt dangerous sports despite the misgivings of parents and partners! In addition, the model does not try to explain adherence or cessation of sporting activity and yet information is needed about these aspects of sporting behaviour.

Expectancy Value Model

Eccles developed a sophisticated and complicated model which attempts to analyse the motivational reasons for sporting behaviour (Eccles and Harold, 1991). The expectancy value model, shown in Figure 3.4, assumes that activities are selected from a range of choices that are influenced by numerous factors such as cultural milieu, previous experience, individual perceptions, personal goals, motivational orientation and expectations of success.

The model contains many of the factors shown in models described earlier in the chapter, although it tends to offer more detail. For example, rather than simply noting that activity choice is affected by self-perceptions, Eccles identified the importance of an individual's perceptions of socialisers' beliefs, gender roles and activity stereotypes. The model is valuable because it illustrates the interrelationship of all factors, a feature that is helpful in understanding sporting behaviour. Once again, however, the model needs to be tested, especially to establish the relative influence of the factors. For example, do previous achievement-related experiences outweigh perceptions of gender roles? It will also be necessary to find out whether the model can be widely generalised, or whether the relative importance of all the factors varies with different individuals, at different times and in different circumstances.

Figure 3.4 Eccles' expectancy value model of activity choice

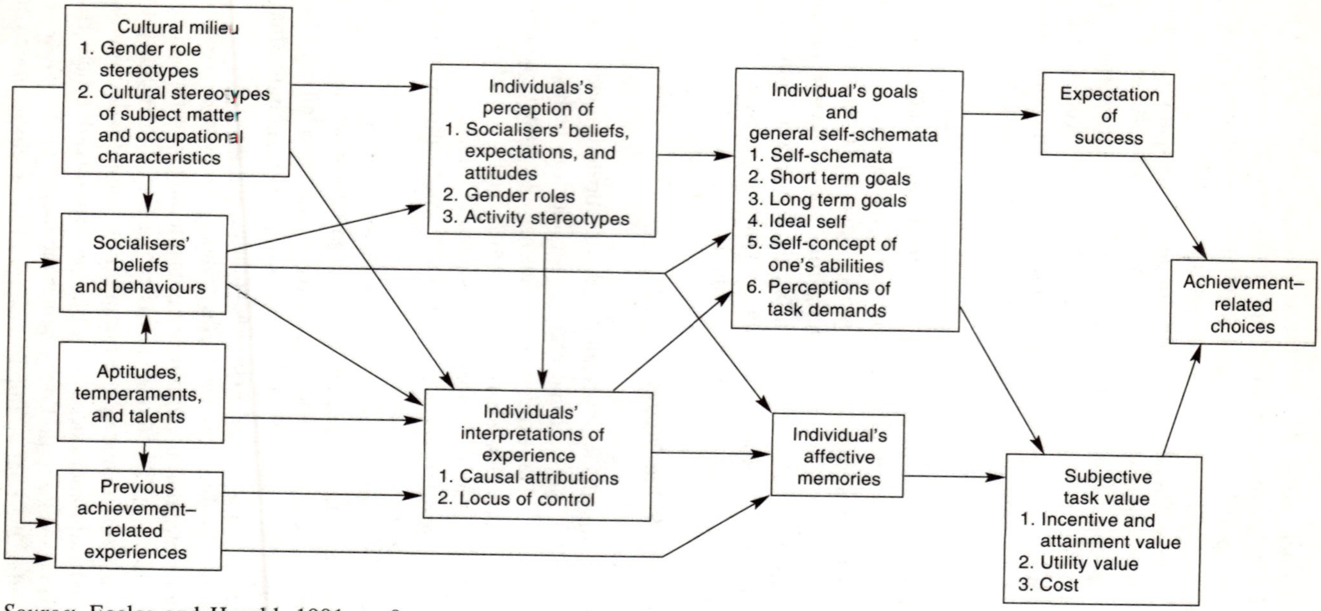

Source: Eccles and Harold, 1991, p. 9.

The ever increasing complexity of these models illustrates the advances that have been made in understanding the many determinants of sporting behaviour. The task ahead is for researchers to test these models and to look for common ground among them.

WITHDRAWAL FROM SPORT

While great attention has been focused on sports participation patterns and ways of encouraging people to take up sport, it should not be forgotten that withdrawal from sport is an important issue. This is especially significant in relation to young people, since a large proportion of them withdraw from sport in their teenage years. If Britain resembles America on this issue, it is likely that 'one-third of all participants between ten and seventeen years of age withdraw from their sport every year' (Lindner, Johns and Butcher, 1991, p. 4). The most frequently mentioned reasons for withdrawal from sport by young people have been summarised by Lindner *et al.* as follows:

'Other things to do' 'It took too much time'
'No longer fun' 'I lost interest'
'I did not get to play enough' (in team sports) 'Did not like the coach'
'Did not like the club' 'Too much pressure'
'I'm not so good as I used to be'

However, these superficial responses often hide the real reasons for dropout and it is more valuable to consider theories which have been developed on this issue.

Perceived Ability Theories

Because perceived ability is an important factor in explaining sport behaviour, its role in relation to withdrawal from sport also needs to be taken into account. If initial participation in sport does not lead to feelings of success and mastery, withdrawal may occur. Equally, if people feel that their ability level is deteriorating, perhaps due to increasing age, there may be a strong temptation to cease participation. However, this theory is not adequate on its own, since individuals with high self-perceptions of competence have been found to be among those who drop out.

Burnout Theory

Burnout refers to athletes who experience chronic stress because of excessive demands placed on them. Little research has been completed on this issue, although it has received a lot of media coverage and has apparently led to withdrawal by high profile stars such as the tennis players Tracy Austen and Andrea Jaeger. This theory mostly relates to élite performers and is not likely to be a major reason for withdrawal from sport among recreational players.

Developmental Theories

This group of theories are concerned with the cognitive, physical, social and psychological changes that occur during life. A youngster may see non-sporting activities as increasingly attractive, while finding the regimen associated with sports participation as increasingly unattractive. School, work and family commitments also increase in significance and have to be balanced with sporting involvement. The extensive work of Hendry (1978, 1983) revealed the many subcultural influences that affect adolescent sports participation, often leading to disaffection with the sporting experience.

Lindner, Johns and Butcher (1991) believed that developmental theories held the most promise in explaining withdrawal from sport, suggesting that alternative activities became important as the needs of the individual matured. They noted that many dropouts had enjoyed their sport experience and thus concluded that it was not necessarily that sport had 'faults', but that other attractions had greater 'strengths'. The *Allied Dunbar National Fitness Survey* (Sports Council and Health Education Authority, 1992) corroborated this, reporting that it was competing pressures, such as career development, finding a partner, getting married, raising a family and setting up home, that interfered with sports participation.

An interesting analysis by Kay and Jackson (1991) of constraints on leisure participation is relevant to sports participation. Many people in their study participated in activities, despite experiencing constraints. In other words, although constraints may exist, they can be overcome and participation can be maintained. Further research is necessary to explore the interrelationship between desire to take part in sport and the strength of the constraint needed to prevent participation occurring.

PROMOTING SPORTS PARTICIPATION

The personal and social benefits of sports participation are wide ranging. However, during the second half of the twentieth century, the sedentary nature of the British population has increased and the potential health benefits of sports participation have been realised. This has led to widespread promotion of 'sport for all' among the general population. The Sports Council introduced promotional campaigns during the 1970s and 1980s that targeted specific groups. These included:

- disabled – *Sport for All Disabled People*
- young people – *Ever Thought of Sport?*
- over-50s – *50+ All To Play For*
- women – Wales, Scotland, N. Ireland only
- people in deprived urban areas – *Action Sport*.

In 1982 the Sports Council identified additional target groups in its Ten-Year Plan (Sports Council, 1982). These included ethnic minorities, parents with young children (especially mothers) and low income households, including the unemployed. In 1985 an evaluation of the Sport For All campaign concluded that, although the amount of sports participation had risen, 'the patterns of participation and non-participation had remained obstinately unchanged' (McIntosh and Charlton, 1985, p. 190). It was also suggested that Sport For All had not reduced coronary heart disease, vandalism or urban boredom. Although the limitations of early campaigns are now recognised, it would be naive to expect them to have impacted significantly on deep-rooted social and health problems, especially after only a relatively short period of time. In the 1990s the Sports Council has maintained its promotion of both élite sport and mass participation and has also been involved in allocating funding for sport from the national lottery. In addition, a major emphasis has been put on the development of sport among young people, embodied in a National Junior Sports Programme.

Most attempts to promote sport have employed educational or general media approaches and, while they have raised awareness, they have not been as successful as might have been hoped. Exercise promotion is now much more soundly based, utilising learning theory, communication theory and social marketing theory (Killoran, Fentem and Caspersen, 1994), and sports promotion is starting to follow suit. For example, theoretical perspectives are beginning to be utilised in promoting lifetime sports participation among young people. Duda (1994) has drawn upon the goal perspective theory of motivation to illustrate how youth can be encouraged to continue engagement in sport. One outcome of this approach is recognition that emphasis upon task-oriented goals (for example, working with, rather than always trying to outdo, others) rather than ego-oriented goals (for example, constant and overt evaluation and comparison among youngsters) is more likely to lead to participation adherence in sport.

Health promotion has long been attempting to convert people to healthier ways and one of the most important developments has been recognition that individuals adopting a new behaviour move through a series of stages of change. Prochaska and Marcus (1994) applied their transtheoretical model of behaviour change to involvement in physical exercise and indicated that, to be effective, intervention needs to match the stages of change:

- *resistance* – no exercise and no intention to begin exercise
- *recruitment* – no exercise but intention to begin exercise
- *retention* – occasional participation in exercise
- *relapse* – cessation of exercise
- *recovery* – recommencement of exercise.

While most studies employing the stages of change model have focused on exercise, it seems reasonable to expect that it would have equal validity for sporting behaviour and, consequently, should be taken into consideration in sports promotion.

Wankel and Hills (1994) proposed that a marketing approach might be combined with the transtheoretical model of behaviour change to increase physical activity involvement. Marketing principles such as product analysis, availability of product, pricing and promotion are combined with the target group's stage of change to ensure physical activity is attractive to potential participants. This approach has a logical appeal to it and studies are eagerly awaited which evaluate its effectiveness. Thus, it would seem that, with increased theoretical underpinning, future sports promotion will perhaps be more successful in encouraging people to be actively engaged in sport on a long term basis.

REFERENCES

Ajzen, I., *Attitudes, Personality, and Behavior* (Milton Keynes: Open University Press, 1988).

Ajzen, I. and Driver, B.L., 'Prediction of Leisure Participation from Behavioral,

Normative, and Control Beliefs: An Application of the Theory of Planned Behaviour', *Leisure Sciences*, 13 (1991), pp. 185–204.

Allen, L.R., 'The Relationship between Murray's Personality Needs and Leisure Interests', *Journal of Leisure Research*, 14 (1982), pp. 63–76.

Atsalakis, M. and Sleap, M., 'Registration of Children in a Physical Activity Program: An Application of the Theory of Planned Behaviour', *Pediatric Exercise Science*, 8 (1996), pp. 166–76.

Bandura, A. *Social Foundations of Thought and Action* (Englewood Cliffs: Prentice Hall, 1986).

Barnett, M.S. and Wright, P., 'Psychological Considerations for Women in Sports', *Clinics in Sports Medicine*, 13 (1994), pp. 297–313.

Boothby, J., Tungatt, M., Townsend, A.R. and Collins, M.F., *A Sporting Chance?* (London: Sports Council, 1981).

Brandenburg, J., Greiner, W., Hamilton-Smith, E., Scholten, H., Senior, R. and Webb, J., 'A Conceptual Model of How People Adopt Recreational Activities', *Leisure Studies*, 1 (1982), pp. 263–76.

Duda, J.L., 'Fostering Active Living for Children and Youth: The Motivational Significance of Goal Orientations in Sport'. In H.A. Quinney, L. Gauvin and A.E. Ted Wall (eds), *Toward Active Living* (Champaign: Human Kinetics, 1994), pp. 123–7.

Eccles, J.S. and Harold, R.D., 'Gender Differences in Sport Involvement: Applying the Eccles Expectancy–value Model', *Journal of Applied Sport Psychology*, 3 (1991), pp. 36–48.

Harter, S., 'Effectance Motivation Reconsidered: Toward a Developmental Model', *Human Development*, 21 (1978), pp. 34–64.

Hendry, L.B., *School, Sport and Leisure* (London: Lepus, 1978).

Hendry, L.B., *Growing Up and Going Out: Adolescents and Leisure* (Aberdeen: Aberdeen University Press, 1983).

Kay, T. and Jackson, G., 'Leisure Despite Constraints: The Impact of Leisure Constraints on Leisure Participation', *Journal of Leisure Research*, 23 (1991), pp. 301–13.

Kelly, J.R., 'Leisure Socialization: Replication and Extension', *Journal of Leisure Research*, 9 (1977), pp. 121–32.

Killoran, A.J., Fentem, P. and Caspersen, C. (eds), *Moving On: International Perspectives on Promoting Physical Activity* (London: Health Education Authority, 1994).

Lindner, K.J., Johns, D.P. and Butcher, J., 'Factors in Withdrawal from Youth Sport: A Proposed Model', *Journal of Sport Behaviour*, 14 (1991), pp. 3–18.

McIntosh, P. and Charlton, V., *The Impact of Sport For All Policy* (London: Sports Council, 1985).

McPherson, B.D., Curtis, J.E. and Loy, J.W., *The Social Significance of Sport* (Champaign: Human Kinetics, 1989).

Matheson, J., *Participation in Sport: General Household Survey 1987* (London: HMSO, 1991).

Prochaska, J.O. and Marcus, B.H., 'The Transtheoretical Model: Applications to Exercise'. In R.K, Dishman (ed.), *Advances in Exercise Adherence* (Champaign: Human Kinetics, 1994), pp. 161–80.

Roberts, K. and Brodie, D.A., *Inner-city Sport: Who Plays, and What are the Benefits?* (Voorthuizen: Giordano Bruno Culemborg, 1992).

Sports Council, *Sport in the Community: The Next Ten Years* (London: Sports Council, 1982).

Sports Council and Health Education Authority, *Allied Dunbar National Fitness Survey* (London: Sports Council and Health Education Authority, 1992).

Tinsley, H.E.A., Barrett, T.C. and Kass, R.A., 'Leisure Activities and Need Satisfaction', *Journal of Leisure Research*, 9 (1977), pp. 110–20.

Wankel, L.M. and Hills, C., 'A Social Marketing and Stage of Change Perspective of Interventions to Enhance Physical Activity: The Importance of PRs'. In H.A. Quinney, L. Gauvin and A.E. Ted Wall (eds), *Toward Active Living* (Champaign: Human Kinetics, 1994), pp. 115–22.

Weiss, M.R. and Glenn, S.D., 'Psychological Development and Females' Sport Participation: An Interactional Perspective', *Quest*, 44 (1992), pp. 138–57.

Yoesting, D.R. and Burkhead, D.L., 'Significance of Childhood Recreation Experience on Adult Behaviour', *Journal of Leisure Research*, 5 (1973), pp. 25–36.

FURTHER READING

The work of Ajzen, Duda, Eccles, Harter, Prochaska and Weiss (cited above) needs to be studied in greater detail.

Explanations of exercise behaviour can be found in Killoran (cited above). See also:

Dishman, R.K., 'Determinants of Participation in Physical Activity'. In C. Bouchard, R.J. Shephard, T. Stephens, J.R. Sutton and B.D. McPherson (eds), *Exercise, Fitness and Health: A Consensus of Current Knowledge* (Champaign: Human Kinetics, 1990), pp. 75–101.

4 Sport and Health

DIMENSIONS OF HEALTH

This chapter is concerned with the role played by sport in the maintenance of health. Initially, consideration is given to research which has investigated the connection between physical activity and various parameters of health. The main part of the chapter then reviews surveys that have examined the health benefits of sports participation. Finally, the harmful effects of sports participation are discussed. It should be emphasised that, where possible, the focus will be on the role of 'sport' rather than exercise, or other physical activities undertaken during work and everyday chores.

There is an increased desire among the general population nowadays to lead healthier lifestyles and people are interested in the potential benefits of being fit. In the past, health was generally viewed as an absence of illness and disease, and yet, in more recent times, it has also come to encompass a feeling of physical, social and emotional well-being. In this chapter, attention will be focused on perceptions of health and functional capacity as well as an absence of illness and disease.

It is now recognised that many health problems in contemporary society are related to sedentary lifestyles. Inactivity has been linked with coronary artery disease, some cancers, stroke, non-insulin dependent diabetes mellitus, overweight, osteoporosis and other health problems (Montoye, 1992). As a consequence, a considerable amount of research has investigated correlations between involvement, or lack of involvement, in physical activity and the type and extent of health problems. Chapter 2 showed that the general population was relatively inactive and therefore at risk of suffering these health problems.

A recent consensus statement (International Scientific Consensus Conference, 1995) has comprehensively outlined the beneficial effects of regular physical activity on atherosclerotic diseases, musculoskeletal health, cancer and immune function, psychosocial health and well-being at different life stages. The Health Education Authority provided a summary of the health benefits of regular exercise, as shown in Table 4.1. It is perhaps reasonable to expect similar health benefits from regular participation in active and energetic sports.

Table 4.1 Health benefits of exercise

Lower all-cause mortality
Reduced risk of heart disease
Reduced mortality after heart attack
Reduced risk of heart attack among the obese
Lowering of high blood pressure
Possible reduced risk of stroke
Lower mortality from colon cancer
Lower incidence of non-insulin dependent diabetes
Better control of non-insulin dependent diabetes
Contributes to weight control
Reduced risk of osteoporosis
Reduced mild anxiety and depression
Improved muscle strength and flexibility among the elderly
Slows age-related deterioration in aerobic fitness
Improved memory among the elderly
Improved self-esteem and confidence among the elderly

Source: Adapted from Health Education Authority, 1995, p. 7.

In addition to objective health and fitness measurements, socio-psychological components also need to be considered. Sports participation may help an individual to feel good, whereas a sedentary lifestyle, although not necessarily producing illness, could leave the individual feeling low and 'under the weather'. Sport can be a means of self-realisation, providing rewards and satisfactions that contribute to enjoyment of life and personal well-being. Unfortunately, these health benefits cannot easily be defined or measured and therefore their validity is open to question.

It has been found that exercise can be useful in counteracting mild to moderate depression and, when combined with other forms of professional treatment, can help to alleviate severe depression. There also seems to be a role for regular physical activity of a rhythmic nature in reducing anxiety (Health Education Authority, 1995). Steptoe and Butler (1996) found that participation in sport and vigorous recreational activity was positively associated with emotional well-being among adolescents. In a review of the relationship between sport, exercise and psycho-social health, Biddle (1995) concluded that exercise offered moderate beneficial effects for depression, and led to improvements on indices of anxiety, mood, self-esteem and other indices of psychological well-being. The question arises as to whether beneficial effects arise from the body's response to participation in physical activity or from other factors. For example, depression may well be eased by the social nature of an exercise class or sporting occasion rather than the physiological changes caused by physical activity.

Most of the above findings have focused on the effects of exercise on health rather than drawing from subjects taking part in sport. However, it would again seem reasonable to expect these benefits to occur as a result of involvement in active and energetic sports.

Level of Physical Activity Needed to Promote Health

Until recently it has been thought that regular and sustained vigorous exercise was necessary to maintain optimum health. It was recommended that people should take part in three 20-minute sessions of vigorous physical activity per week. Regular participation in many forms of sport fulfilled this recommendation and there developed an association between taking part in sport and staying healthy. Two issues have emerged in relation to this. First, the three times 20-minute vigorous activity recommendation was mainly conceived as a measure to prevent heart disease, and therefore other forms of physical activity which could prove beneficial to health tended to get overlooked. Second, for a variety of reasons, only a small percentage of the population adopted the recommended activity levels.

As a result of increased knowledge about the relationship between physical activity and health, a new set of recommendations have been proposed for England:

- 30 minutes of moderate intensity physical activity, such as a sustained brisk walk, on at least five days of the week.
- One 30-minute period of sustained activity is best, but two bouts of 15 minutes are also beneficial.
- Moderate intensity physical activities raise the heart rate to leave you warm and slightly out of breath, such as brisk walking, climbing stairs, swimming, social dancing, exercises and heavy household activities (adapted from Killoran, Fentem and Caspersen, 1994, p. 215).

These recommendations encompass a broad range of everyday activities and also mean that participants in less vigorous sports like golf and sailing could fulfil the criteria. However, sports like snooker and darts do not provide the activity levels needed to achieve the above mentioned health benefits.

Whereas, in the past, promotional campaigns have given sports participation a highly prominent position as a means of achieving physical activity objectives, the emphasis has now moved to everyday activities which can contribute to an active lifestyle (Health Education Authority, 1996). Nevertheless, the Health Education Authority (1995, p. 5) stated that 'for health-related benefits, aerobic exercise should be the focus of attention' and therefore sports involving aerobic exercise are clearly important in this context.

Activity Levels in Different Sports

There are four main aspects of physical activity that need to be taken into account when considering the relationship between sport and health.

1 Frequency of Participation
Health benefits will accrue only if individuals engage in physical activity regularly, and this principle will apply whichever sport is involved. Thus, a 30-minute game of tennis played every few days will be more beneficial than a game played only once a month.

2 Type of Physical Activity
Some sports like swimming involve the whole body, while others like archery only involve parts of the body. It is known that whole body movement is likely to be most valuable for general health benefits and to decrease the risk of atherosclerotic diseases. However, specific advantages, such as improvement in bone density and development of shoulder strength, can be gained from sports like archery.

3 Duration of Physical Activity
It would seem that sports involving sustained activity for 30 minutes or longer are ideal, while those requiring shorter bouts are still valuable. In fact, research indicates that the accumulation of short bursts of activity may promote health in the same way (Debusk *et al.*, 1990).

4 Level of Intensity of Physical Activity
Sports such as squash require vigorous activity, some like golf involve low levels of activity, while others like fishing need almost no physical activity at all. Energy expenditure for different sports was calculated for the *Allied Dunbar National Fitness Survey* (Sports Council and Health Education Authority, 1992) and is shown in Table 4.2. The energy cost will depend upon the amount of effort expended by an individual and therefore a high and low cost score was provided. For example, there is a considerable difference between swimming continuous lengths in a pool and paddling around on holiday.

Table 4.2 Energy expenditure in different sports

Sport	Energy cost score (kcal/min.)	
	High	Low
Squash, jogging/running	13	8
Football, weight training	10	6
Swimming, tennis, aerobics, Badminton, keep fit	8	5
Cricket, exercises	6	4
Table-tennis, golf	5	3
Bowls, fishing, Ten-pin bowling	3	3
Snooker, darts	2	2

Source: Adapted from Sports Council and Health Education Authority, 1992, p. 13.

Dose–Response Relationship between Physical Activity and Health

Although research evidence is limited, it appears that most health parameters are related to the amount and intensity of physical activity undertaken within an individual's lifestyle. This is known as the dose–response relationship and it is an important consideration, since sports participation can vary greatly in terms of the amount and intensity of physical activity involved. In his review of the issue, Pate (1995) indicated that specific health outcomes such as cardiorespiratory fitness, chronic disease risk factors, morbidity from chronic diseases and all-cause mortality were related in different ways to the dose–response relationship between physical activity and health. For example, an increase in physical activity in an individual's lifestyle has been associated with a lower risk of all-cause mortality.

Sports which fulfil the physical activity recommendations described earlier will clearly contribute towards optimum health and help to prevent chronic diseases. No studies have examined the specific health benefits accruing from different sports, although it is possible to speculate on the issue. For example, the body parts involved in a particular sport could contribute towards mobility of those body parts in old age. All sports probably have the potential to contribute towards psychological well-being, since even an inactive sport such as fishing may help to alleviate stress and thus provide a useful health benefit. It is anticipated that future research findings could illustrate specific health benefits of levels of participation in different sports.

SURVEYS INVESTIGATING THE RELATIONSHIP BETWEEN SPORTS PARTICIPATION AND HEALTH

Physiological evidence and epidemiological studies have comprehensively established the health value of an active lifestyle. However, active lifestyles can be made up of occupational physical activity, everyday chores and recreational exercising, as well as sports participation. The small number of studies that have isolated the independent influence of sports participation upon health status will be considered here.

University rowers were some of the first sports participants to be studied and early findings suggested that former athletes lived longer than non-athletes, although the comparison of university rowers, a highly select group, with the general population undermined the credibility of the results. According to Montoye, recent studies with sound methodology have 'revealed no important difference in life expectancy of former college athletes compared to their classmates' (1992, p. 76). This is not necessarily surprising since most physiological effects of sports participation are lost within a few days and former college athletes may have been less active than their non-athlete counterparts in later life.

The importance of physical activity in later life was demonstrated by a study in which former Harvard University athletes and their classmates were compared (Paffenbarger, Wing and Hyde, 1987). Figure 4.1 shows that, in relation to prevention of first heart attack, involvement in lifetime activity was more important than sporting experiences at university.

The above studies are limited to a small, select group of college sportsmen who have often only participated competitively in the early part of their lives. Non-athletic counterparts may have taken part in sport at school and in intermural sport. The varying activity demands of different sports may also have been significant, since the physiological demands of a football player will contrast with those of a competitor in an athletic field event. Present knowledge regarding the health benefits of an active lifestyle reinforce the notion that, if sport and other physical activities are given up during youth, early experiences will contribute little, if at all, to health status in later life.

Figure 4.1 Comparison of former Harvard University athletes and their classmates in incidence of first heart attack

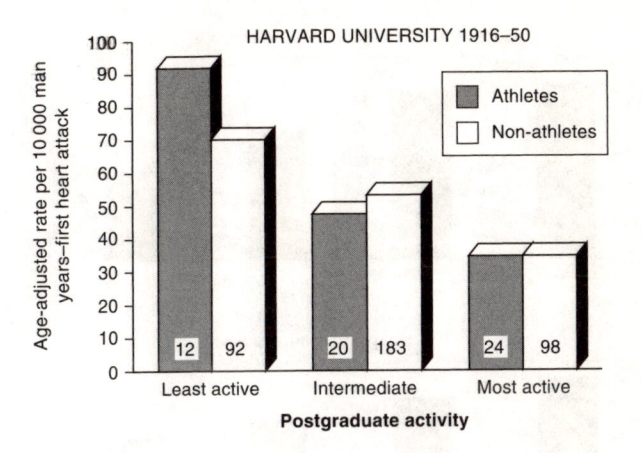

HARVARD UNIVERSITY 1916–50

[Bar chart: Age-adjusted rate per 10 000 man years–first heart attack, by Postgraduate activity]

- Least active: Athletes 12, Non-athletes 92
- Intermediate: Athletes 20, Non-athletes 183
- Most active: Athletes 24, Non-athletes 98

Source: Paffenbarger, Wing and Hyde, 1987, p. 77.

General Household Survey and Health and Lifestyle Survey

Gratton and Tice (1989) undertook an analysis of data from the 1980 *General Household Survey* and the *Health and Lifestyle Survey* to explore the relationship between sports participation and health. Although these surveys investigated a wide range of leisure activities, Gratton and Tice focused on active sport, omitting physically passive activities such as darts, billiards and snooker. Additionally, they incorporated data on frequency of participation and estimated energy expenditure according to the activity demands of the sports played.

Figure 4.2 shows that, at all ages and in all income groups, sports participants rated their health higher than non-participants, while it is also revealing to see that non-participants missed substantially more work than sports participants. Gratton and Tice also found a positive correlation between frequency of participation in strenuous sports and belief about being in good health, as shown in Table 4.3.

Sports participants were also less likely to suffer from chronic and short term illnesses than non-participants and, after the age of 40 years, fared much better on a whole range of health indicators. In addition, sports participants were less likely to smoke than non-participants, but curiously, although they believed that drinking damaged health, they

Figure 4.2 Sports participation in relation to health rating and absence from work

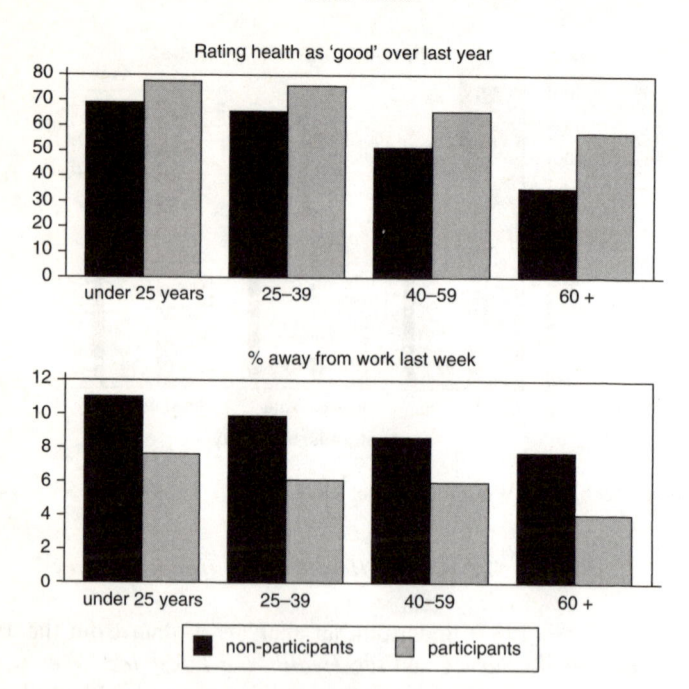

Source: Gratton and Tice, 1989, pp. 80–1.

were more likely to be moderate or heavy alcohol drinkers than non-participants. Gratton and Tice (1989, p. 92) concluded that:

> participation in sport not only makes the participant healthier, but also provides an enriched quality of life by stimulating participation in a whole range of non-sport leisure activities.

This is one of the few studies that has considered the relationship between sports participation and health, but the findings need to be treated with caution since the data were taken from general surveys that did not aim to study this particular issue. There are many ways of assessing health and, while personal ratings and absence from work are useful indicators, they can also be misleading; there can be many reasons other than poor health for absence from work. The authors themselves acknowledged that the cross-sectional nature of the data limited the analysis. For example, many people who take part in competitive

Table 4.3 Level of participation and belief about being in good health: health on the whole over last year

	No participation	Low participation	Medium participation	High participation
Males % in good health	56	69	75	78
Females % in good health	48	65	69	71

Source: Gratton and Tice, 1989, p. 86.

sport tend to be mesomorphic in physique (slim with broad shoulders) and it has been suggested that this could give a natural resistance to some health problems (Montoye, 1992).

The Liverpool Study

The most extensive study on this issue in Britain was conducted by Brodie, Roberts and Lamb (1991) at the University of Liverpool. It involved more than 4000 adults and focused on the seven sports of swimming, keep fit, martial arts, indoor bowls, badminton, five-a-side football and snooker. The research methodology included a questionnaire survey, home-based interviews and a comprehensive health-related fitness assessment. Respondents were allocated participation scores according to number of sports played and frequency of participation. In addition to questions about sports participation, the authors tried to collect information about personal circumstances and everyday lifestyles that could have a bearing on health. In all, 32 indicators of health were incorporated, although analysis showed that most indicators were not discrete, but part contributors of broad, underlying health states.

Thus, four main factors were identified:

- *strength* – grip strength and lung function
- *cardiovascular* – blood pressure and pulse rate
- *self-assessment* – attitudes and feelings about health
- *illness-free* – doctor's visits and use of medicines.

Health-related Fitness Assessment
Three hundred and seventy-one adults were assessed on measurements of blood pressure, resting pulse rate, body mass index, lung function and flexibility. Highly active sports participants had superior lung function,

Figure 4.3 Sports participation and cholesterol levels

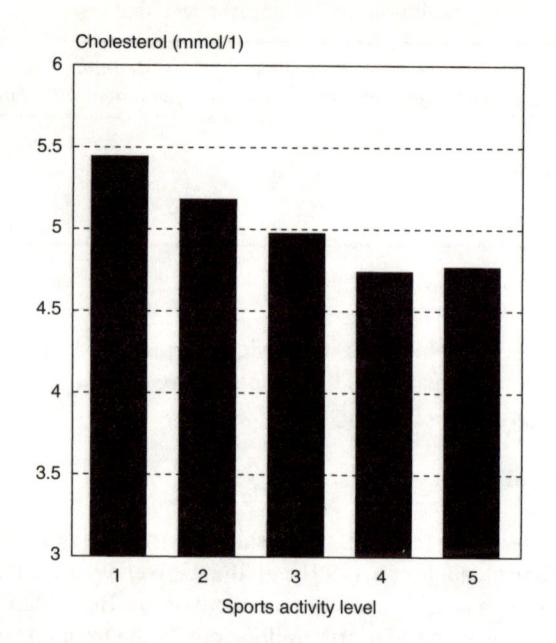

Source: Brodie, Roberts and Lamb, 1991, p. 100.

lower resting pulses, increased flexibility and greater strength than less active participants. Sports participants were also compared with members of the general public, as assessed in the *Health and Lifestyle Survey* (Cox et al., 1987). Sports participants had more favourable blood pressures, pulse rates and body mass indexes than the general population (Lamb et al., 1991). The differences might have been greater but for the fact that there were undoubtedly people who were physically active in the *Health and Lifestyle Survey* and people who were minimally active (for example, snooker players) among the Liverpool sample.

Coronary Risk

Coronary risk was assessed according to body mass index, systolic blood pressure, diastolic blood pressure, gender, smoking behaviour and family history of heart disease. Coronary risk was found to be generally low among sports participants, with 90 per cent of males and 96 per cent of females within the 'low' and 'moderate' risk categories. Although the role of cholesterol levels in coronary heart disease is not totally clear, it is assumed that higher cholesterol levels increase coronary risk. Figure 4.3 shows that the more active sports participants generally exhibited lower cholesterol levels than less active participants.

Despite the above findings, a clear pattern did not emerge in terms of higher sports participation scores being associated with higher cardiovascular scores (that is, with less coronary risk). It appears that other health-related behaviours, such as diet, tended to confound the issue.

Health Scores
Sports participants were allocated a 'health score' based upon perceptions of their own health, their fitness, sleep patterns, doctor's visits, height, weight and medicines taken. Interestingly, participants in the martial arts had higher health scores than participants in other sports, although it can be seen in Figure 4.4 that most participants had relatively high scores.

Participants in the less physically demanding sports of bowls and snooker recorded lower health scores, but the older average age of bowlers and higher proportion of manual workers among snooker players may have confounded the results.

Perceived Health
Most health statistics are formulated from objective measures such as hospital admissions or incidence of disease and, as a consequence, personal feelings about health are not usually recorded. Thus, it is interesting to note that over 80 per cent of sports participants considered their health to be either 'good' or 'excellent' and perceptions improved with age. Thirty-three per cent of participants over 34 years of age rated their health as excellent, compared with 22 per cent of participants under 25 years of age (Lamb, Roberts and Brodie, 1990). Health perceptions were also higher among sports participants than among those of the general population, as surveyed in the *Health and Lifestyle Survey* (Cox *et al.*, 1987).

Sport Careers
The study investigated the sport careers of the sample to explore whether a lifetime of sport offered particular health benefits. The indications were that current participation was an important factor in current health status and, as noted earlier in the chapter, previous sporting activity did not confer lasting health benefits. These findings were quite tentative, however, since the sample contained relatively few non-participants.

Figure 4.4 Sports participation and health score

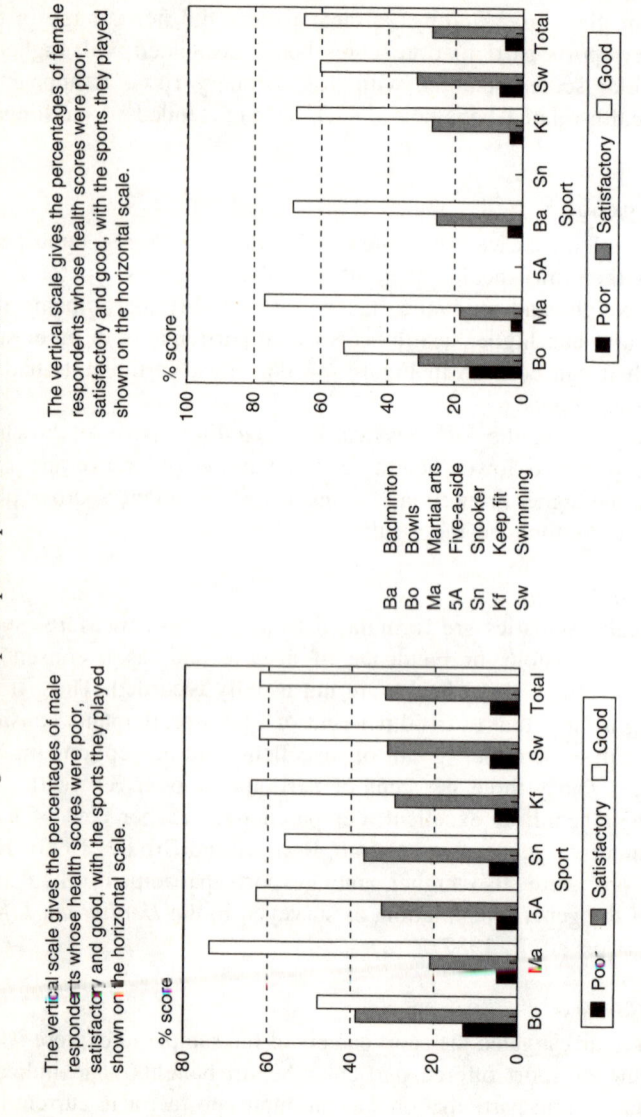

The vertical scale gives the percentages of male respondents whose health scores were poor, satisfactory and good, with the sports they played shown on the horizontal scale.

The vertical scale gives the percentages of female respondents whose health scores were poor, satisfactory and good, with the sports they played shown on the horizontal scale.

Ba	Badminton
Bo	Bowls
Ma	Martial arts
5A	Five-a-side
Sn	Snooker
Kf	Keep fit
Sw	Swimming

Source: Brodie, Roberts and Lamb, 1991, p. 37.

Sports Injuries
Nineteen per cent of sports participants in the Liverpool study suffered sports injuries and almost half of these lasted for longer than one month. Injuries varied considerably between sports, ranging from 38 per cent of participants in martial arts to 3 per cent of bowls players. However, a sports injury is a specific loss of health which is relatively minor in comparison with chronic illness and generally does not last for more than a few months at most.

Conclusions about the Liverpool Study

The Liverpool study demonstrated a positive correlation between sports participation and health, which held constant when analysed in terms of sex, age and socio-economic status. Because the study was mainly of a cross-sectional nature, it is not possible to say whether sport caused good health, since it may be that healthier people were more likely to take part in sport. It is also the case that the study did not include outdoor sports, although the sports in the study involved a range of physical activity demands – from keep fit to snooker – and a similar picture is likely to have emerged if outdoor sports had been included.

The findings demonstrated a relationship between energetic sports activity and health benefits and yet it did not show benefits on all health indicators. For example, playing sport did not reduce the need for medical care since participants were presumably still vulnerable to infections and illnesses. An additional twelve-month longitudinal analysis also produced equivocal results in respect of the effects of sporting activity on health indicators. The authors concluded that other lifestyle factors, such as diet, smoking and alcohol consumption, interfered with the relationship between sports participation and health. In other words, the health status of a regular sports participant could have been adversely affected by smoking or a poor diet.

The Liverpool sample was heavily biased in favour of frequent sports participants and the relatively small number of non-participants may not have been representative of the general population. Nevertheless, this study offers a strong indication that sports participation contributes to health, concurring with other surveys showing the health benefits of an active lifestyle. Further research is needed, in the form of longitudinal studies, to corroborate these findings and to examine whether particular sports are more beneficial than others and whether there are differences in respect of benefits to males and females.

HARMFUL EFFECTS OF SPORTS PARTICIPATION

The harmful effects of gruelling exercise date back to 490BC when Pheidippides is believed to have died after having run 22 miles from Marathon to Athens to announce an Athenian victory against opposing forces. Nowadays, widespread media coverage of injuries to high profile élite athletes suggests that sports participation is particularly hazardous, although the danger to the average sports participant is not so dramatic. Nevertheless, in England and Wales 19 million injuries occur during sport and exercise each year, although only 5 million necessitate treatment (Health Education Authority, 1995). Highest death rates and most serious injuries occur in air sports, water sports, climbing and motor racing, while the risk of serious injury is extremely low for all other sports and can be reduced even further by the use of appropriate clothing and equipment. The incidence of heart attack and sudden death during or following strenuous exercise is rare and mostly limited to normally sedentary individuals:

> Sedentary individuals were found to be at 30 times greater risk of suffering a primary cardiac arrest during unaccustomed vigorous exertion than frequently active subjects. (Sports Council and Health Education Authority, 1992, p. 34)

Heart problems seem to occur if individuals who have underlying heart disease subject the body to a sudden intolerable burden. Many competitors also seem to ignore the body's warning signs and continue participating until a serious incident occurs.

'Wear and tear' on musculo-skeletal function is not a problem for the vast majority of recreational sports enthusiasts, but adverse effects may be experienced by élite competitive performers. For example, athletes involved in strenuous exercise seem to suffer from accelerated development of osteoarthritis. In addition, it is estimated by the Health Education Authority (1995) that up to 50 per cent of high level female runners, cyclists and rowers suffer from amenorrhoea (cessation of periods). For all sports participants, injury is most likely if an activity is not built up gradually, if minor problems are ignored and if people run in poor quality shoes or on hazardous surfaces.

The harmful effects of sports can be regarded in a different way, however. Part of the reason for a sedentary adult population is the negative perception that many people have about taking part in sport and exercise (Wankel, 1988), perhaps because it has been embarrassing, or painful, or because it put them in a failure situation. If this leads to the abandonment of all forms of physical activity, they become long term sedentary adults who run the risk of suffering from the health problems cited earlier.

It would appear that a true assessment of the harmful effects of sports participation is not possible at the present time. Koplan, Siscovich and Goldbaum (1985) highlighted problems which have not yet been addressed, showing that existing studies lacked rigour – there was lack of controls, selection bias and looseness of definition. For example, although injury figures are available for cyclists, it is not known whether the injuries occurred when cycling for transportation reasons or whether they happened in a sporting context!

CONCLUSIONS

The beneficial effects of regular exercise on health are now well documented and the indications are that sports participation plays a similar, positive role in maintaining health. However, there is a pressing need to isolate the independent effect of sport, since it has mostly been mixed up with the exercise literature. Does sport provide health benefits over and above those gained from the body's responses to participation in physical activity: for example, in terms of psychological advantages? While the harmful effects of sports participation cannot be ignored, it would seem that most problems are short term and relatively minor, and many injuries could be avoided if appropriate safety measures were taken.

REFERENCES

Biddle, S., 'Exercise and Psychosocial Health', *Research Quarterly for Exercise and Sport*, 66 (1995), pp. 292–7.

Brodie, D., Roberts, K. and Lamb, K., *Citysport Challenge* (Cambridge: Health Promotion Research Trust, 1991).

Cox, B.D. et al., *The Health and Lifestyle Survey* (Cambridge: Health Promotion Research Trust, 1987).

Debusk, R.F., Stenestrand, U., Sheehan, M. and Haskell, W.L., 'Training Effects of Long Versus Short Bouts of Exercise in Healthy Subjects', *American Journal of Cardiology*, 65 (1990), pp. 1010–13.

Gratton, C. and Tice, A., 'Sports Participation and Health', *Leisure Studies*, 8 (1989), pp. 77–92.

Health Education Authority, *Health Update 5: Physical Activity* (London: Health Education Authority, 1995).

Health Education Authority, *Active For Life Newsletter* (London: Health Education Authority, 1996).

International Scientific Consensus Conference, 'Consensus Statement', *Research Quarterly for Exercise and Sport*, 66 (1995), pp. v–viii.

Killoran, A.J., Fentem, P. and Caspersen, C. (eds), *Moving On: International Perspectives on Promoting Physical Activity* (London: Health Education Authority, 1994).

Koplan, J.P., Siscovick, D.S. and Goldbaum, G.M., 'The Risks of Exercise: A Public Health View of Injuries and Hazards', *Public Health Reports*, 100 (1985), pp. 189–95.

Lamb, K.L., Brodie, D.A., Minten, J.H. and Roberts, K., 'A Comparison of Selected Health-related Data from Surveys of a General Population and a Sporting Population', *Social Science and Medicine*, 33 (1991), pp. 835–9.

Lamb, K.L., Roberts, K. and Brodie, D.A., 'Self-perceived Health among Sports Participants and Non-sports Participants', *Social Science and Medicine*, 31 (1990), pp. 963–9.

Montoye, H.J., 'The Raymond Pearl Memorial Lecture, 1991: Health, Exercise, and Athletics: A Millennium of Observations – A Century of Research', *American Journal of Human Biology*, 4 (1992), pp. 69–82.

Paffenbarger, R.S., Wing, A.L. and Hyde, R.T., 'Physical Activity as an Index of Heart Attack Risk in College Alumni', *American Journal of Epidemiology*, 108 (1987), pp. 161–75.

Pate, R.R., 'Physical Activity and Health: Dose–Response Issues', *Research Quarterly for Exercise and Sport*, 66 (1995), pp. 313–17.

Sports Council and Health Education Authority, *Allied Dunbar National Fitness Survey* (London: Sports Council and Health Education Authority, 1992).

Steptoe, A. and Butler, N., 'Sports Participation and Emotional Wellbeing in Adolescents', *The Lancet*, 347 (1996), pp. 1789–92.

Wankel, L.M., 'Exercise Adherence and Leisure Activity: Patterns of Involvement and Interventions to Facilitate Regular Activity'. In R.K. Dishman (ed.), *Exercise Adherence: Its Impact on Public Health* (Champaign: Human Kinetics, 1988), pp. 369–96.

FURTHER READING

For exercise and health:

Bouchard, C. *et al*, (eds), *Physical Activity, Fitness and Health: International Proceedings and Consensus Statement 1992* (Champaign: Human Kinetics, 1994). Also, many articles in *Research Quarterly for Exercise and Health*, and a useful review in Killoran, Fentem and Caspersen (cited above).

For sport and health: books and articles by Brodie, Roberts and Lamb (cited above).

5 Women and Sport

INTRODUCTION

This chapter examines women's involvement in sport. It is generally assumed that women do not take part in sport as much as men and are also limited in the kinds of sport they play. The first part of the chapter therefore sets out to examine the extent and nature of female participation in sport in Britain. Then a brief description of the physical differences between males and females prepares the way for consideration of the performance potential of men and women. The main part of the chapter explores various factors that can inhibit women's involvement in sport. Prompted by researchers with a critical feminist perspective, this topic has generated extensive debate and a dynamic situation is revealed wherein female involvement is affected by a complex interplay of historical, cultural and psychosocial influences. Finally, there is a review of initiatives and developments that aim to improve sporting opportunities for women.

PARTICIPATION RATES OF FEMALES IN SPORT

Sports Participation of Girls

Recently, the Sports Council (1995) commissioned a national survey of over 4400 young people aged 6–16 years to investigate their involvement in sport. In relation to sports participation outside of school PE lessons during the previous year, boys in each age group spent more time on sport, played a greater number of sports and competed at higher levels than girls. Figure 5.1 shows the difference between boys and girls, and it can be seen that a relatively small percentage of girls took part in sport in most age groups, with boys participating approximately twice as much as girls.

Table 5.1 shows sports played most regularly by girls of primary and secondary school ages, revealing that traditional, competitive sports were not popular with either age group.

Activities like cycling, swimming, walking and aerobics clearly have excellent health and social benefits, and yet it is unlikely that they

Figure 5.1 Boys' and girls' participation in sport out of school

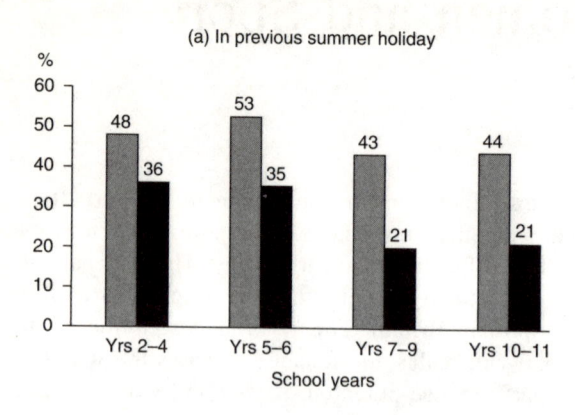

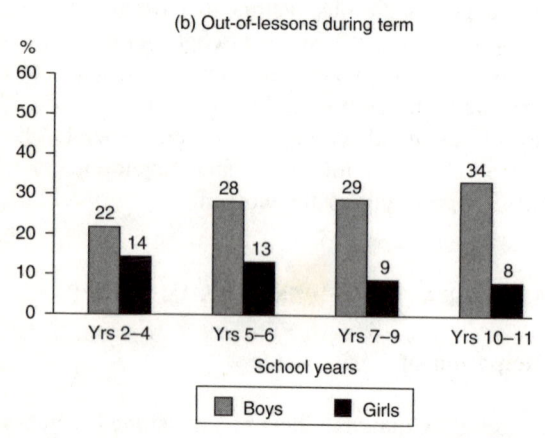

(a) In previous summer holiday

School years	Boys	Girls
Yrs 2–4	48	36
Yrs 5–6	53	35
Yrs 7–9	43	21
Yrs 10–11	44	21

(b) Out-of-lessons during term

School years	Boys	Girls
Yrs 2–4	22	14
Yrs 5–6	28	13
Yrs 7–9	29	9
Yrs 10–11	34	8

Source: Sports Council, 1995, p. 19.

were genuine sporting situations, since very few girls would have been involved, for example, in competitive walking or cycle racing. Interestingly, almost all girls said that they enjoyed sport, both in PE lessons and in other settings, and yet they demonstrated relatively low participation rates. The reason for this anomaly will be explored later in the chapter. The research of Armstrong *et al.* (1990) demonstrated the disturbingly low levels of physical activity among adolescent girls. These assessments mean that girls could not have been involved in any more than a minimal amount of sport.

Table 5.1 Rank order of sports played by girls out of PE lessons at least ten times in previous year

Primary age		Secondary age	
1. Cycling	(65%)	1. Swimming	(42%)
2. Swimming	(59%)	2. Cycling	(38%)
3. Games skills	(37%)	3. Tennis	(24%)
4. Aerobics/skipping	(29%)	=4. Walking [>1hr]	(19%)
5. Walking [>1hr]	(27%)	=4. Aerobics	(19%)
6. Gymnastics	(24%)	6. Badminton	(15%)
7. Dance	(21%)	7. Roller-skating	(14%)
8. Athletics	(16%)	=8. Rounders	(13%)
=9. Tennis	(15%)	=8. Horse riding	(13%)
=9. Rounders	(15%)	=8. Dance	(13%)
=9. Football	(15%)		

Source: Adapted from Sports Council, 1995, pp. 87–9.

Sports Participation of Women

General Household Survey
Based on a representative sample of more than 17 000 adults, the *General Household Survey* (Office of Population, Censuses and Surveys, 1993) provided a reasonably accurate profile of sports involvement in Britain. In 1993, 39 per cent of women had engaged in at least one sporting activity in the four weeks prior to the survey, compared with 57 per cent of men. The rank order of the most popular sports for men and women is shown in Table 5.2. It is interesting to note that no competitive team sports figured on the women's list and only soccer was on the men's list. The popularity among women of snooker, ten-pin bowling and darts is perhaps unexpected, although each of these activities involved fewer than 5 per cent of women. Women had a substantially higher participation rate than men in keep fit/yoga (17 per cent to 6 per cent) and slightly higher in swimming (16 per cent to 15 per cent).

In addition to investigating sports participation in the previous four weeks, the *General Household Survey* also examined involvement in the twelve months before interview. Table 5.3 provides a comparison of women's sports involvement four weeks and twelve months prior to interview. The higher percentages for the twelve month period indicate a substantial amount of casual participation in sport by women.

Table 5.2 Most popular sports of men and women: rank order for the percentage of men or women participating in the activity in the four weeks before interview

Men	Women
Walking	Walking
Snooker/pool/billiards	Keep fit/yoga
Swimming	Swimming
Cycling	Cycling
Soccer	Snooker/pool/billiards
Golf	Tenpin bowls/skittles
Weight lifting/training	Darts
Darts	Weight lifting/training
Running (exc. track)	Badminton
Keep fit/yoga	Running (exc. track)

Source: Office of Population Censuses and Surveys, 1993, p. 141.

Table 5.3 Comparison of women's four-week and twelve-month involvement in selected sports

	% participating four weeks before interview	% participating twelve months before interview
Swimming	16	43
Keep fit/yoga	17	29
Cycling	7	14
Snooker/pool/billiards	5	9
Darts	3	6
Weight lifting/training	3	6
Tenpin bowling/skittles	3	13
Badminton	2	6
Tennis	2	6
Golf	2	5
Running (jogging, etc.)	2	5

Source: Adapted from Office of Population, Censuses and Surveys, 1993, p. 149.

Allied Dunbar National Fitness Survey

The *Allied Dunbar National Fitness Survey* studied a representative sample of 6000 adults (16 years and over) to measure the physical activity levels of the English population. It was found that the difference in activity levels between men and women was relatively small, with 44 per cent of men and 40 per cent of women taking part in sport or active recreation at a vigorous or moderate intensity. In the light of

Table 5.4 Activity levels for men and women

Frequency and intensity of activity 20-minute occasions in previous four weeks	Men %	Women %
Level 5 – 12 or more occasions of vigorous activity	14	4
Level 4 – 12 or more occasions of moderate and vigorous activity	12	10
Level 3 – 12 or more occasions of moderate activity only	23	27
Level 2 – 5–11 occasions of moderate and vigorous activity	18	25
Level 1 – 1–4 occasions of moderate and vigorous activity	16	18
Level 0 – None	17	16

Source: Adapted from Sports Council and Health Education Authority, 1992, p. 48.

this, it is surprising to find that the aerobic fitness of women was disturbingly low. It was estimated that two-thirds of women would find it difficult to sustain walking at a reasonable pace up a 1 in 20 slope for any more than a few minutes, and more than half of women over the age of 55 years were considered to be particularly unfit.

These results may be explained by Table 5.4, which shows that women were not as regularly involved as men in high intensity physical activity. Interestingly, over two-thirds of women in Activity Level 0 believed they were very or fairly fit! Women rated 'looking good' and 'controlling and losing body weight' as the most important benefits of taking exercise. 'Having fun' and 'relaxing' were considered most important for men.

It is revealing to see the sports and recreations which contribute to the activity levels shown in the *Allied Dunbar Survey*. Table 5.5 compares participation between men and women, and illustrates that, while women were more active than men in some activities such as social dancing, they were clearly less involved in traditional sports like football, golf and squash.

Health and Lifestyle Survey
The *Health and Lifestyle Survey* (Cox *et al.*, 1993) investigated the activity levels of more than 3000 adults in England, Scotland and Wales. Figure 5.2 shows a comparison of the percentage of men and women taking part in activities involving physical effort, at least once in the two weeks prior to interview. The activities were mainly sporting activities,

Table 5.5 Sports and recreations played by men and women

Sport/recreation	Past four weeks Men %	Past four weeks Women %	Past year Men %	Past year Women %	Intensity category
Swimming	17	19	45	44	(Vig./mod.)
Exercises	18	18	24	24	(Mod./light)
Social dancing	12	18	21	31	(Mod./light)
Cycling	16	12	30	22	(Vig./mod.)
Snooker	16	2	27	5	(Light)
Darts	10	3	17	6	(Light)
Jogging/running	9	2	17	6	(Vigorous)
Rambling	6	5	12	9	(Mod./light)
Football	10	1	20	3	(Vig./mod.)
Weight training	8	2	13	6	(Vig./mod.)
Keep fit	2	7	3	14	(Vig./mod.)
Golf	9	1	17	3	(Mod./light)
Badminton	3	3	10	9	(Vig./mod.)
Aerobics	1	5	1	10	(Vig./mod.)
Squash	4	1	11	3	(Vigorous)
Tennis	3	2	11	7	(Vig./mod.)
Table tennis	3	1	10	5	(Mod./light)
Tenpin bowling	3	3	11	9	(Light)
Fishing	4	–	10	1	(Light)
Cricket	3	–	10	1	(Mod./light)
Bowls	2	1	7	3	(Light)

Source: Sports Council and Health Education Authority, 1992, p. 62.

apart from keep fit and yoga, and did not include non-sporting physical activities such as gardening, walking or dancing.

It can be seen that, although male participation is higher in all age groups, the difference is not large. However, the most popular activities among females were keep fit and yoga, and if these non-sporting activities were omitted, the difference would be considerably greater.

Conclusions about Women's Sporting Involvement

While the methodology was slightly different in each of the above studies, a noticeable pattern does emerge. In general, women seemed to be only slightly less active than men, but if competitive, active sports are compared, the difference becomes much greater. Thus, although the surveys showed that female participants were involved in a relatively wide range of activities, regular participation in traditional sports

Figure 5.2 Men's and women's participation in activities requiring physical effort

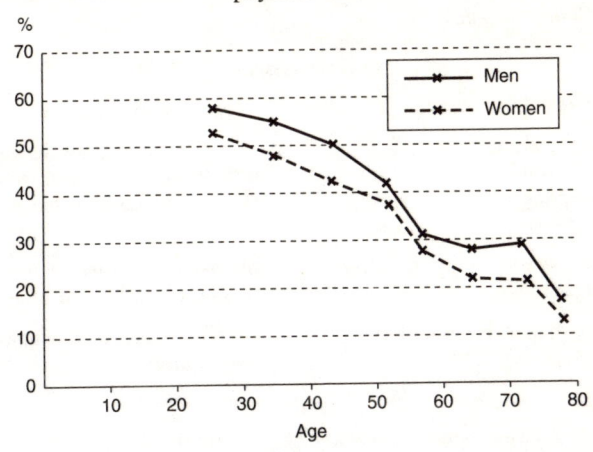

Source: Adapted from Cox *et al.*, 1993, p. 258.

was limited to a small minority of younger women. Apart from the growth in aerobics, women's sports participation has changed little over the past ten years and it will be interesting to see if the decline in women's sports participation recently noticed in America (Robinson and Godbey, 1993) occurs in Britain.

PHYSICAL FACTORS

It is clear that there are morphological (form and structure of the body) differences between males and females which affect sporting performance. These are summarised in Table 5.6.

There are also physiological differences between men and women, as shown in Table 5.7, which are of equal significance for sporting performance. However, both morphological and physiological differences are smaller among highly trained male and female athletes, which suggests that there are behavioural influences involved as well as biological states.

Performance Potential of Males and Females

What effect do the above physical differences have on sporting performance potential?

Table 5.6 Morphological differences between men and women

Characteristics	Results
Skeletal system	
Women are usually smaller and shorter.	Lighter body frame.
Women have a wider pelvis, the thighs slant inward toward the knees, and the lower leg bones are less bowed than in men.	Different running mechanics; some believe more prone to injury because of knee instability.
Women have shorter limbs (relative to body length).	Shorter lever arms for movement (important for use of implements).
Women have narrower shoulders with more slope.	Different mechanics of upper limb musculature.
Body composition	
Women have a larger percentage body fat and concentration of subcutaneous adipose tissue.	Contours more rounded and less angular.
Women have less LBM (less bone and muscle).	Physique less mesomorphic and more endomorphic. Less metabolically active tissue. More buoyant.
Women have a smaller muscle mass.	Lower absolute strength.

Source: Wells, 1991, p. 17.

- *Strength events*. The female has only 65 per cent of the strength of a man and therefore the strength potential of men will be higher.
- *Anaerobic events (requiring power for less than one minute)*. The female has a lower proportion of muscle tissue, which reduces high energy phosphates, and may be less able to tolerate a lactacid debt. Men will therefore have an advantage in short events such as sprint athletics.
- *Aerobic events (between one minute and one hour)*. Man's larger heart and higher haemoglobin content and haematocrit can increase his rate of oxygen uptake. The male's larger proportion of total body weight ensures rapid metabolism during exercise, offering a better power to weight ratio. Men will therefore have an advantage in these events.
- *Ultra-long distance events*. Women are better at utilising fat as a fuel for exercise, giving greater capacity for endurance events. Where total capacity is stretched and thermal balance becomes a factor, females may have the edge.

Table 5.7 Physiological differences between men and women

Characteristics	Results
Cardiovascular system	
Women have lower blood volume, fewer RBCs (= 6% fewer) and fewer HBs (= 15% fewer).	Lower total oxygen-carrying capacity of blood.
Women have smaller hearts.	Higher HR, smaller SV, and lower oxygen pulse for given Q and VO_2.
Women have lower Qmax.	Lower VO_2max (20–25% lower).
Respiratory system	
Women have a smaller thorax.	Lower VC, TV, RV and MBC.
Women have less lung tissue.	Lower $V_e$max.
Muscular system	
No differences in the distribution of slow- and fast-twitch fibres.	
Women have smaller muscle mass (fewer fibres and smaller fibres)	40–60% weaker in upper body strength, 25% weaker in lower body strength.

Source: Wells, 1991, p. 34.

It has been rumoured that women risk a wide range of medical problems if they take part in sport. Table 5.8 shows that there is little substance to these rumours.

Women's Performances

Thomas and French (1985) performed a meta-analysis of studies that investigated gender differences in sports skills. They found that males outperformed females on 17 out of 20 motor tasks. They concluded, however, that a biological contribution was indicated only in throwing skills. The superiority of males on motor tasks would thus seem to be influenced by boys' early introduction to sport and the encouragement they are given to develop sports skills.

It is interesting to compare the relative performances of men and women in sporting events such as running and swimming. In all but ultra-long distance swimming and walking, men exceed women in absolute time. This is mainly because of physiological differences between the sexes, but also because of the comparatively recent emergence of women's

Table 5.8 Myths and facts about women's participation in sport

Myth	Fact
Sport causes pregnancy and child birth problems.	No pregnancy problems found among sportswomen – exercise has favourable effects on pregnancy and childbirth.
Sport upsets normal patterns of menstruation.	Normal cycle of menstruation only affected at highest competitive levels
Sports performance is adversely affected during the menstrual cycle.	Performance variation can occur during menstrual cycle, but only of significance at highest competitive levels.
Sport causes substantial injuries to females.	Sportswomen suffer relatively the same number of injuries as sportsmen.
Sport produces unattractive, bulging muscles.	Extensive increase in muscle mass does not normally occur with females who participate in sport.

Source: Adapted from Mees, 1979.

participation, the small number of females competing and the limited training resources of females.

It is fascinating to observe in Figure 5.3 that 'the rate of improvement curves for women are consistently higher than those of men for all distances in swimming and running' (Chatterjee and Laudato, 1995, p. 130).

The question arises as to the extent to which present day performances are due to the smaller number of female participants and restricted training opportunities, as opposed to physical differences between the sexes. Although physical factors may account for performance differences in sport, they do not prevent females being involved. The next part of the chapter explores reasons for the reluctance of females to participate in sport.

FACTORS AFFECTING FEMALE SPORTS INVOLVEMENT

Historical Influences

Present day behaviour is affected by happenings in the past, and an understanding of women and sport can be informed by the historical background to this issue. The origins of women's limited involvement in sport can be traced back to the Ancient Olympics where women

Figure 5.3 Comparison of men's and women's sporting improvement

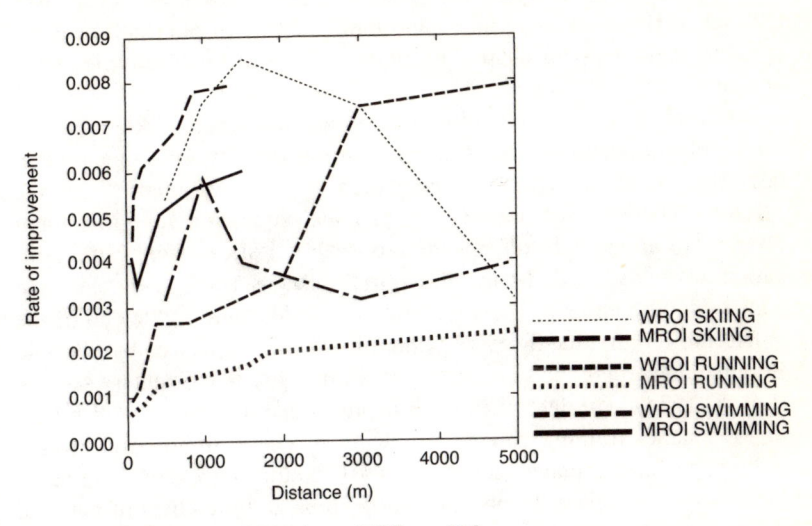

[Graph with x-axis "Distance (m)" from 0 to 5000, y-axis "Rate of improvement" from 0.000 to 0.009. Legend: WROI SKIING, MROI SKIING, WROI RUNNING, MROI RUNNING, WROI SWIMMING, MROI SWIMMING]

Source: Chatterjee and Laudato, 1995, p. 128.

were excluded both as performers and as spectators (Finley and Pleket, 1976). This kind of discrimination continued throughout history and into the nineteenth century when men were seen as competitive and were characterised by physical prowess, aggression and leadership, while women were considered to be emotional, docile and passive. Boys and men could acquire a masculine and muscular identity by taking part in games that had been organised and institutionalised in boys' public schools, whereas women were expected to bear children and/or stay quietly in the home.

These expectations were further reinforced by the view of the medical profession that sport was harmful to the female body, and it was thought that procreation was so demanding that women should preserve their strength for childbirth and not waste their energies on other activities. Thus, there developed a vicious circle. Women were not seen to be involved in sport and therefore it was considered unnatural for them to do so. Their inactivity often led to fainting and ill-health, reinforcing the stereotype of the frail nature of the female body.

The increased affluence of the Edwardian middle classes led to wealth being exhibited, in part, by conspicuous demonstrations of leisure: for example, in physical recreations. However, with corsets, fine shoes and fancy hats, Edwardian women were prevented from anything other than minimal physical movement (Dobbs, 1973). In contrast, many working class women undertook strenuous physical labour in factories and fields. However, long hours and family duties meant that, for these women, there was no chance to engage in spare time activities such as sport.

While the passiveness of middle class women was a strong theme in the nineteenth century, the seeds of sporting activity for women were, nevertheless, sown within the education system. Although there was certainly no universal approval of physical education for girls, there often were attempts to offer some physical activities where girls' education was advanced. Many élite girls' schools tried to emulate the games-playing ethos of the boys' public schools, and by the end of the nineteenth century, the Swedish gymnastic system, introduced by Madame Bergman Osterberg, was taught to girls in many state elementary schools (Smith, 1974). The late nineteenth century also saw the establishment of PE teacher training colleges for women where, in addition to providing specialist female teachers of physical education, there originated many women's sports teams and sports clubs and members of national women's sports teams.

The Twentieth Century

In the early twentieth century, middle class women engaged in field sports such as riding, hunting, rifle shooting and even kangaroo hunting (in Australia), but were still expected to retain their femininity and maintain a respectable, high moral image. Strangely, the popularity of cycling among women at this time, and the necessary changes in dress, have been linked with an accelerated development of female sport. Shortened and divided skirts, knickerbockers and bloomers were introduced for the bicycle, providing bodily freedom and, at the same time, attracting strident criticism on the grounds of indecency and impropriety. Despite this censure the precedent had been set and more appropriate clothing for women gradually spread to other sports.

Hargreaves (1994, p. 97) highlighted the problems associated with another sporting recreation:

> Although early swimming costumes covered as much of the body as was reasonable for safety, nevertheless, the shape of the woman's body was visible, and the closeness of male and female bodies in the water smacked of depravity and was anathema to middle-class ethics.

Croquet and archery were considered 'safe' for mixed competition, while strenuous activities like tennis had separate competitions for many years. Hockey, with its aggressive contact and muddy image, illustrated the position at the turn of the century. Despite the enthusiasm of some women to play hockey, especially in colleges and universities, the public image of respectability was maintained by dressing with decorum and playing in a ladylike manner. During the early years of the twentieth century, efforts to provide PE for girls at school probably stemmed from a desire to promote healthy motherhood as opposed to any thoughts of feminine liberation (McCrone, 1982, p. 7).

The Inter-war Years
During the inter-war years a relatively wide range of sports were taught and played in schools for middle class girls and at colleges and universities. However, moral rectitude, in the form of exemplary standards and behaviour, was still an important consideration and, in order to achieve this, sport and PE was portrayed as sexless. In contrast, sporting opportunities for working class girls were sparse. Despite an acceptance of the therapeutic value of exercise for girls, and official recognition of games in the school curriculum, the lack of gymnastics and games facilities and of specialist teachers meant that PE often consisted of stilted exercises and, in some cases, the games of netball and rounders. After leaving school and college, those with the skill and determination could continue playing in a modest number of sports clubs which catered for female sports enthusiasts.

However, sport itself underwent a transformation during this period which influenced the gender issue. The first tentacles of commercialism established sports as forms of entertainment and this opened up opportunities for women, while also introducing some obstacles. An example was the case of Suzanne Lenglen, the French tennis player, who won six Wimbledon and six French Championships. In contrast to the staid appearance of most female tennis players of the time, Lenglen dressed and acted flamboyantly on and off court. For many women, she was a fresh and exciting new image, but in some quarters she was rebuked and accused of indecent behaviour. Lenglen was the archetypal sports heroine and, like a small number of others, undoubtedly must have inspired many young girls to take part in sports and aspire to reach similar heights. Even so, it was mostly the middle class and wealthy who could realistically participate in most sports, since cost and lack of time still blocked widespread involvement on the part of the masses. In addition, men held all the administrative positions and this tended to restrict sporting opportunities for women.

Added to educational and commercial opportunities, there also emerged a political influence which proved beneficial to the acceptance and proliferation of women's sport. In the 1930s there was considerable concern about the low fitness levels of the general population, especially with storm clouds gathering over Europe. A government-supported fitness campaign, involving propoganda films and evening fitness classes, promoted exercise for all, and women joined (with gusto) in large numbers. All in all, women's involvement in sport was patchy: while some women engaged in physical recreations, there was scepticism about their participation and the vast majority remained inactive.

PE in the 1950s and 1960s
During the 1950s and 1960s, boys' and girls' PE followed different routes, mostly being taught separately. Developing from a scientific background, boys' PE focused on skill acquisition, competitive games and fitness training. In contrast, girls' PE embraced Laban's philosophy, which emphasised creative movement principles and aesthetic appreciation (Foster, 1977). These distinct emphases had a significant influence: boys and men were given a good grounding in competitive sports, especially team games, whereas girls experienced PE which de-emphasised competition and ignored the majority of sports. This had a significant impact on the later, adult generation since men tended to engage in competitive sports, especially team games, whereas women tended to lack interest in them.

This brief historical overview reveals that females today do not start on a level playing field. There are many attitudes and traditional practices which hinder their sporting involvement and a closer examination of how this legacy relates to other factors will now be undertaken.

Social Influences

Sex Typing
Babies have a biological sex when born, but no masculine or feminine identity. They rapidly develop their identity through the psychological, social and cultural world, to the extent that a fairly mature understanding of gender is reached by the age of 8–9 years. Socialisation involves modelling and reinforcement from significant others such as parents, peers and teachers. Later, it may also take the form of a socialising

situation, such as a basketball club, where there may be a negative ethos about girls playing basketball.

The behaviour of parents is critical in this process since boys are often encouraged to be adventurous and active, while girls are given less physical freedom. Girls with supportive parents, peers, teachers or coaches are more likely to initiate and continue sports participation than girls with little or no support. For example, if parents feel that it is inappropriate for girls to play contact sports then they are unlikely to encourage their daughter to play them.

The work of Brown, Frankel and Fennell (1989) in Canada is interesting because it involved investigation of competitive and recreative forms of sport in both school and community. They found that female sport involvement was restricted because sports participation:

- violated gender appropriate behaviour
- inhibited involvement in other activities
- did not lead to strong social reinforcement.

Gender stereotypes exist because there are particular qualities that are perceived as typically masculine and feminine. In most western European countries, men are perceived as aggressive, independent, dominant, active, adventurous and competitive, while women are seen as gentle, emotional, understanding, tactful, quiet and dependent. Stereotypical views of femininity and masculinity reinforce expectations of appropriate behaviour for males and females. Thus, it is the social construction of gender and not biological differences which need to be examined to understand inequalities in sport and PE.

Appropriate and Inappropriate Sports
Definitions of masculinity and femininity have also been ascribed to sporting activities. In the 1960s, Metheny (1965) originally described sports as 'acceptable' or 'unacceptable' for female involvement, depending on the characteristics of the sports. For example, sports involving bodily contact were inappropriate for females, while sports involving aesthetic movement were considered appropriate.

Recent research by Colley *et al.* (1987), involving the perceptions of male and female 16–18-year-olds in Britain, suggests that many sports are still strongly sex-typed. Activities considered appropriate for males included traditional male, competitive team sports like rugby, high-risk sports such as mountaineering, water sports involving strength/risk like rowing and those activities requiring direct bodily contact such as boxing. Activities sex-typed for females included traditional

Figure 5.4 Appropriate and inappropriate sports

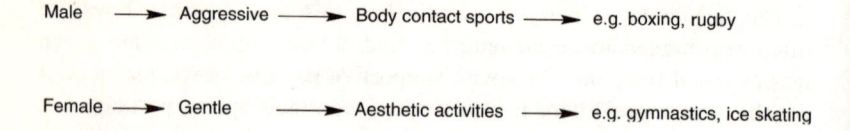

Male ⟶ Aggressive ⟶ Body contact sports ⟶ e.g. boxing, rugby

Female ⟶ Gentle ⟶ Aesthetic activities ⟶ e.g. gymnastics, ice skating

female sports like netball and some non-competitive activities like aerobics. Figure 5.4 provides an illustration of this idea.

Engel (1994) confirmed that these divisions had persisted into the 1990s with a study of the views of 12/13 and 15/16-year-old girls. One slight difference was that some high risk sports were rated as neutral, whereas in previous studies they had been considered as masculine type activities. Engel concluded that the lack of variety, low status and small number of female-appropriate sports led to a 'persisting subordination of women in sport' (1994, p. 447).

A related point is that there is a positive relationship between a female's self-confidence and participation in physical activity – that is, girls and women who are confident about their ability in sport will participate. However, as might be expected, females are less confident in 'masculine' sports than in 'feminine' or 'neutral' sports. Similarly, girls lack self-confidence in competitive sports and activities if they believe they are being evaluated (Stewart and Corbin, 1989). Girls with low self-confidence may decide not to take part in activities, may choose less demanding activities and may be easily discouraged by failure. Increased female self-confidence could therefore lead to greater involvement in sport. To achieve this there is a need to:

- teach girls skills that enhance their chance of success
- increase role models for females in the media
- give positive feedback emphasising that success is due to skill and failure is due to lack of effort.

A question that might be asked is whether social expectations vary across social groups (for example, low income females, senior citizens) and whether they differ between high level competitive sport and recreational sport. For example, is it considered acceptable for women to play recreational basketball, while inappropriate for them to engage in high level, competitive basketball? Another matter to consider is the extent to which social evaluations change. For example, women's golf has recently received exposure on television and this may have changed social evaluations about women playing golf.

Role Conflict

Role conflict occurs when there is psychological concern that behaviour does not match up to social expectations. Masculinity associated with many sports is in conflict with sex-role socialisation for females. It has been assumed that the sex typing of sports produced role conflict and apologetic behaviour for female sports participants. In her review of this issue, Allison (1991) found that, although role conflict did exist among female athletes, it was at a relatively low level. However, it may be that females who experienced serious role conflict opted out of sport, while those who persevered with sport were socialised to see no contradiction between their sport behaviour and social expectation. It should also be remembered that this finding mainly related to American sportswomen and the situation may be different in Britain.

Images of Femininity in Contemporary PE and Sport

This section examines how PE and sport experiences during childhood and adolescence can affect self-perceptions and have a long term effect on attitudes to sporting involvement. It was shown in the historical background that boys and girls were treated differently in physical education and sport at school. It could be speculated that there has been some erosion of gender differences in primary school PE in the 1980s and 1990s. Many schools have taught creative movement and small-sided games to mixed classes, especially with children up to the age of about 9 years. However, girls and boys may be treated differentially, albeit unknowingly, in mixed classes. For example, boys may be encouraged to perform strong, powerful actions in movement, while girls are given limited opportunities in games like soccer and cricket.

Until the advent of the National Curriculum for PE (National Curriculum Council, 1995), secondary school PE teachers had relative freedom with regard to the content and delivery of PE. Thus, although there have undoubtedly been exceptions, traditional gender differences seen in the 1950s and 1960s have persisted into the 1990s. Scraton (1992) confirmed these gender differences when she examined images of femininity in contemporary secondary school PE. She found that PE teachers and PE advisers accepted physical differences in sporting ability and physical capacity between boys and girls, and were willing to accommodate these differences in the teaching of PE. For example, images of femininity and masculinity were such that many activities were still considered unsuitable for girls (for example, football) and boys (for example, educational dance). Girls were expected to have an attractive appearance and were protected from overt physical contact, leading to damage of the sexual parts of the body; a confirmation of female sexuality in a sporting context. Although some boys find masculine-type sports brutalising and some girls enjoy them, these individuals can be viewed as abnormal and labelled jokingly, and seriously, as 'poofs' or tomboys.

In response to the apathy shown by girls for traditional PE activities, and the desire to offer education for leisure, 'options' have become a feature of PE in the upper secondary age range. Attempts have been made to make options attractive to adolescent girls and thus they have often been individually based (avoiding large team situations), non-competitive, indoor (avoiding mud and mess) and appearance related (for example, aerobics). Scraton made the point, however, that, although options often have more appeal for adolescent girls, 'they reinforce the cultural expectations of femininity' (Scraton, 1992, p. 121). In essence, females remain limited to certain 'appropriate' activities. Thus, it would seem that PE teachers are in a catch-22 situation. If they offer a broad PE curriculum, they meet reluctance on the part of many girls towards activities which do not have feminine characteristics, but if they give more time to 'appropriate' activities, they perpetuate gender divisions existing in sport.

Scraton (1992) concluded that gender-specific subcultures still existed in the teaching of secondary school PE, thus upholding gender differences in sport. Boys are judged in terms of their sporting accomplishments, while girls opt out as part of their efforts to appear attractive to boys. The culture of femininity reinforces a social expectation for adolescent girls to be presentable through being inactive. Embarrassment caused by pubertal body changes make matters worse, and peer pressure will consolidate the inactive ideology and convert waverers who might otherwise have enjoyed some form of sport involvement. Sport becomes incompatible with an adolescent girl's expected lifestyle and images of womanhood.

Leaman and Carrington (1985) expressed a similar view in relation to the notion of education for leisure within school PE. Many males can envisage sport playing a significant role in future leisure, whereas females may see little time available for sport in the future due to the prospect of the 'double shift' scenario where domestic and child-rearing responsibilities have to be fulfilled in addition to employed work. Leaman and Carrington claimed that most young women put sport in the category of childish activities to be discarded as soon as possible in favour of the more socially acceptable roles of wife and mother. Antagonism to physical activities symbolises the 'exchange' of leisure potential for a subservient but socially acceptable role as wife and mother in the home.

Coakley and White (1992) came to a similar conclusion after conducting semistructured interviews with 60 young men and women aged 13–23 years, in an attempt to discover events and situations associated with decisions to participate or not participate in sport. Their findings also provide a useful insight into the reasons for female antipathy towards sports involvement. In accord with Leaman and Carrington (1985), they found that young women considered that sport had little or nothing to do with adulthood: in other words, they maintained traditional views of femininity where they were more concerned with their appearance and with becoming wives and mothers. Second, their perception of low self-competence in sporting activities led to them feeling stupid and embarrassed and, consequently, unenthusiastic about participation. This was partially linked to negative PE experiences at school where they had been bored, lacked choice, felt incompetent and met with critical reactions from peers. Discomfort and embarrassment were caused by changing, getting cold, being self-conscious about their body and being in losing situations – a situation summed up by a young woman who remembered that they had to 'go running round the streets in these horrible short skirts' (Coakley and White, 1992, p. 31).

The protective attitude of parents, mostly accepted by the young women, meant close monitoring, accounting for behaviour and dependence upon parents for lifts, all factors which constrained involvement in sport. Coakley and White concluded (1992) that sports participation was sidelined by their social world because it was not a central part of their lives. For girls, sport had nothing to do with their identified role of becoming a partner or child rearing. Traditional cultural practices related to gender were not questioned, to the extent that girls were not aware of it as an issue. Many girls rejected sports participation long before leaving school, while those with positive sporting experiences at school mostly continued only if someone close to them (for example, a parent) supported and protected them (for example, escorted them to the venue). Coakley and White (1992, p. 34) concluded that:

> Sports participation is the result of decisions negotiated within the context of a young person's social environment and mediated by the young person's view of self and personal goals.

Female adolescent culture revolves around spending time in bedrooms trying on clothes, experimenting with make-up, reading magazines, listening to pop music and chatting with friends. Sport is on the periphery and often a girl's only contact with sport is when she spectates in the hope of meeting boys. Teenage magazines in the 1990s focus on fashion and beauty features where healthy living, diet and exercise are described. This leads to some interest and involvement in activities like aerobics, but very little engagement in competitive sport. In the end, the basic question might be whether traditional female roles are innate rather than created parts of the human condition. Can women gain equity in sporting opportunities if such roles are to continue?

Religious and Cultural Influences

Women from ethnic minority groups in Britain have to face additional constraints in relation to sports participation. Religious beliefs of Muslims, for example, mean that Muslim women are unable to expose their limbs to play sport, and fasting in daylight hours during Ramadan can seriously impair a sports training regime. The cultural traditions of some ethnic groups mean that females are not allowed to participate in mixed activities, while extensive family duties may deny others the opportunity to engage in sport.

Contextual Influences

Sporting behaviour will always be affected by practical issues such as the availability of facilities, the cost of participation and the existence of domestic duties. It is often argued that women are disadvantaged because they have traditionally shouldered the responsibility of domestic duties and child rearing, making it more difficult to take part in sport. Jackson and Henderson (1995) have suggested that cultural expectations of biological sex lead to gendered decisions. Women do not participate in sport because they are expected to undertake domestic chores, not because they are female. Within-gender differences can be as great as between-gender differences – since participation rates in hockey are as great between old and young male players as between young male and female players. 'Most men and women make sports choices because of context and relationship not because they are biologically male or female' (Jackson and Henderson, 1995, p. 48).

Power Situations in Sport

Power structures in sport have traditionally favoured men. Men have held important positions within sports clubs, and female sports have

Table 5.9 Percentages of male and female Olympic athletes and coaches, 1976–88

	Athletes		Coaches	
	Male %	Female %	Male %	Female %
1976	73	27	96	4
1980	68	32	91	9
1984	68	32	98	2
1988	66	34	92	8

Source: White, Maygothling and Carr, cited in Hargreaves, 1994, p. 201.

generally had a lower status socially and financially. Private and single-sex clubs and voluntary associations are exempt from the 1975 Sex Discrimination Act (Pannick, 1983) and, because many sports clubs are private, single-sex and voluntary, it is possible for them to pursue sexist policies and practices. Lack of opportunities for women have been particularly severe in sports like golf, snooker and cricket where men have traditionally controlled the clubs. This has taken the form of limited access to facilities, less playing time and lack of voting rights. However, an interesting development is that National Lottery funds will not be granted unless sports clubs provide equal opportunities for men and women. This has already resulted in improvements for women in sports clubs where opportunities were previously unequal.

The underrepresentation of women in sports coaching roles, as shown in Table 5.9, demonstrates the structural power held by men. This analysis illustrates the very low number of female coaches in high level competitive sport, to the extent that male coaches predominate even in sports like tennis and badminton, which have relatively large numbers of female players. The imbalance of male sports coaches has a number of effects. For example, there are very few role models to attract girls into coaching, and male coaches have power over female participants. A disturbing illustration of the latter issue is the recent court case where male swimming coaches were found guilty of sexually abusing girl swimmers.

In summary, power is related to school, media, state and the existing male domination of much of sport's administrative structure. Overcoming inequalities involves unravelling not just sporting contexts, but wider social and cultural traditions and practices.

Media Influences

The mass media is one of the most powerful institutional forces in society, portraying both written and visual messages to the general public. Hargreaves (1994, p. 196) commented that 'Sports media shape public consciousness about gender', and an examination of the media is one way of assessing the extent to which women's sport has gained widespread acceptance. For example, it is assumed that media coverage of sport can encourage young people to participate in sport, with successful sports stars acting as significant role models. It is therefore valuable to explore whether there are gender differences in media coverage of sport.

Children and Adolescents
According to Young (1990, p. 158), 'Children are thirteen times more likely to see a vigorously active man than a vigorously active woman' in children's textbooks. This bias is replicated in comics since sports, and in particular football, have a prominent profile in boys' comics, while girls' comics focus mainly on stories about the home and relationships. The situation is the same in magazines for 12–16-year-olds, where boys' predominate in sports-related content. Thus, young people's print media mirror sport-related gender differences in life, perpetuating them in children's minds.

Visual images have greater power than written texts, and in a study of the American magazine *Young Athlete*, Rintala and Birrell (1984) found that men appeared in more sporting photographs than women. They also noticed that there was a difference in the style of the photographs, with men appearing in more sports leadership, strength and risk-taking roles than women. This type of finding was replicated by Duncan (1990) in a review of the American publication *Sports Illustrated for Kids*.

Adults
In the case of adults, it appears that women's sport receives limited print media coverage across the globe. In Australia, women's sport has been found to account for only 1.3 per cent of total sports news (McKay and Rowe, 1987); in Germany, Klein (1988) found a similar situation with women receiving 4.3–6.7 per cent of total sports coverage; while in America, a study by Lumpkin and Williams (1991) revealed that only 9 per cent of articles in *Sports Illustrated* focused on women. In Britain the Sports Council (1992) estimated that only ½–5 per cent of space given to sport in newspapers was allocated to women's

Table 5.10 Television coverage of the 1991 World Athletic Championships and the 1992 Summer Olympic Games

Broadcasting time (minutes) devoted to each track and field event for men and women at two major athletics championships

	\multicolumn{4}{c}{World Athletic Championships}		
	Live		Highlights		Olympic Games	
Event	Male	Female	Male	Female	Male	Female
100 m	92.43	60.38	66.71	9.83	235.40	106.62
200 m	73.12	21.54	18.03	4.39	101.47	76.85
400 m	61.58	41.27	23.82	7.73	117.83	67.99
800 m	54.95	64.51	30.94	17.36	92.37	72.80
1500 m	97.48	39.88	18.74	1.04	74.58	59.47
5000 m	54.81	72.03	15.89	38.34	84.97	75.03
10 000 m	34.70	79.48	44.94	36.16	76.31	140.73
110 m hurdles	67.27	15.07	10.53	2.24	109.11	58.28
400 m hurdles	40.30	51.13	24.82	13.77	86.83	100.46
4 × 100 m	43.52	31.09	14.00	4.13	73.27	22.23
4 × 400 m	66.44	31.95	35.20	7.61	46.60	36.06
20 km walk	5.97	3.52	6.12	3.19	12.19	16.42
Marathon	161.17	169.32	8.35	42.47	159.20	51.32
Long jump	58.16	34.57	21.39	0.35	60.25	44.57
High jump	45.63	9.42	5.33	0.28	33.20	29.00
Shot putt	3.22	19.47	0.23	1.50	18.92	10.02
Discus	21.43	6.12	0.28	0.95	16.62	13.82
Javelin	41.38	10.30	26.65	1.22	71.23	22.57
Decathlon	60.65	28.42	8.45	3.02	136.38	47.07
Mean	57.06	41.55	20.02	10.29	84.56	55.33

Source: Alexander, 1994a, p. 651.

sport. Where included, women's sport tended to be briefly mentioned, located in obscure parts of the page and without photographs.

Alexander (1994b) examined newspaper coverage of athletics at the 1991 World Athletics Championships and the 1992 Summer Olympic Games. She found that women received approximately a quarter of the total written coverage of athletics and that there were substantially fewer photographs of women than men. A similar picture emerged in relation to television coverage. Table 5.10 shows the greater amount of time devoted to men at both the 1991 World Athletic Championships and the 1992 Summer Olympic Games.

It is interesting to note that, in the 1992 Olympic Games, Linford Christie (100 m) and Sally Gunnell (400 m hurdles) both won individual gold medals and yet, on the day after their wins, the BBC devoted 38.42 minutes to Christie and 2.54 minutes to Gunnell. According to Alexander (1994a, p. 654), 'gender inequalities established in this and other similar television studies influence public opinion and hence socialisation'.

It seems as if television coverage concentrates on male-dominated sports which are shown at peak viewing times, while women's sport is limited to about 10 per cent of total sport coverage. Additionally, Kane (1989) noted that females in 'feminine' sports (for example, figure skating) received significantly more coverage than female participants in 'masculine' sports (for example, football). The implication of this is that the female stereotype in relation to 'feminine' sports is reinforced. Even the long-running BBC quiz programme *A Question of Sport* is male dominated, with only a few token women invited to join the panel. Is the bias in favour of male sport because men are faster, stronger and more skilful, thus offering a more exciting spectacle? Television producers have to attract as many viewers as possible and they will broadcast programmes that people want to watch rather than respond to an ideal of sexual equality.

Commercialisation of the Female Body in Sports

Commercial pressures concerning the ideal image of the female body, as illustrated in the media, have an additional, influential effect. Thus, a girl will be loath to display her body in a sports situation if it does not match up to the ideal image. Sportswear is now promoted to display a sexy image and this has implications for participation in sport by women. A minority of females fit the ideal body image and may be quite active, although this is mainly in keep fit activities and not sport. The majority may be discouraged from playing sport because their bodies do not fit the ideal form.

Some female sports stars, such as Sharron Davies and Gabriela Sabatini, portray images of femininity and sexuality far removed from the staid Victorian image of sportswomen. This would appear to be an attractive image which young girls and women might wish to emulate, and, more importantly, it ought to produce a perception that involvement in sport does not contravene femininity, but is an appropriate form of behaviour for females. However, Gabriela Sabatini participates in tennis, an acceptable type of sport for females. Other sports lead to different problems for women, as Tracy Edwards, the captain of an all-female yachting crew explained:

All-male crews have been yacht-racing for centuries and no-one has ever suggested they're a bunch of raging queers. But the moment an all-women crew gets together it's assumed we're all lesbians. (Cited in Hargreaves, 1994, p. 171)

Photographic Images
Another viewpoint exists in relation to images of the female body in sport. Despite their realism, photographs are never neutral images, since photographers make decisions about subject and setting, editors make their selections and a degree of artificial touching up can be done. Femininity is often highlighted in sports pictures of women, with a preponderance of photographs highlighting hips, thighs, buttocks and breasts. Sometimes, a promotional photograph of a sportswoman will show her pouting, suggesting a kind of feminine teasing with sexual undertones. The position of the body may portray an image of submissiveness, signalling femininity, while dominating poses of men illustrate masculinity. It has even been suggested that 'Female athletes are sometimes photographed in poses that bear a striking resemblance to those of women in soft-core pornography' (Duncan, 1990, p. 29).

There can be no doubt that female sport involvement receives limited attention and coverage in the media. Although fewer women take part in sport, their media coverage seems disproportionately small. In addition, it appears that there is a certain amount of trivialisation of female sports stars, both in written text and in photographic images. There are a number of reasons for this situation. In practical terms, men's sport has far greater organisational and institutional resources than women's sport. For example, there are far more male sports reporters and male sports editors. Of the 120 British journalists and photographers accredited at the 1988 Seoul Olympic Games, only two were women. Press boxes can be places of male intimidation and late night deadlines can lead to safety problems for women. Since features about men's sport sell newspapers and magazines and men's sport attracts greater numbers of television viewers, editors fear that newspaper sales would fall and television ratings drop if women's sport were given wider coverage in the media.

The implications of limited media coverage of women's sport are that:

- there are fewer role models in sport for girls
- female athletes seem not to be as important as male athletes
- women find sponsorship harder to get due to reduced media exposure.

Consequently, women's sporting chances will continue to be more restricted than those of men.

SPORTING OPPORTUNITIES FOR WOMEN

Innovative ideas and schemes attempt to improve sporting opportunities for women and this section illustrates how change is taking place.

School PE and Sport

Previous sections have shown that problems still exist in respect of girls' PE at school. A number of progressive ideas were suggested in the Final Report of the Physical Education Working Group, which was set up by the government to make recommendations for the PE National Curriculum:

> it would be a mistake to equate *access* with *opportunity*, and it is important to appreciate the distinction between the two. It is for teachers... to question the stereotypes which limit children's behaviour and achievements; and to challenge, whenever necessary, instances of sexism...
>
> Equality of opportunity... requires an understanding and appreciation of the range of pupils' responses to femininity, masculinity and sexuality... willingness to question long-held beliefs and prejudices... [and] avoid future undesirable sex stereotyping activities. (Department of Education and Science, 1991, pp. 15 and 57)

Although not published in the final National Curriculum documents, these comments highlighted the need to go further than providing mixed PE lessons and simply offering girls physical activities previously limited to boys. For example, girls may be as severely constrained as before if disregarded in a lesson of mixed football.

Improvements in PE can also be made in the following ways:

- phasing out boys' and girls' PE departments
- eradicating sexist language
- taking care not to reinforce stereotypes – for example, by encouraging competition among girls as well as boys
- arranging visits to school by both male and female sports stars
- taking sex differences into account in assessment, such that males do not have an unfair advantage over females due to physical differences.

Women and Soccer

Soccer provides an example of how sporting opportunities have, to some extent, been improved for women. In 1921 the Football Association banned organised women's football matches and it was not until 1969 that a Women's Football Association was formed; the ban was rescinded a year later. Progress has continued with an England Women's Football team being formed in 1972, the Women's European Football Championships commencing in 1982 and the Women's World Football Championships now in existence. Section 44 of the 1975 Sex Discrimination Act states that mixed competitions are not allowed where 'strength, speed and physique' are important. This led to one of the most publicised court cases about sex discrimination when Theresa Bennett, a 12-year-old girl, was prevented by the Football Association from playing football with boys in a local league.

> Women have many other qualities superior to those of men but they have not got the strength and stamina to run, kick, to tackle and so forth. (ILEA, 1984, p. 23)

This attitude meant that girls were not able to take part in mixed football teams until 1990 when the Football Association agreed to mixed football for children under 11 years of age. There are now Development Officers for girls' and women's football, the FA and Regional Sports Councils have Development Plans for women's football and it is possible for women to take the FA Full Coaching Badge. Women's football does not perhaps have the prestige found in some other countries, but progress has been made.

Brighton Declaration of Women and Sport, 1994

A watershed was reached in 1994 when an international conference set a new agenda for women's sport. The Brighton Declaration of Women and Sport was agreed by 280 delegates from 82 countries, representing both governmental and non-governmental organisations. The declaration aimed 'to develop a sporting culture that enables and values the full involvement of women in every aspect of sport' (Sports Council, 1994, p. 18).

The declaration stated that appropriate policies, structures and mechanisms should be developed to:

- ensure that all women and girls have the opportunity to participate in sport in a safe and supportive environment which preserves the rights, dignity and respect of the individual;
- increase the involvement of women in sport at all levels and in all functions and roles;
- ensure that the knowledge, experiences and values of women contribute to the development of sport;
- promote the recognition of women's involvement in sport as a contribution to public life, community development and in building a healthy nation;
- promote the recognition by women of the intrinsic value of sport and its contribution to personal development and healthy lifestyle. (Sports Council, 1994, pp. 18–19)

The Women's Sports Foundation

The impetus for improving women's sport in Britain is being maintained by an organisation called the Women's Sports Foundation. Founded in 1984, the Women's Sports Foundation seeks to promote sporting opportunities for women in Britain through regional development work, publicity projects, seminars and resource materials. The Foundation aims to:

- increase awareness about the issues surrounding women's involvement in sport
- support women to become involved in sport at all levels and in all capacities
- encourage organisations to improve access to sporting opportunities for women
- challenge instances of inequality in sport and seek to bring about change
- raise the visibility of British sportswomen. (Women's Sports Foundation, undated)

Making a Difference

During the 1980s and 1990s, the Sports Council (1988) has adopted policies and strategies to increase sports participation among women. Recently, it has acknowledged the need for organisational change and that 'achievement of equality of opportunity requires unequal distribution of effort and resources' (Sports Council, 1992, p. 29).

Local authorities have begun appointing Sports Development Officers with responsibility for women's sport, while measures such as the organisation of 'women only' sessions and the provision of crèche facilities have clearly alleviated some barriers to involvement. Initiatives which target specific groups, like young mothers, are known to be effective (Sports Council, 1991) and it is recognised that a more sensitive understanding of women's lives is needed, since lifestyle changes are much more frequent and subtle than had been previously appreciated or acknowledged (for example, differing childcare responsibilities).

Some important ingredients for success have been as follows:

- Convenient *timing* to match lifestyle circumstances (for example, lunchtime sessions for young city centre working women).
- Flexibility of *payment*.
- *Any activities* are viable, but the women themselves need to be involved in the decision-making process.
- A welcoming, hospitable *social setting* with safe and easy access is needed to overcome psychosocial inhibitions concerned with confidence, competence and social expectations (Sports Council, 1991).

REFERENCES

Alexander, S., 'Gender Bias in British Television Coverage of Major Athletic Championships', *Women's Studies International Forum*, 17 (1994a), pp. 647–54.
Alexander, S., 'Newspaper Coverage of Athletics as a Function of Gender', *Women's Studies International Forum*, 17 (1994b), pp. 655–62.
Allison, M.T., 'Role Conflict and the Female Athlete: Preoccupations with Little Grounding', *Journal of Applied Sport Psychology*, 3 (1991), pp. 49–60.
Armstrong, N., Balding, J., Gentle, P. and Kirby, B., 'Patterns of Physical Activity among 11 to 16-year-old British Children', *British Medical Journal*, 301 (1990), pp. 203–5.
Brown, B.A., Frankel, B.G. and Fennell, M.P., 'Hugs or Shrugs: Parental and Peer Influence on Continuity of Involvement in Sport by Female Adolescents', *Sex Roles*, 20 (1989), pp. 397–412.
Chatterjee, S. and Laudato, M., 'Gender and Performance in Athletics', *Social Biology*, 42 (1995), pp. 124–32.
Coakley, J. and White, A., 'Making Decisions: Gender and Sport Participation among British Adolescents', *Sociology of Sport Journal*, 9 (1992), pp. 20–35.
Colley, A., Nash, J., O'Donnell, L. and Restorick, L., 'Attitudes to the Female Sex Role and Sex Typing of Physical Activities', *International Journal of Sport Psychology*, 18 (1987), pp. 19–29.
Cox, B.D. et al., *Health and Lifestyle Survey: Seven Years On* (Aldershot: Dartmouth, 1993).

Department of Education and Science, *Physical Education for Ages 5–16* (London: HMSO, 1991).
Dobbs, B., *Edwardians at Play: Sport 1890–1914* (London: Pelham, 1973).
Duncan, M.C., 'Sports Photographs and Sexual Difference: Images of Women and Men in the 1984 and 1988 Olympic Games', *Sociology of Sport Journal*, 7 (1990), pp. 22–43.
Engel, A., 'Sex Roles and Gender Stereotyping in Young Women's Participation in Sport', *Feminism and Psychology*, 4 (1994), pp. 439–48.
Finley, M.I. and Pleket, H.W., *The Olympic Games: The First Thousand Years*, (London: Chatto and Windus, 1976).
Foster, J., *The Influence of Laban* (London: Lepus, 1977).
Hargreaves, J., *Sporting Females* (London: Routledge, 1994).
ILEA, *Providing Equal Opportunities for Girls and Boys in Physical Education* (London: Physical Education Teachers Centre, 1984).
Jackson, E.L. and Henderson, K.A., 'Gender-based Analysis of Leisure Constraints', *Leisure Sciences*, 17 (1995), pp. 31–51.
Kane, M.J., 'The Post Title IX Female Athlete in the Media', *Journal of Health, PE, Recreation and Dance*, 60 (1989), pp. 58–62.
Klein, M.-L., 'Women in the Discourse of Sports Reports', *International Review for Sociology of Sport*, 23 (1988), pp. 139–51.
Leaman, O. and Carrington, B., 'Athleticism and the Reproduction of Gender and Ethnic Marginality', *Leisure Studies*, 4 (1985), pp. 205–17.
Lirgg, C.D., 'Girls and Women, Sport, and Self-confidence', *Quest*, 44 (1992), pp. 158–78.
Lumpkin, A. and Williams, L.D., 'An Analysis of Sports Illustrated Feature Articles 1954–1987', *Sociology of Sport Journal*, 8 (1991), pp. 16–32.
McCrone, K., 'Victorian Women and Sport: The Game in Colleges and Public Schools', *Canadian Historical Association* (1982), pp. 1–39.
McKay, J. and Rowe, D., 'Ideology, the Media and Australian Sport', *Sociology of Sport Journal*, 4 (1987), pp. 258–73.
Mees, A., 'Women in Sport: A Review of Physiological Factors', *Physical Education Review*, 2 (1979), pp. 44–9.
Metheny, E., 'Symbolic Forms of Movement: The Feminine Image in Sports'. In E. Metheny (ed.), *Connotations of Movement in Sport and Dance* (Dubuque: W.C. Brown, 1965), pp. 43–56.
National Curriculum Council, *Physical Education in the National Curriculum* (London: HMSO, 1995).
Office of Population, Censuses and Surveys, *General Household Survey* (London: HMSO, 1993).
Pannick, D., *Sex Discrimination in Sport* (Manchester: Equal Opportunities Commission, 1983).
Rintala, J. and Birrell, S., 'Fair Treatment for the Active Female: A Content Analysis of *Young Athlete* Magazine', *Sociology of Sport Journal*, 1 (1984), pp. 231–50.
Robinson, J.P. and Godbey, G., 'Sport, Fitness and the Gender Gap', *Leisure Sciences*, 15 (1993), pp. 291–307.
Scraton, S., *Shaping Up to Womanhood* (Buckingham: Open University Press, 1992).
Smith, D., *Stretching Their Bodies: The History of Physical Education* (Newton Abbot: Abbot and Charles, 1974).

Sports Council, *Sport in the Community: Into the Nineties – A Strategy for Sport 1988–1993* (London: Sports Council, 1988).
Sports Council, *Participation Demonstration Projects: Activities Promoter for Women – Norwich City Council* (London: Sports Council, 1991).
Sports Council, *Women and Sport: A Consultation Document* (London: Sports Council, 1992).
Sports Council, *Sport 2*, magazine of the Sports Council, May/June, 1994.
Sports Council, *Young People and Sport* (London: Sports Council, 1995).
Sports Council and Health Education Authority, *Allied Dunbar National Fitness Survey* (London: Sports Council and Health Education Authority, 1992).
Stewart, M.J. and Corbin, C.J., 'Self-confidence of Young Girls in Physical Activity', *The Physical Educator*, 46 (1989), pp. 64–8.
Thomas, J.R. and French, K.E., 'Gender Differences across Age in Motor Performance: A Meta-analysis, *Psychological Bulletin*, 98 (1985), pp. 260–82.
Wells, C.L., *Women, Sport, and Performance: A Physiological Perspective* (Champaign: Human Kinetics, 1991).
Women's Sports Foundation *Women's Sports Foundation Publicity Leaflet* (London: Women's Sports Foundation undated).
Young, I., *Throwing Like a Girl and Other Essays in Philosophy and Social Theory* (Bloomington and Indianapolis: Indiana University Press, 1990).

FURTHER READING

Creedon, P.J. (ed.), *Women, Media and Sport* (Thousand Oaks: Sage, 1994).
Leaman, O., *Sit on the Sidelines and Watch the Boys Play: Sex Differentiation in Physical Education* (York: Longman, 1984).
Women's Sports Foundation, *Women and Sport Syllabus Guide* (London: Women's Sports Foundation).

6 Social Class Issues in Sport

INTRODUCTION

In an ideal world everyone would have the freedom to take part in any sport; in the real world, where resources are limited, this does not happen. However, a simple comparison with previous periods of history shows that there are now far more opportunities for people to participate in sport and, instead of being a privilege of class and status, sport is claimed as a right of citizenship. The chapter opens with a brief historical snapshot to provide an insight of how class differences have evolved in sport. Then, present day patterns of sports participation are explored in relation to social groupings, and the reasons for continuing class differences are analysed. Finally, consideration is given to the claim that upward social mobility can be achieved through sport.

Most people have a vague idea of the meaning of social class and yet it has also been the subject of many sociological theories and ideas. Over the years, sociologists have considered social class to be based on social honour, authority, ownership of property and market capacity, although most sports surveys have simply tended to differentiate people according to their occupational status or place of residence. For example, the *General Household Survey* (Office of Population, Censuses and Surveys, 1993) aggregates occupations into socio-economic groups such as: professional, employers and managers, intermediate and junior non-manual, skilled manual, semi-skilled manual and unskilled manual.

SPORT AND SOCIAL CLASS IN THE NINETEENTH AND EARLY TWENTIETH CENTURIES

The Upper Class

Upper class involvement in sport during the nineteenth century was given a fascinating interpretation by Thorsten Veblen (1953). His theory of social class is based upon the historical association between property ownership and social honour. Manual labour and productive work held an inferior status and those who did not need to work illustrated their lofty position with a conspicuous display of involvement in leisure activities. Idleness was not enough to exhibit upper class status; conspicuous consumption was needed and sports were an ideal demonstration of wasting time and money.

During the nineteenth century rowing held a high social cachet, with regattas on the Thames becoming pre-eminent social occasions, and, of course, Henley regatta is still one of the highlights of the social calendar for the élite classes. At the turn of the century, horse racing was strongly class bound, with a high proportion of owners being titled and, because of this, new rich businessmen saw it as an expensive hobby which could gain them access to high society. Golf clubs were also infiltrated by businessmen, not just because they had been established by aristocrats and had a social value, but because the clubhouse offered the opportunity to secure business deals with like-minded business people. Although it was usually less expensive than golf, tennis was also favoured by the upper classes because they could gain prestige from being a member of an exclusive club, especially one like the All-England Tennis Club at Wimbledon.

Veblen's theory needs to be set in the context of the nineteenth century since both sport and the class structure of western capitalist societies have changed significantly. Critics have suggested that, as a theory of class analysis, Veblen's work has many limitations and yet it was a perceptive view of meanings attached to sport and it is clear that conspicuous consumption of leisure has continued into the twentieth century, albeit in a diluted fashion. The ability to be seen in the Members' Enclosure at Ascot Races or to play golf during the working week has vestiges of conspicuous display over and above the potential pleasure obtained from such activities.

In the 1980s Bourdieu (1984) believed that Veblen's notion of conspicuous consumption was still relevant since the dominant classes favoured sports which distinguished them from the rest of society. If a particular sport like tennis became democratised and popularised, the upper classes turned to a new sport like power boat racing, which continued to set them apart from the crowd. Gruneau (1983, p. 80) suggested that Veblen's ideas formed a baseline upon which recent developments in sport and class have been judged. For example, mass participation in sport during the second half of the twentieth century has meant that class inequality in sport has apparently declined and there is now a 'leisure mass' instead of a 'leisure class'.

The cult of athleticism in nineteenth century public schools was an important feature in the preparation of the upper class for prestigious social positions and élite careers. In contrast, the working class were subjected to drill in order to produce a fit, disciplined workforce which could be mobilised for the armed forces if war threatened. During this period there was a rigid distinction between 'professionals', who played sport for money, and 'amateurs', who took part in sport for enjoyment, status and other reasons; the professionals were mainly working class and the amateurs upper class. Interestingly, the upper class looked down upon the professionals, not just because they were from a lower class, but 'because they allegedly cheated, and outclassed amateurs by extra training and superior strength' (Riess, 1994, p. 144).

The Middle Class

The Victorian middle class was enthusiastic about sport since many of them saw it as a way of contributing to the good of society. In addition to bringing order and suppressing violence among the working class, they thought that organised sport could fashion 'loyal and brave muscular Christians who could exercise social control over their sexual impulses, including homosexuality' (Riess, 1994, p. 155). In addition, the middle class embraced the concept of the sports club since it provided status, order and dignity, while also offering a venue for socialising.

The middle classes became involved in nearly all sports, often aping the upper class, and if entry to exclusive sports clubs was barred, they would organise their own clubs, as exemplified in the case of tennis. The middle classes even infiltrated supposedly working class sports. For example, in addition to playing the game of football, many became major shareholders and directors of professional football clubs. Between 1870 and 1914, upper middle class women played a major role in the development of women's sport. An important reason for their involvement was the potential of sport as a means of liberation. As noted in Chapter 5, although women's sports participation met with opposition, activities like tennis and cycling became beacons for women because these sports offered the chance of taking part in recreation outside the home.

The Working Class

In the early part of the nineteenth century, the working classes were induced to give up disruptive and disorganised forms of sport and to adopt less brutal sporting activity. If moral persuasion did not work, laws were introduced to quell the violent excesses of rough, chaotic sports. By the end of the nineteenth century, there was widespread interest in organised sports clubs among the upper, respectable, economically secure section of the working class. Hargreaves (1992) noted that the growth of commercialisation in sport offered further opportunities for the working class to participate in sport. For example, football, a formerly violent and chaotic game enjoyed by the working class, was by the early twentieth century well organised and structured. Some working class men became football professionals and they played an influential role in the inspiration of young working class men to take part in games of recreational football.

There is disagreement over the extent to which the working classes determined their own sporting destiny during this period. On the one hand, it appears that, during the nineteenth century, the middle class influenced working class sport. First, there was concern about the morals and behaviour of large numbers of unchurched urban workers and, in response, various charitable and religious groups established football and cricket clubs to try and regulate behaviour and secure conversions. Second, many businesses invested in sports facilities to increase fitness and productivity, while also encouraging a sense of loyalty. Riess (1994, p. 164) remarked upon:

> the noteworthy efforts of Cadburys and Rowntree chocolate factories to provide substantial facilities for male and female physical training in the late nineteenth century. For example, girls under sixteen were given time off to swim and exercise at the company gym under professional instructors, and encouraged to play team sports after work.

It is also possible that sport reflected the attempts of a not inconsiderable number to aspire to middle class status. While the middle class used sport to mimic upper class behaviour, the same process existed vis-à-vis the working class and middle class recreations.

However, Holt (1989) expressed a different view, believing that the working class instilled their own traditional values of toughness, persistence and loyalty, while their sports clubs, unlike the widespread geographical catchment areas of the middle class, were based on close-knit street and neighbourhood groups. Holt claimed that the muscular Christians and social reformers were ineffectual in achieving social control. This line of thought is supported by the inclusion within working class sport of values such as winning, partisanship, earning money, disdain for authority and rules, mutual solidarity through teamwork and vulgar crowd behaviour – values directly opposed to those espoused by the middle class. Roughness and rudeness prevailed while fair play and sportsmanship floundered!

The socialist movement of the late nineteenth century was split on the issue of sport. Socialist critics claimed that consumerism and profiteering in sport was yet another means of exploiting the working classes, while, in contrast, some leading socialists saw intellectual, moral and health values in sport, and labour organisations like the National Clarion Cycling Club used sport 'to propagate Socialism and Good Fellowship' (Jones, 1992, p. 32).

Hargreaves (1986) noted a significant rise in working class sports participation in the 1920s and 1930s, stimulated by developments such as the inclusion of sport in schools, improved living standards, commercial and media expansion in sport and the advent of the half-day holiday on Saturdays. Although the sporting culture of the working class was, to some extent, influenced by the ruling classes, Jones (1992) maintained that proletarian meanings and attitudes were retained and reproduced during the inter-war years. An important focus for working class sport was the pub. Sports like backroom boxing, football and bowling, with their associated gambling exploits, were promoted by publicans who saw the commercial benefits of regular custom arising from sports events. The pub was also the base for traditional working class sports like angling and pigeon racing, each of which could boast more than half a million participants by the 1930s.

Class polarisation occurred across and within sports. The upper classes retained exclusivity by means of excessive cost or through restricted membership of golf and sailing clubs, while the working classes were attracted to the raw excitement of sports like boxing, wrestling and greyhound racing. However, polarisation occurred within a sport like rugby. Although there were a number of exceptions, amateur gentlemen developed the game of rugby union, while working class professionals went their separate way with rugby league. The crossing of players between the two codes in the 1990s offers the prospect of a fascinating social mix. Thus, during the last century, sport has not been a site of total class domination. The socialist movement has campaigned to bring about sporting reforms which have led to improvements in sports provision for the working class. At the same time, although middle class values have been incorporated, certain working class characteristics such as partisanship, the pre-eminence of winning and vulgar hedonism have clearly survived.

SCHOOL PHYSICAL EDUCATION AND SPORT

It was noted earlier that, during the nineteenth and early twentieth centuries, children had different sporting experiences according to the type of school they attended. The comprehensive school system of the late twentieth century aims to give children similar sporting experiences. The extent to which this has been achieved is not easy to evaluate, but there appears to have been differential involvement in extra-curricular sport. Saunders (1979), for example, found that participation of working class pupils in secondary school sport was substantially lower than that of their middle class peers. Participation of working class girls was very low throughout secondary school, and although sport was popular among working class boys during the first year, their involvement fell away as they got older. Extensive work undertaken in the 1970s led Hendry (1978) to conclude that the middle class values of schools alienated working class pupils from school sport. It is possible that this is still the case today.

Equality of opportunity in physical education was an important feature of proposals for the National Curriculum (Department of Education and Science, 1991). It was envisaged that all children would receive more or less the same physical education and sporting experiences, with no differentiation according to class, sex or race. However, the notion of equity, where the educational results are just and fair, also needs to be considered here. Thus, if the physical education curriculum is biased in favour of a particular class, equity will not have been achieved. For example, if the sports offered in a school are the domain of a particular social class, then other social classes will not receive an equitable entitlement.

Dodds (1993) warned about the dangers of biases and prejudices in sport when a person is judged according to stereotypes of a particular group. A physical education teacher or sports coach may have the following expectations about disadvantaged young people from a deprived area:

- Particular sports may be considered inappropriate for them.
- They are not expected to be given the family support needed to pursue sport.
- They will be disruptive in lessons or coaching sessions.
- They will not be reliable or show long-term commitment.

These young people may therefore be discriminated against in physical education and sport, with rights denied and choices restricted.

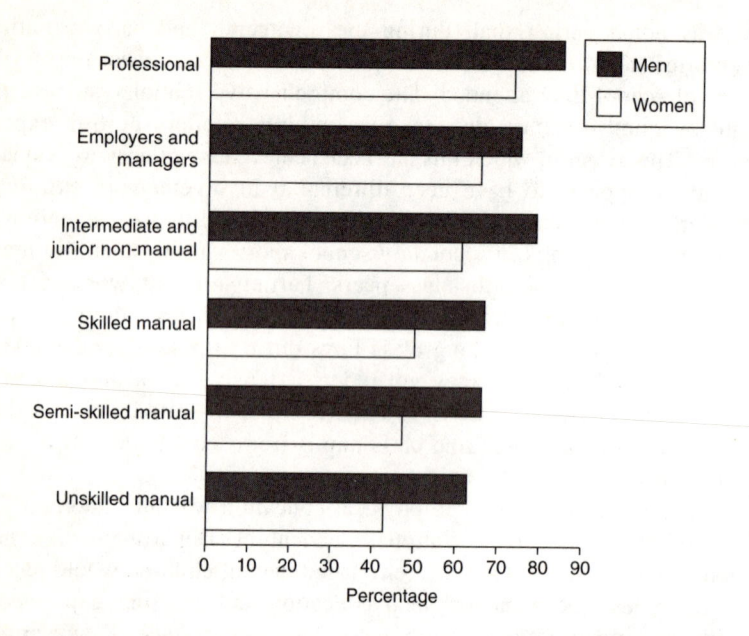

Figure 6.1 Sports participation by socio-economic group and sex

Source: Office of Population, Censuses and Surveys, 1993, p. 143.

SPORTS PARTICIPATION AND SOCIAL CLASS

A relatively clear picture of sports participation among members of different social groupings can be obtained from recent surveys. However, this is qualified by the fact that no research has specifically set out to investigate the relationship between sport and social class, and data have been retrieved from general participation surveys. Inevitably, there is the issue of how social class has been defined and the possibility of variance across surveys. In essence, the Registrar General's classification of occupations is invariably used, sometimes with categories merged to form a larger grouping such as the working class.

General Household Survey

It was seen in Chapter 2 that the *General Household Survey* (Office of Population, Censuses and Surveys, 1993) provided useful data in relation to sports participation among the general population. Figure 6.1

shows participation in the four weeks prior to interview in terms of socio-economic group and sex. There was a distinct variation in participation between socio-economic groups, with participation being higher among non-manual groups than manual groups. The difference was even more striking in the case of women, with a steady decline from professional to unskilled manual occupations.

When specific activities are analysed, as in Table 6.1, both expected and unexpected features emerge. Those in non-manual occupations tended to participate more in activities such as keep fit/yoga, golf, running, badminton, tennis and squash, but they were also well represented in darts, soccer, fishing and cue sports.

The *General Household Survey* requests information on economic status, and when this was analysed, it was found that men and women in paid employment had relatively high participation rates in comparison to the unemployed. Interestingly, there was also:

> evidence that those in part-time work had the highest participation rates, which perhaps reflects the greater amount of leisure time available to them than to those in full-time work. (Office of Population, Censuses and Surveys, 1993, pp. 143–4)

Brodie, Roberts and Lamb (1991) conducted a study of more than 4000 adult sport centre users and particularly focused on the seven activities of badminton, bowls, keep fit, martial arts, snooker, soccer and weight training. Apart from a few exceptions, they categorised respondents with non-manual occupations as middle class and manual workers as working class. All local authorities in the study made special efforts to provide access to sports centres for all social groups and this was most evident in terms of financial concessions (for example, discounts for the unemployed), sensitive programming and the provision of appropriate services (for example, crèche facilities). Despite the acknowledged trend for affluent individuals to travel many miles to use sports centres, it was the case that nearly half of the sports centre users lived within 2 miles of the facility. Thus, where sports centres had been sited in so-called working class areas, manual workers were relatively well represented.

There were only small differences between working class and middle class users of sports centres. For example, working class participants spent slightly less on sport and were likely to be playing fewer sports, but they participated in as much sport overall as those from the middle class. Similarly, there were few differences in the types of sport played. The seven sports attracted players from all social classes, although

Table 6.1 Participation in specific activities according to socio-economic group: persons aged 16 and over, Great Britain, 1993 (% participating in the four weeks before interview)

Active sports, games and physical activities*	Professional	Employers and managers	Intermediate and junior non-manual	Skilled manual and own account non-professional	Semi-skilled manual and personal service	Unskilled manual	Total**
Walking	57	46	42	39	36	31	41
Any swimming	27	19	18	10	11	8	15
Snooker/pool/billiards	11	12	8	17	10	9	12
Keep fit/yoga	13	12	18	6	9	8	12
Cycling	14	9	9	10	8	9	10
Darts	6	5	4	8	6	6	6
Weight lifting/training	7	5	5	6	4	3	5
Golf	9	10	5	6	2	2	5
Running (jogging, etc.)	11	6	4	3	2	2	5
Any soccer	6	3	3	6	3	3	4
Tenpin bowls/skittles	5	5	4	4	3	2	4
Badminton	5	3	3	1	1	1	3
Tennis	5	2	2	1	1	1	2
Fishing	3	3	1	3	2	1	2
Any bowls	1	2	2	2	2	2	2

Squash	4	3	2	1	1	0
Table tennis	3	2	1	1	1	1
Horse riding	1	1	1	0	1	1
Cricket	2	1	1	1	0	1
At least one activity (exc. walking) ††	64	53	49	46	36	31
At least one activity ††	82	71	65	63	54	48
Base = 100%	708	2362	5608	3486	2978	1164	17 552

* Includes only activities in which more than 1.0% of all adults participated in the four weeks before interview.
† Socio-economic group is based on the person's current or most recent job.
** Total includes full-time students, members of the Armed Forces, those who have never worked, and those whose job was inadequately described.
†† Total includes those activities not separately listed.

Source: Adapted from Office of Population, Censuses and Surveys, 1993, p. 153.

the working class was not quite so well represented among keep fit, weight training and badminton participants. Brodie, Roberts and Lamb (1991) argued that working class participants were more likely to drop out from sport during youth and young adulthood because of certain crucial factors. For example, they lacked encouragement and support from their families to play different sports during childhood, while middle class adolescents maintained involvement in sporting activities by effective management of time available for study, work and leisure. The middle class also benefited from heavily subsidised and convenient sporting opportunities in higher education and through the old boy/girl network of their schools.

It must be remembered that this study focused mainly on inner-city sports centres and therefore offers only a limited view of sports participation patterns. However, the study reveals many valuable insights into the relationship between sports participation and different social groupings. The variability of findings between sports centres indicates that different factors are significant in different circumstances and there is no single or simple explanation. Follow-up investigation is clearly needed.

The correlation between social class and sports participation seems to have diminished in America according to a fifteen-year study undertaken by Anderson and Stone (1979) between 1960 and 1975. Since this work is more than twenty years old, it would be valuable to see if their findings are still relevant today. In Britain there has been a more restrained assessment of progress. McIntosh and Charlton (1985, p. 89) identified a number of social filters which discouraged sports participation and concluded that '[sports] centres are still predominantly designed and run by the middle-classes, consequently attracting the middle-classes.'

WHY DO SOCIAL CLASS DIFFERENCES STILL EXIST IN SPORT?

There appear to be many practical barriers which restrict freedom of choice in sports participation. Factors such as lack of convenient facilities, shortage of time and work commitments prove a hindrance to many, and only the wealthiest can afford to engage in sports like flying and equestrian events. Even sports like swimming and squash can be prohibitive in cost to the poorest in society if participation is desired on a frequent basis. Undoubtedly, other factors such as cost of

Table 6.2 The constraints affecting leisure participation

Constraints	Constraint 'most affecting leisure' %
Financial	53
Time	36
Family commitments	16
Work	13
Transport problems	12
Health-related	7
Lack of provision	7
Domestic commitments	6
Age	4
Being too tired	4

Source: Adapted from Kay and Jackson, 1991, p. 306.

equipment and lack of transport also prove a hindrance to many. The fact that public sports centres are now run on a commercial basis will not ease the problem of cost. Although discount schemes still exist for disadvantaged groups, there will be pressures to attract full fee-paying custom. While there have been extensive attempts to create equality on the basis of race, sex and disability, it could be argued that social class has only been acknowledged in terms of concessionary rates and that even financial disgression comes under threat when sports centres are run on a commercial basis.

Although cost has not always been highlighted in surveys as a major hindrance to sports participation, this may have been due to a reluctance to admit that money was a problem. A recent thorough investigation by Kay and Jackson (1991) demonstrated the pre-eminence of cost as a major constraint on leisure participation.

While the financial constraints shown in Table 6.2 reduced leisure participation to some extent, Kay and Jackson found that individuals continued to participate in activities to which the constraint applied. Sleap and Duffy (1982) conducted an investigation of factors affecting active participation in sport by the working class. They found that, although lack of facilities and lack of time were given as major barriers to participation, the reality was that both facilities and time were available to the respondents. Sleap and Duffy (1982, p. 18) thus concluded that, while practical constraints could not be ignored, a legacy remained of 'a sporting ethos which is still permeated by middle class values and which is, thus, still alien to working class lifestyles'.

Shilling (1993) addressed the issue by proposing that different social classes perceived the body in different ways and therefore preferred different sporting activities. He suggested that members of the working class have an instrumental orientation to the body and, consequently, sports such as football, motor-cycling and boxing are a means to experiencing excitement. The dominant classes, in contrast, treat the body as an end in itself, engaging in sports which develop physique or contribute to health. This view is not entirely convincing, however, since there is surely an instrumental element to the development of a healthy and beautiful body and many wealthy people are extensively involved in exciting sports like motor racing.

Chapter 3 showed how sporting behaviour involved a complex array of psychological, sociological and cultural factors, enmeshed with very real practical constraints. This suggests that socio-cultural factors and financial considerations bias many working class individuals towards certain sports rather than others. As a result, the easy access and relatively modest cost of pub-centred sports activities mean that they retain their traditional popularity among the working class.

SOCIAL MOBILITY THROUGH SPORT

The rise to stardom of a number of sportsmen from working class origins has led to speculation that sport offers a route to upward social mobility. Prior to the First World War, it was possible for working class men to improve their circumstances through professional football, cricket, rugby league and car racing, and as jockeys in horse racing. Financial returns varied, however. At the turn of the century, while jockeys could earn more than £1000 in a good year, football players were restricted to a maximum wage of £4 per week, and many worked a second job. The career prospects for most footballers were poor, with drawbacks such as lack of long-term security, little control over working conditions and slender opportunities for further social advancement.

In the late nineteenth and early twentieth centuries, it became possible for working class men to gain financial and status advantages through a career in cricket. However, for much of the twentieth century, the professional game of cricket has largely been monopolised by the middle and upper classes from grammar or public schools, leaving very few opportunities for members of the working class. On the other hand, it is possible that professional football has been a means of upward social mobility for the working class. The prominence among professional footballers of railway workers, clerks and boys from industrial areas suggests that many had working class origins, but Chappell (1985) considered that the evidence was not comprehensive enough to be conclusive.

In recent years there has been a dramatic increase in the financial rewards for élite sportsmen and sportswomen. Chapter 10 illustrates how relatively large sums of prize money can be substantially boosted by commercial enterprise such as product endorsement. This means that, assuming reasonable financial management, a successful sportsperson can become financially secure for life. Sports such as boxing, snooker, football and rugby league appear to have enabled individuals from working class origins to improve their financial standing and possibly their social status.

There is very little evidence in Britain in relation to the status of working class sportsmen after the end of their playing careers. In America, Riess (1994) established that, although sports differ, the significant advantage gained by many working class entrants to professional sport was that they benefited from a college education and invariably obtained a white collar position later in life. Since Britain does not have the same sports scholarship system, these educational benefits in most cases will not be present. Riess also commented that, despite financial parity with the middle classes, many black sportsmen had not been integrated into white middle class society because of racial segregation. Although black sportsmen experienced upward social mobility, it was restricted to the separate class structure of American black society.

The issue of social mobility through sport is plagued by the use of conjecture and anecdotes, which means that firm conclusions cannot be drawn. While sport may offer a relatively small number of opportunities for financial advancement, there is little evidence to show whether upward social mobility has been achieved on a long term basis. Questions still remain about the extent to which financial improvement has led to social integration and whether or not the end of a playing career has resulted in a return to working class origins. An accurate assessment of social mobility in sport needs to be set within the overall class and mobility structure. For the time being, the advice given to parents in the 1970s by Arthur Ashe, a former Wimbledon tennis champion, may still be worth heeding:

> I have often addressed high school audiences and my message is always the same. For every hour you spend on the athletic field,

spend two in the library. Even if you make it as a pro athlete, your career will be over by the time you are 35. So you will need that diploma... (Cited in Snyder and Spreitzer, 1978, p. 83)

THE FUTURE

With regard to school physical education and sport, the National Curriculum should ensure that sporting experiences within the curriculum are equal for all pupils attending state schools. However, the market-led approach to school management, where schools compete with one another to attract pupils (or rather their parents), could lead to a return to traditional, team games that are admired by the middle classes. In its efforts to regain sporting traditions of the past, the government (Department of National Heritage, 1995) supported this approach in schools, extolling the virtues of competitive team sports for children.

Giddens (1991) talked of the emancipation of the individual, of being free from constraints imposed by unequal conditions. In sport there still seems a long way to go. Despite the apparent affluence of postindustrial society and the democratisation of some sports, there are many restrictions which limit involvement in sport. While the cost of sport continues to inhibit participation, social barriers also need to be acknowledged. Some sports clubs operate exclusive procedures and certain classes feel uncomfortable in relation to particular sports. While the law apparently offers access to all sports, psychosocial barriers still seem to foreclose particular sports. McIntosh and Charlton (1985) recommended that the causes of inequality in sports participation should be explored and that providers should be helped to understand why inequalities exist and shown how to overcome them.

REFERENCES

Anderson, D.F. and Stone, G.P., 'A Fifteen Year Analysis of Socio-economic Strata Differences in the Meaning Given to Sport by Metropolitans'. In M.C. Krotee (ed.), *The Dimensions of Sport Sociology* (West Point, NY: Leisure Press, 1979), pp. 167–84.

Bourdieu, P., *Distinction: A Social Critique of the Judgement of Taste* (London: Routledge and Kegan Paul, 1984).

Brodie, D., Roberts, K. and Lamb, K., *Citysport Challenge* (Cambridge: Health Promotion Research Trust, 1991).

Chappell, R., 'A Preliminary Investigation into Sport as a Means of Social Mobility', *British Journal of Physical Education*, 16 (1985), pp. 36–7.

Department of Education and Science, *Physical Education for Ages 5 to 16* (London: HMSO, 1991).

Department of National Heritage, *Sport: Raising the Game* (London: Department of National Heritage, 1995).

Dodds, P., 'Removing the Ugly "Isms" in Your Gym: Thoughts for Teachers on Equity'. In J. Evans (ed.), *Equality, Education and Physical Education* (London: Falmer Press, 1993), pp. 28–39.

Giddens, A., *Modernity and Self Identity*, (Oxford: Blackwell, 1991).

Gruneau, R., *Class, Sports, and Social Development* (Amherst: University of Massachusetts Press, 1983).

Hargreaves, J., *Sport, Power and Culture: A Social and Historical Analysis of Popular Sports in Britain* (New York: St Martin's Press, 1986).

Hargreaves, J., 'Sport and Socialism in Britain', *Sociology of Sport Journal*, 9 (1992), pp. 131–53.

Hendry, L., *School, Sport and Leisure* (London: Lepus, 1978).

Holt, R., *Sport and the British: A Modern History* (Oxford: Oxford University Press, 1989).

Jones, S.G., *Sport, Politics and the Working Class* (Manchester: Manchester University Press, 1992).

Kay, T. and Jackson, G., 'Leisure Despite Constraint: The Impact of Leisure Constraints on Leisure Participation', *Journal of Leisure Research*, 23 (1991), pp. 301–13.

McIntosh, P. and Charlton, V., *The Impact of Sport For All Policy – 1966–1984* (London: Sports Council, 1985).

Office of Population, Censuses and Surveys, *General Household Survey* (London: HMSO, 1993).

Riess, S.A., 'From Pitch to Putt: Sport and Class in Anglo-American Sport', *Journal of Sport History*, 21 (1994), pp. 138–84.

Saunders, C., 'Pupil Involvement in Physical Activities at School', *Bulletin of PE*, XV (1979), pp. 28–37.

Shilling, C., 'The Body, Class and Social Inequalities'. In J. Evans (ed.), *Equality, Education and Physical Education* (London: Falmer Press, 1993), pp. 55–73.

Sleap, M. and Duffy, P., 'Factors Affecting Active Participation in Sport by the Working Class', *International Review of Sport Sociology*, 1 (1982), pp. 5–21.

Snyder, E.E. and Spreitzer, E., *Social Aspects of Sport* (Englewood Cliffs: Prentice Hall, 1978).

Veblen, T., *The Theory of the Leisure Class* (New York: Mentor, 1953).

FURTHER READING

Dunning, E. and Sheard, K., *Barbarians, Gentlemen and Players* (Oxford: Martin Robertson, 1979).

Gruneau, R., *Class, Sports, and Social Development* (Amherst: University of Massachusetts Press, 1983).

Jones, S.G., *Sport, Politics and the Working Class* (Manchester: Manchester University Press).

McPherson, B.D., Curtis, J.E. and Loy, J.W., *The Social Significance of Sport* (Champaign: Human Kinetics, 1989).

7 Racial Issues in Sport

INTRODUCTION

> Some people think it's all over . . . but it hasn't gone away. (Ouseley, 1995, p. 1)

This chapter investigates the relationship between race and sport. Racism in Britain has a long history, being rooted in the power structure of the colonial period. As a consequence, racist attitudes and practices have become entrenched in the fabric of society. In recent years, many people in Britain may have thought that, in general, a climate for good race relations had been achieved. This misconception was vividly exposed by the violent incidents in Bradford in 1995, which appeared to be racially motivated. If racial conflict is powerful enough to erupt into violence in Bradford, it is likely that racial tensions exist to a greater or lesser extent in many other areas of the country. It is also likely that they impinge upon all aspects of life, including sport.

The chapter first explores the nature of racial issues in British sport, with special consideration given to the situation that exists in school physical education and sport. Racial abuse and discrimination in sport is then discussed, before we turn to more positive aspects, with a review of efforts being made to improve sport for ethnic minority groups in Britain.

Clarifying Terms

As in other chapters, it is necessary to clarify the terms that are used in order to ensure a meaningful discussion. For example, there is often confusion over the words 'race' and 'ethnicity'. *Race* is usually considered to be a biological category, with people socially distinct from others by birth. A racial group originates from a specific country, although nowadays the boundaries of countries change rapidly and there is a constant migration of people from one part of the world to another. Racial groups share common values, traditions and interests, and have a common identity. Racism occurs when systematic practices exclude certain racial groups from access to social resources.

Ethnicity is associated with a group of people differentiated not by birth but by their cultural heritage. Thus an *ethnic group* is a group of people who share a common cultural background. Despite the difference in meaning, the terms *racial group* and *ethnic group* tend to be used interchangeably in the literature. In everyday life, racial classification is often determined by skin colour. This makes little sense in Britain where families of Afro-Caribbean and Asian origin have lived for two or three generations, where mixed relationships are commonplace and where there are many variations in skin colour.

The histories, ideologies and practices of different ethnic groups mean that it is inappropriate to talk in terms of a single problem in relation to race and sport. For example, issues concerning black professional footballers will be different from those concerning Muslim girls playing sport at school. As with other topics, it is also important to differentiate between élite sport and recreational sport. It may be incorrect, for example, to accept that, because a high proportion of British international athletes are black,[1] sporting opportunities are freely available at all levels of sport. It may also be misleading to see this as significant in terms of racial integration for British society in general. The study of race and sport is not limited to black and white, since there are many ethnic groups to be taken into consideration. However, it should be recognised that white cultural norms are usually the yardstick for judgements about all kinds of sporting situation.

Sociological Studies of Race and Sport

Two kinds of writing are noticeable in relation to race and sport:

- that which boasts of the potential of sport to help racial integration
- that which challenges the above idea, exploring sporting reality.

Maguire (1991) maintained that the sociological study of sport has largely been empirical in nature, neglecting theoretical discussion. As a result, racial sporting issues have not usually been viewed as part of a broader, structural dimension of inequality. In effect, the interrelationship between sport and race cannot be separated from the structure of society. The clearest illustration of this was in South Africa, where full sporting integration between whites and blacks had to wait until the chains of apartheid were broken. Any conflicts that occur in sport may be symptomatic of wider social issues which exist when different ethnic groups try to live together. For example, it is essential to be alert to the complex interrelationship between social class, race and sport.

---

[1] The terms 'Afro-Caribbean' and 'black' are used interchangeably in this chapter, since this has been done in the literature on the topic.

Birrell (1989) also commented on the lack of theoretical analysis in the study of race and sport. She acknowledged, however, that some work was implicitly set within certain theoretical approaches. For example, the extensive writing on 'stacking' in America (that is, the study of team positions in relation to ethnic groups) fell within a discrimination model, while other writing which recognised the loss of ethnic identity as a result of sports participation was consistent with assimilation theory. She also asserted that, rather than remaining at the level of description, a more useful approach would be to adopt a cultural studies model which sought:

> to conceive of race as a culturally produced marker of a particular relationship of power, to racial identity as contested, and to ask how racial relations are produced and reproduced through sport. (Birrell, 1989, p. 214)

RACIAL ISSUES IN BRITISH SPORT

There has been relatively little systematic investigation of the nature and extent of racial problems in British sport. Most writing on the topic has been based on anecdotal evidence, local reports or case studies (Parry, 1989) and, therefore, although problems clearly exist, it is not possible to assess their significance in the country as a whole. Walsh (1991) claimed that racial abuse in football dated back to the 1960s, with the arrival in professional football of the first black footballers, Ces Podd and Clyde Best. A recent Premier League football survey (Sir Norman Chester Centre for Football Research, 1996) revealed that nearly four out of ten fans had heard racist comments or chants at least 'sometimes' during their home matches. Interestingly, the survey reported that:

> it is no coincidence that the *lowest* reported rates of overt racism ... do tend to occur at clubs which are regularly fielding black footballers and for whom black players have become a very 'normal' part of the playing cultures at those clubs. (Sir Norman Chester Centre for Football Research, 1996, p. 111)

Racist remarks and racist incidents also appear to have occurred in sports like boxing, rugby and athletics, although the extent of the problem is not easy to gauge. Anecdotal accounts of racist episodes are given by the sportsmen in Cashmore's (1982) work and considerable attention has been paid to racial problems arising in school sport (Carroll and

Hollinshead, 1993). However, one of the difficulties is that many individuals prefer not to draw attention to themselves or feel that racist problems will disappear if they are ignored. As a result, the extent of the problem may be underestimated.

One of the few pieces of empirical work conducted in Britain was undertaken by Manchester University (Carroll, 1993) to investigate ethnic minority participation in sport in ten local authorities. A white control group was selected and a wide range of ethnic groups were studied, including African, Afro-Caribbean, Asian, Bangladeshi, Chinese, East African, Indian and Pakistani communities. It was found that, although local authorities had equal opportunity policy statements, there was little specifically related to leisure provision and there were no policies to deal with racial harassment or abuse in sport.

Among all ethnic groups, sport was considered to be an important leisure activity, and especially so for males. Interestingly, the most popular sports were the same for all ethnic groups, although most sports participation was segregated into ethnic-related groups, which seems to run counter to the view that sport can be a vehicle for racial integration. Higher sports participation rates were evident among Christians and non-believers, with lower rates among Muslims, Sikhs and Hindus. It was also found that the greater the importance placed on religion by an ethnic group, the lower the participation rate. A recommendation from the researchers was that sports governing bodies and sports clubs ought to be more sensitive to the needs of ethnic minority groups.

The Manchester University study confirmed the widely held view that ethnic minority groups engaged in sport less than their white counterparts. David (1990) identified three ways in which low sports participation rates of ethnic minorities have been explained:

- *Social deprivation.* This explanation sees race as indistinguishable from class. Sports participation is prevented by social disadvantages like lack of money and lack of access.
- *Ethnicity.* Ethnicity influences the leisure choices people make, assuming that sporting meanings and preferences are not accommodated by traditional sporting availability.
- *Racial discrimination.* This acknowledges historical racial discrimination in all areas of social life, including sport and recreation. It highlights the need to investigate power in the form of representation, access to resources and expertise, and ability to make decisions.

If elements of all three exist, there will undoubtedly be great barriers to participation in sport among members of ethnic minorities.

Table 7.1 Popular sporting misconceptions about ethnic minority groups

---
Afro-Caribbeans are poor swimmers because they have heavy bones.
Afro-Caribbeans have weak ankles and therefore cannot play hockey.
Asians are too frail for contact sports.
Asians can only play hockey.
Blacks are good at boxing because they can absorb a heavier beating.
Blacks are good at sport because slavery weeded out the weak.
Blacks have an extra muscle at the top of their legs which helps them to run faster.

Stereotyping

Minority representation is strikingly visible in sporting spectacles, expressing symbolic significance. The media put the spotlight on the athletes, with the result that their performances and behaviour are watched closely. The image portrayed by athletes may be represented as a stereotype for their race, with the general public thinking that the attributes of a famous black boxer, athlete or footballer are typical of all black people. For example, the image demonstrated by the black footballer John Barnes probably has a significant influence on the way white people perceive blacks in general.

> Indeed, he [John Barnes] was fast and skilful. He was also laid-back and inconsistent. He seemed to fit all the requirements of the stereotype. (Hill, 1989, p. 57)

Looking at the issue from a different perspective, black sportsmen like John Barnes and Linford Christie probably act as role models for black youth, encouraging sports participation. In contrast, the absence of black sportsmen and sportswomen from swimming and gymnastics means that few black youngsters will aspire to become international athletes in these sports. McPherson, Curtis and Loy (1989) refer to this as *minority group socialisation*, wherein youths from minority groups seek to play specific sport roles of élite sportsmen and sportswomen from their ethnic group. Thus, an Afro-Caribbean youngster will aspire to become successful like Linford Christie in athletic sprint events, but not in field events like hammer throwing where there are no black role models.

Bayliss (1989, p. 20) listed a number of popular misconceptions about the sporting abilities of ethnic minority groups and these are shown in Table 7.1.

A stereotype which exists about Afro-Caribbeans is their exceptional physical ability. Their prowess is considered to be relatively narrow, however, being mostly associated with speed. Thus, a parallel seems to exist between their representation in sport and the significance of speed in a sport. In some athletic events like the sprints, where speed is paramount, there is a high representation of Afro-Caribbeans, while in football and rugby, where speed in certain positions is vital, they are also well represented.

Scientific Racism

Superior performances by blacks in some sports and their absence from others has been explained in terms of innate differences. The fallibility of this explanation can be demonstrated by considering water sports. The dearth of black, competitive swimmers at international level has been attributed to their lack of buoyancy. If true, this might account for a lack of international breast stroke swimmers, but it would hardly hinder the progress of aspiring high board divers! The achievements of black athletes have been demeaned by the assertion that they are due to genetic factors rather than dedication and intelligence. No consistent relationship has been found between external physical features and mental attributes such as dedication, intelligence, temperament and personality. It is therefore inappropriate to predict that individuals of a certain skin colour will have a potential advantage or disadvantage in particular sports.

It is never suggested that white Scandinavians have a gene in their make-up that helps them to become excellent skiers. It is similarly inappropriate to envisage certain races with a gene which helps them to become excellent boxers. The combination of physical, psychological and experiential factors that are needed to attain sporting prowess leads the social scientist to explore historical, social and cultural influences, rather than a genetic component. For example, McPherson, Curtis and Loy (1989) reported that, in America, élite black athletes had contrasting early sporting experiences (socialisation into sport roles) to élite white athletes. Interaction with significant others such as parents, peers and coaches clearly affected the types of sport and the kinds of event in which black youngsters made progress.

A puzzling feature of sport in Britain is that many, perhaps most, Afro-Caribbean young people engage in sport with little support or encouragement from their parents. This is in direct contrast to most research findings which indicate that parental support is usually an important factor in young people's perseverance in sport. This may be one of the reasons why black youths are limited to certain sports, with financial support and practical assistance (for example, lifts to training) not forthcoming for other sports. It also emphasises the vital supportive role played by schoolteachers, coaches and other adult figures connected with the development of sport among black youth.

It may be that the main reason for racial variation in sports participation is related to differential opportunities. Blacks excel in sports like athletics and basketball because their talent can be nurtured in schools, while they do not have ready access to club settings where sports like tennis, golf, swimming and gymnastics prosper. The differentiation in athletic events is not explained by this, however, since black athletes excel in sprints and jumps but do not feature in throws and long distance events. Nevertheless, the eminence of African long distance runners illustrates that black sportsmen and sportswomen can reach the highest levels in these events.

Coakley (1994, p. 247) suggested that achievement by African Americans in track and field, basketball, football and boxing might be related to interpretations of their own physical abilities and potential:

> when a group of people feel destined to greatness in an activity, when their feelings are grounded in an ideology emphasizing the 'naturalness' of their achievements, and when their social worlds are structured so those feelings make sense in their lives, *it shouldn't be surprising when they achieve notable things.*

This self-fulfilling prophecy may also be relevant for Afro-Caribbeans living in Britain.

SCHOOL PHYSICAL EDUCATION (PE) AND SPORT

Evidence of racial problems in sport can be identified in the school setting. The significance of these should not be underestimated because of the impact that childhood experiences have on future life. The size of the potential problem can also be gauged by the fact that, in London alone, there are around 180 languages among 280 000 pupils. Sporting opportunities and constraints for ethnic minorities exist at school in PE lessons, in extra-curricular clubs and during play situations. Bayliss (1989) claimed that PE had not responded to policies relating to anti-racism and multicultural education, and considered that, during the 1970s and 1980s, a problematic approach had developed whereby superficial remedies were suggested to overcome cultural and religious problems, such as Asian girls not being able to uncover their legs during PE lessons. This can be interpreted as an assimilationist approach, where problem children are integrated into traditional curricula, rather than trying to confront racism and attempting to amend inappropriate curricula.

Fleming (1991) undertook a case study which identified the sporting problems of Asian males in a state comprehensive school. Fleming's interpretation of comments by Asian pupils highlights some important issues:

- *Value of sport.* Muslims do not value sport as much as other aspects of life, such as prayer and, for some, studying.
- *Role models.* There are very few high profile Asian international sportsmen and, therefore, Asian pupils feel that they are no good and sport is 'not for them'.
- *Dance.* Although their own cultural dance is significant for Asian pupils, British dance forms are problematic, leading to apprehension and embarrassment.
- *Showering.* Because of shyness, Asian males often miss physical education to avoid the embarrassment of undressing in front of others.
- *Self-defence.* Some sporting activities like the martial arts are seen as useful, but mainly in protecting them from physical attacks of a racist nature.

For Afro-Caribbean pupils, sport is seen as a route to social acceptance by peers and a possible career pathway, but for Asian males, sport does not seem to offer this prospect. Sport does not have a strong historical tradition for Asians and parental attitudes are mostly negative. Fleming found that the celebrated success of some Asians in cricket, hockey and squash was of little interest to his sample. The traditional, élitist selection process in these sports usually limits entry to relatively affluent young people and not to the majority of Asians attending state schools. The social isolation of Asian pupils at school leads to separation in sporting play situations, which, in turn, hinders development of their sports skills. In addition, the strong influence of family, religious and cultural commitments severely constrains sporting activities outside of curriculum time.

Fleming detected the existence of a self-fulfilling process where Asian males were not expected to take part or succeed in sport and, for one reason or another, lived up to this expectation. He went further, however, viewing sport in a very negative way:

> The reality is that sport, popularly conceived as providing minority groups with equal opportunity, is not only failing to integrate them,

but is a vehicle for the expression of ethnic antagonism and racial tension, and is consolidating and even exacerbating social division. (Fleming, 1991, p. 53)

Although it may not be widespread, a disturbing possibility is that physical violence against ethnic minorities occurs and is legitimised through sport in school. This may be another reason why pupils from ethnic minorities vote with their feet and forget their PE kit. It should be remembered that Fleming's study was limited to Asian males in one comprehensive school and that further studies are needed to evaluate the extent of problems identified.

Afro-Caribbean pupils tend to respond to sport more enthusiastically than their Asian peers and have been found to gain a disproportionate number of school sports team places (Carrington, 1983). This is despite emanating mostly from working class origins and achieving, on average, lower academic attainment levels. Thus, while disadvantaged and disillusioned white pupils can be very negative about PE and school, Afro-Caribbeans are more positive. Teachers may reinforce this with a covert control mechanism, since they can avoid trouble from potentially difficult pupils by offering sporting opportunities. Leaman and Carrington (1985, p. 210) interpreted enthusiasm for sport as a means of 'establishing an aspect of school life, namely sport and dance, as primarily their territory and so display symbolic control of some features of their school lives', thus helping black pupils overcome the imposed marginality which would otherwise be their lot in school life.

Daley (1991) identified other issues that influence school sports participation on the part of ethnic minorities:

- *Language.* Pupils who experience difficulty with the English language will not understand terminology in sporting situations and, consequently, may find it harder to make progress.
- *Fasting.* Fasting will mean that vigorous sporting activity is not advisable.
- *Mixed PE.* Strict religious codes may not allow mixed physical activity.
- *Dress.* Muslim girls may need to be fully covered at all times and sport may have to be done by both boys and girls without removing headwear and jewellery.
- *Parents.* Sport may not be valued by many parents, leading to lack of support for PE and extra-curricular sport.

A tension often develops between the values and cultural convictions of minority ethnic groups and the traditional values of PE in British schools. Giving way to religious beliefs and cultural traditions of minority groups may be seen by teachers as unfair to the majority white pupils. Carroll and Hollinshead (1993, p. 165) commented that PE:

> poses the moral dilemma of individual freedom, equality of opportunity and life-chances in society against the rights of the group to maintain cultural tradition and control over its members in the political context of white domination.

It would seem that equal opportunities policies will not succeed unless ethnic minority cultural and religious traditions and values are acknowledged. This is even more significant in the case of females, since the principle of equal opportunities for women conflicts with Muslim cultural values:

> The teachers are in the middle of this ... They are in danger of being accused of being sexist if they accept cultural tradition and do not operate policies of equality of opportunity, and of being racist if they do not accept cultural tradition and go for equal opportunities. (Carroll and Hollinshead, 1993, p. 165)

In an attempt to make progress on the issue, Bayliss (1989, p. 21) identified four key questions that needed to be asked in order to counteract racial stereotyping and cultural coercion in school PE:

- *Entitlement*. Are the school's aims rooted in individual need?
- *PE*. Does the PE department have specific multicultural aims that are related to the crosscurricular thread?
- *Delivery*. Do staff teaching styles, grouping, attitudes, relationships and expertise reconcile the needs of all ethnic groups?
- *Monitoring*. Is there evaluation to see if racial issues have been addressed?

RACIAL ABUSE AND DISCRIMINATION IN SPORT

It was reported by Cashmore (1982) that, for some famous black sportsmen, skin colour was not an issue during childhood and was only recognised as a problem by remarks or incidents when approaching adulthood. However, these sportsmen came from relatively affluent families and it may have been different for those who grew up in the inner cities. Although no large scale studies have been published on the topic, there are indications that racial abuse has been widespread in sport. Hill's (1989) biography of the footballer John Barnes illustrated the racial abuse that black footballers have had to face in Britain. Despite his undisputed talent, Barnes has encountered racist graffiti, abusive chanting and banana missiles throughout his career. Hill even asserted that the right-wing National Front organisation recruited from the white working classes on the terraces and encouraged fans to support their racist aims. Another disturbing feature is that black football spectators can experience greater problems than black players because of their proximity to the white crowd. Black spectators not only face ugly invective, but can have objects thrown at them and have to cope with white fans picking fights.

In relation to recreational sports participation, Lashley (1991) claimed that racism and racial discrimination in Britain have affected the use of sporting facilities by ethnic minorities. He pointed out that, although the desire for use of sporting facilities by ethnic minorities is high, uptake is low. Thus, despite a legal guarantee in Britain of equal services in public places, the fear of racial discrimination and harassment forms a barrier to participation.

Power

Sport may appear to be open and freely chosen in Britain and yet it will only be within socially produced constraints and pressures. One key issue is the organisation of power in sport: the control, decision making and resource allocation. Is it the case that the hegemonic (power) system disadvantages ethnic minorities, with whites trying to retain an unequal status quo since they are the main beneficiaries? Do whites define sport to their advantage by, for example, changing the rules to prevent black domination?

One way of investigating this issue is to study representative and organisational positions such as coaches and governing body officers. It would appear that much of the discussion on race and sport has failed to differentiate between issues of sports participation and issues related to organisational leadership. A high proportion of British athletes may be black, but their representation in coaching and management is almost non-existent. It is not just in athletics either, since ethnic minorities are underrepresented in all sports in terms of administrative positions.

Both Lovell (1991) and Fleming (1991) claimed that hierarchical arrangements and resource distribution in sports organisations remain within white supremacy, thus determining overall sporting opportunities in British society. While legislation attempts to eliminate racial discrimination in respect of employment matters, it does not cover the service delivery side of sport. In terms of recreational provision it is therefore possible for a public sports centre to find ways of covert discrimination against racial groups. David (1990) warned that the advent of cost effective sports services (that is, competitive tendering) could mean that certain groups in society will suffer, since a provider will attempt to attract people who can pay full rates rather than offer schemes involving subsidies or concessions. If those from ethnic minorities fall into the latter group, as they often do, then their opportunities will inevitably be curtailed.

Unequal Opportunity for Equal Ability

Racial discrimination in sport occurs when differential opportunities exist among individuals who are equal, apart from race. It has been suggested that individuals from ethnic minorities need superior ability to their white counterparts if they are to succeed in sport. The difficulty arises in deciding whether or not people are indeed equal in ability. There may be little ambiguity in an event like the 100 metre sprint, but in team games, evaluation of ability is to a certain degree subjective and discrimination may be concealed by the latitude allowed for subjectivity. In America, Coakley (1994) showed that blacks needed to be better than whites to play representative sport. Scoring averages in basketball, for example, were significantly higher for blacks, and college recruitment profiles showed that blacks demonstrated superior achievement records to whites, prior to being accepted by colleges.

Racial discrimination is difficult to prove in Britain because of ambiguous and subjective performance criteria in many sports. Although a football forward may be assessed objectively by the number of goals scored, there are many other subjective attributes that might be considered. For example, maintaining possession and tackling back are important factors in deciding the best person to select for their contribution to the team. The comments of the black boxer Herol Graham illustrate how inequality may have spurred many aspiring black sportsmen and sportswomen to strive even harder to reach higher standards than their white peers:

> Because they're black they've got to try four times as hard as the white guy. The white people control and I think sometimes they can't accept that blacks are coming up and they've got to live with

them. This makes it tougher for the black guy to make it. (Cited in Cashmore, 1982, p. 114)

Maguire (1991) speculated that the 'unequal access for equal ability' hypothesis could exist in professional football since the proportion of Afro-Caribbean players in the upper divisions of the football league was higher than in the lower divisions. Afro-Caribbean players needed to outperform white peers to succeed, while mediocre Afro-Caribbean footballers were overlooked or rejected.

A substantial amount of work in America has investigated 'stacking', the allocation of black players to certain positions in sports teams. There is an assumption that black players lack the mental acuity to play in important decision-making positions. Maguire (1991) found that black players in English football were less likely to be in positions needing greater judgement and decision making (for example, midfield), positions of responsibility (for example, captain) and positions influencing the flow and pattern of the game (for example, midfield), but were overrepresented in forward positions where speed and flair were primary assets. He also found that similar situations existed in rugby, although, as captain of the England rugby league team, Ellery Hanley did a lot to dismantle this idea, while the England rugby union forward Victor Obogu has done much to negate the idea that black players are unwilling to get involved in the physical side of the game.

Gender Issues

Chapter 5 explored factors that influence women's involvement in sport. A complex interplay of historical, sociological and psychological considerations were identified as important, but it should be recognised that women's sporting experiences are also mediated by racial issues. Sports participation among South Asian women is particularly low in Britain and is restricted to fringe sporting activities like exercise and dance classes. Sport has traditionally held an inferior cultural value for women from South Asian families, with religious affairs occupying almost all of their domestic free time. While white women have few sporting role models to inspire them, role models are virtually non-existent for Asian women. Lovell (1991) suggested that these factors have been reinforced by racist views that label South Asian women as passive and lacking in physical ability.

Interestingly, Asian women do not necessarily feel deprived of sporting opportunities, since sport is not deemed to have an important role in their lives. In contrast, sport is perceived differently by Afro-Caribbean women. Traditionally, Afro-Caribbean women have been more assertive physically in the family setting, since they have had a stronger economic role. They are also perceived as being good at sport because of the high profile media coverage given to élite athletes such as Florence Griffith Joyner and Tessa Sanderson. However, despite their strong tradition in sports like athletics, they are noticeably absent from other sports like swimming and gymnastics. As with men, Lovell (1991) believed it was a combination of cultural identity and racism that allowed Afro-Caribbean women access to particular sports and excluded them from others.

Protest

A cultural arena like sport offers ethnic minorities almost unlimited publicity for their causes:

> in an age when power and capital have developed sophisticated techniques to insulate themselves against traditional, materialistic forms of protest and challenge, cultural arenas provide one of the few public spaces in which otherwise marginalized and disempowered groups can express social grievances and begin to fashion some sort of mobilisation on their behalf. (Hartmann, 1996, p. 549)

The black power salute by Tommie Smith and John Carlos at the 1968 Mexico Olympic Games was organised by the Olympic Project for Human Rights to raise awareness about four main issues:

- persistent violation of black people's human rights in the USA
- the historical exploitation of US black athletes as political propaganda tools
- establishing a standard of political responsibility among black athletes
- raising awareness, particularly in developing African nations, of hidden political dynamics and consequences of established sport institutions.

Smith and Carlos were permanently suspended from Olympic competition and received savage critical attacks from the American press, although in the eyes of many black Americans they were revered as heroes. The importance and prestige of élite black athletes in America had led Smith and Carlos to think that, through non-violent protest, they might induce social change.

Hartmann (1996) argued that global revulsion at the protest was strong because, even among blacks, sport was seen as sacrosanct and not a forum for racial protest. Sport was idealistically considered to be open to all people of all races and, furthermore, valued as a vehicle for racial integration. It was an arena where blacks could engage in collective action and where they had enjoyed considerable success. Sport was considered to be an example of liberal, democratic ideology in practice and the Olympic protest seemed to be an attack on the one channel open to ethnic minorities for social integration. It is difficult to judge the effect of the protest and, while many might say that it changed nothing of substance, it has become 'an icon of popular culture' (Hartmann, 1996, p. 563) and in future generations may be seen as a landmark in race relations.

SPORT AS AN AVENUE OF SUCCESS

Sport provides an avenue of success for young people from ethnic minorities who may have found relatively little success in other spheres of life. This is not just concerned with the achievement of international status in sport, but could help in giving any individual a psychological boost or possibly enhancing self-esteem. Sport can be an 'alternative channel for the fulfilment of their achievement needs and a potential source of status, prestige and self-esteem' (Carrington, 1986, p. 16). Gallop and Dolan (1981) referred to the need for people to define a social and personal role for themselves in society and this may be especially true for individuals from minority ethnic groups. Sport can act as a source of self-identity, especially if employment lacks importance and leisure is a central life interest. Gallop and Dolan (1981, p. 64) commented that 'for second generation ethnic minority members their use of leisure time is likely to become a touch stone of their psycho-social well-being'. In contrast, failure in sport, which is far more common than success, has a profound effect and may lead to premature withdrawal from participation. In turn, early withdrawal from sport may reinforce the stereotype of black people generally lacking resilience and reliability.

It was noted in the earlier section on school PE that Afro-Caribbean youth showed a keen interest in sport. Carrington (1983) and Cashmore (1982), among others, have suggested that, while schoolteachers tend to support and encourage sports participation among black youths, they are less enthusiastic about their academic potential, turning it into a self-fulfilling cycle. Carrington (1983) initially found that Afro-Caribbeans did not seem to aspire to careers in professional sport, although later he acknowledged that many had a '*chimerical* view that sport can provide a *viable* route to fame and fortune' (Carrington, 1986, p. 10). For the majority of black youths, the prospects on leaving school range from unemployment to a mundane job with little or no promotional prospects. In this context a black youth with sporting talent may well see sport as a central life interest, a means of self-expression, a way of building relationships with others in sport and the chance of a rewarding career; in effect, a means of upward social mobility. If black youths believe that career pathways other than sport have racial barriers, even though they may not have, they will lean towards sports careers rather than others.

The high media profile of successful black sportsmen like Linford Christie and Frank Bruno reinforces the attraction of this route to success. Carrington (1986, p. 11) reported the view of black boxer John Conteh:

> Boxing was a quick way out of being poor. I hadn't time for five year apprenticeships and no-one was going to send me to Hollywood.

While many may have aspirations of sporting success, very few will earn a living from sport, let alone find fame and fortune. As we saw in Chapter 6, it is also questionable whether sporting success leads to upward social mobility and, if so, whether it persists after retirement from competition. This was underlined by Carrington (1986), who indicated that, although the evidence was quite limited, it showed that professional sportsmen generally experienced downward social mobility after retirement from competition. There is no substantive investigation of this issue, although Maguire (1988) noted that, while Afro-Caribbeans see sport as a way of achieving status and social mobility, access to coaching, administrative and management positions seems remote after retirement from competitive play. It would seem that Afro-Caribbeans have been the 'workhorses of sport' (Leaman and Carrington, 1985, p. 212), disappearing from the scene once their playing days were over.

Social Integration

In theory, the sporting arena offers opportunities for integration that do not always exist in other spheres of life. The organisational features of sport mean that sportsmen and sportswomen from different ethnic groups can be utilised for their sporting performances without a direct threat to the existing power hierarchy in sport or society as a whole. For example:

- An individual's achievements benefit the whole team.
- Superior performances do not usually lead to athletes having power or authority over other team members.
- Friendship between team members is not essential to the success of a team on the field.
- The relatively powerless status of athletes in the rest of society ensures that there is not a threat to the status quo (that is, white control).

It is thought that the integration of minority ethnic groups into a society involves four stages: contact, competition, accommodation and assimilation. Many Afro-Caribbeans and Asians who were born and educated in Britain have been assimilated into British sport. Nevertheless, this has to be qualified by the fact that they are mostly confined to particular sports, particular events and even particular positions within teams. It appears that, in Britain, while assimilation has certainly taken place, there are groups that try to maintain their separateness and their eventual assimilation is not guaranteed.

In America, Chu and Griffey (1985) examined the *contact hypothesis*, where personal interaction between racial groups with shared group goals is thought to lead to positive changes in intergroup attitudes and behaviours. In respect of recreational sport, Chu and Griffey concluded that few, if any, long term changes in attitude or prejudices occurred as a result of membership of interracial sports teams. Also in America, McPherson, Curtis and Loy (1989) reported that sports teams that were exclusively made up of one ethnic minority group did not get assimilated into mainstream society, but tended to adopt ethnic solidarity. On the other hand, teams composed of individuals from diverse ethnic backgrounds were more likely to be successfully assimilated. Cashmore (1982) found that black and white sportsmen in Britain mixed within the sports setting despite holding opposing racial views, but he acknowledged that it was not known whether tolerance existed before, or developed as a result of, the sporting experience.

Progress towards racial integration can be easily undermined by inflammatory journalism in the media, especially newspapers. The ball-tampering issue of the 1992 England versus Pakistan cricket matches provoked the following comment in the *Sun* newspaper from Bob Willis, an ex-captain of England:

> It's just the way the Pakistanis are brought up to play their cricket. It's the nature of the beast. Everything is confrontational. They don't say sorry willingly and don't often accept they are in the wrong... it's not part of their character. (Cited in Searle, 1993, p. 48)

The ball-tampering accusations were countered by suggestions that they were motivated by 'racism and colonial rivalry' (Searle, 1993, p. 50). The affront to the Pakistani people not only slighted those in Pakistan, but also invited a racist backlash from the Pakistani community living in Britain.

MAKING PROGRESS

Equal opportunity was a guiding principle of the National Curriculum Working Group for PE (Department of Education and Science 1991, p. 15), which declared 'that all children should be allowed access to and given confidence in the different activities involved, regardless of their ability, sex, or cultural/ethnic background'. The Working Group went further by stating that PE was an apt opportunity to counter racist thinking through provision of information, by acquainting pupils with one another, through organisation of crosscultural and inter-ethnic activities and by promoting interculturalism through a residential experience. However, Figueroa (1993) pointed out that, although the Working Group seriously addressed issues of cultural diversity, equity and racism, the Statutory Orders for PE in the National Curriculum (Department of Education and Science, 1992) made hardly any reference to them, thus offering little direction for teachers.

Ethnic minorities were targeted for special attention by the Sports Council in their 1982 strategy *The Next Ten Years* (Sports Council, 1982) and in their 1988 strategy *Into the 90s* (Sports Council, 1988). As a result, the Action Sport scheme, along with other local and regional initiatives, tries to cater for the sporting needs of ethnic minorities. A significant step forward was also made by the Sports Council with a Participation Demonstration Project which focused on ethnic minorities (Sports Council, 1991). The project aimed to identify the needs of ethnic minorities, provide suitable sporting opportunities, develop cooperation between appropriate agencies and train sports leaders from ethnic minorities. Although the project team found that leisure was often sacrificed for homework in the case of young people, and for religious and family duties by adults, progress was made in a number of ways. For example, innovative developments included:

- linking sporting opportunities to national celebrations such as the Hindu and Sikh Diwali Festival of Light
- sports literature published in ethnic minority languages

- full consultation within the community on sports issues
- multicultural awareness training given within the Leisure Services Department
- promotion of inter-agency cooperative work: for example, from adult education to health promotion.

Despite its good intentions, there is a sense here of British culture being imposed on ethnic minorities in the form of sport. Sport has not traditionally featured strongly in the cultures of many ethnic minorities and yet projects such as this attempt to shift priorities, raising the importance of sport and lowering the significance of other values.

David (1990) suggested two ways to improve racial equality in sport. First, there was a need to ensure that racial discrimination was not tolerated by sports policy makers and providers. Second, there was a need to enlarge on the outreach concept whereby schemes enhanced the sporting opportunities of ethnic minorities. For example, he claimed that sports participation by Asian women could be substantially increased by initiatives such as 'women only' sessions. However, David believed that this approach, while helpful, was only a short term measure and that progress in the long term required the removal of institutionalised racism, as expressed by lack of appropriate publicity, failure to tackle racial harassment and the need to amend racial stereotypical beliefs held by sports centre staff.

A notable development in Britain has been the inauguration of sports organisations that serve to promote the interests of ethnic minorities. One example is the Birmingham Pakistan Sports Forum (Chisti, 1991), which was launched in 1988 to promote the sport and recreation needs of the Pakistani community in Birmingham. In one sense these organisations can help to identify the needs of an ethnic group and ensure that suitable sporting opportunities are considered. On the other hand, they also lead to a certain degree of sporting separation, as in this case where the Forum organises 'Pakistani only' tournaments and encourages the national games of Pakistan such as Kabbadi and gulli danda.

In 1992 the Sports Council adopted a 'racial equality in sport policy' and now aims:

> To work towards the elimination of racial disadvantage and discrimination in order to achieve better quality sport for black and ethnic minority people. (Sports Council, 1994, p. 7)

In professional football, certain developments have occurred to curb racism. The 1991 Football Offences Act made the chanting of racial abuse a criminal offence, and Walsh (1991) claimed that progress had been made, with racists dwindling to a small minority. However, a few voices were becoming increasingly loud and a problem still existed. In 1995 the Advisory Group Against Racism and Intimidation (AGARI) initiated a new campaign against racism and intimidation in football. With joint themes of 'Let's Kick Racism' and 'Respect All Fans', the campaign aims 'to ensure that all people who play or watch football can do so without fear of racial abuse, either in verbal or physical form' (AGARI, 1995, p. 2). AGARI has united all major organisations involved in football and attracted a large number of football stars to publicise the campaign. Target audiences for the initiative include schools, football clubs, supporters' groups and youth clubs, while a number of cultural activities and anti-racist activities were organised during the European Football Championships held in Britain in 1996.

CONCLUDING COMMENTS

If progress is to be made on this issue, it will be necessary to view people from ethnic minorities as full members of society and not simply as athletes. Racial sporting issues need to be addressed in relation to structural dimensions of inequality and, consequently, the power systems that underlie all social relations. It would appear that three types of acculturation are presently taking place in Britain. Total acculturation occurs in some instances, especially with less devout cultures, while partial acculturation takes place where British values are adopted, but certain cultural traditions are retained. Finally, separate development occurs where particular groups reject erosion of their traditions and values, electing for totally segregated sporting situations.

In capitalist society, sport is often considered to be a conservative force, supporting and reinforcing the established social order. However, sport is also a site of struggle where individuals and organisations attempt to break down racial barriers to expand sporting opportunities for ethnic minority groups. As Donnelly (1996, p. 237) concluded:

> Although sport has been an important agent in the production and reproduction of social inequality, democratizing actions on the part of individuals and organizations have sensitized us to sport's potential to be an equally important agent of social transformation for the production of social equality.

REFERENCES

AGARI, *Let's Kick Racism Newsletter* (London: Commission for Racial Equality, 1995).
Bayliss, T., 'PE and Racism: Making Changes', *Multicultural Teaching*, 7 (1989), pp. 19–22.
Birrell, S., 'Racial Relations Theories and Sport: Suggestions for a More Critical Analysis', *Sociology of Sport Journal*, 6 (1989), pp. 212–27.
Carrington, B., 'Sport as a Side-track: An Analysis of West Indian Involvement in Extra-curricular Sport'. In L. Barton and S. Walker (eds.), *Race, Class and Education* (London: Croom Helm, 1983).
Carrington, B., 'Social Mobility, Ethnicity and Sport', *British Journal of Sociology of Education*, 7 (1986), pp. 3–18.
Carroll, R., 'Factors Influencing Ethnic Minority Groups' Participation in Sport', *Physical Education Review*, 16 (1993), pp. 55–66.
Carroll, R. and Hollinshead, G., 'Equal Opportunities: Race and Gender in Physical Education: A Case Study'. In J. Evans (ed.), *Equality, Education and Physical Education* (London: Falmer Press, 1993).
Cashmore, E., *Black Sportsmen* (London: Routledge and Kegan Paul, 1982).
Chisti, M., 'Birmingham Pakistan Sports Forum', *Sport and Leisure*, 32 (1991), p. 28.
Chu, D. and Griffey, D., 'The Contact Theory of Racial Integration: The Case of Sport', *Sociology of Sport Journal*, 2 (1985), pp. 323–33.
Coakley, J.J., *Sport in Society* (St Louis: Mosby, 1994).
Daley, D., 'Multi-cultural Issues in Physical Education', *British Journal of PE*, 22 (1991), pp. 31–2.
David, C., 'Equal Opportunities?', *Sport and Leisure*, 31 (1990), pp. 32–3.
Department of Education and Science, *Physical Education for Ages 5 to 16* (London: HMSO, 1991).
Department of Education and Science, *Physical Education in the National Curriculum* (London: HMSO, 1992).
Donnelly, P., 'Approaches to Social Inequality in the Sociology of Sport', *Quest*, 48 (1996), pp. 221–42.
Figueroa, P., 'Equality, Multiculturalism, Antiracism and Physical Education in the National Curriculum'. In J. Evans (ed.), *Equality, Education and Physical Education* (London: Falmer Press, 1993), pp. pp. 90–102.
Fleming, S., 'Sport, Schooling and Asian Male Youth Culture'. In G. Jarvie (ed.), *Sport, Racism and Ethnicity* (London: Falmer Press, 1991), pp. 30–57.
Gallop, D. and Dolan, J., 'Perspectives on the Participation in Sporting Recreation amongst Minority Group Youngsters', *Physical Education Review*, 4 (1981), pp. 65–70.
Hartmann, D., 'The Politics of Race and Sport: Resistance and Domination in the 1968 African American Olympic Protest Movement', *Ethnic and Racial Studies*, 19 (1996), pp. 548–66.
Hill, D., *Out of His Skin: The John Barnes Phenomenon* (London: Faber and Faber, 1989).
Lashley, H., 'Promoting Anti-racist Policy and Practice', *Sport and Leisure*, 32 (1991), pp. 16–17.

Leaman, O. and Carrington, B., 'Athleticism and the Reproduction of Gender and Ethnic Marginality', *Leisure Studies*, 4 (1985), pp. 205–17.
Lovell, T., 'Sport, Racism and Young Women'. In G. Jarvie (ed.), *Sport, Racism and Ethnicity* (London: Falmer Press, 1991), pp. 58–73.
McPherson, B.D., Curtis, J.E. and Loy, J.W., *The Social Significance of Sport* (Champaign: Human Kinetics, 1989).
Maguire, J.A., 'Race and Position Assignment in English Soccer: A Preliminary Analysis of Ethnicity and Sport in Britain', *Sociology of Sport Journal*, 5 (1988), pp. 257–69.
Maguire, J.A., 'Sport, Racism and British Society: A Sociological Study of England's Elite Male Afro-Caribbean Soccer and Rugby Union Players'. In G. Jarvie (ed.), *Sport, Racism and Ethnicity* (London: Falmer Press, 1991), pp. 94–123.
Ouseley, H., *Let's Kick Racism Newsletter*, 2 (1995), October, Advisory Group against Racism and Intimidation.
Parry, J., *Participation by Black and Ethnic Minorities in Sport and Recreation* (London: London Research Centre, 1989).
Searle, C., 'Cricket and the Mirror of Racism', *Race and Class*, 34 (1993), pp. 45–54.
Sir Norman Chester Centre for Football Research, *FA Premier League Fan Surveys 1995/96* (Leicester: University of Leicester, 1996).
Sports Council, *Sport in the Community: The Next Ten Years* (London: Sports Council, 1982).
Sports Council, *Into the 90s* (London: Sports Council, 1988).
Sports Council, *Ethnic Minorities Recreation Project* (London: Sports Council, 1991).
Sports Council, *Black and Ethnic Minorities in Sport: Policy and Objectives* (London: Sports Council, 1994).
Walsh, M., 'Coming Through the Hard Way', *Sport and Leisure*, 32 (1991), pp. 26–7.

FURTHER READING

Jarvie, G. (ed.), *Sport, Racism and Ethnicity* (London: Falmer Press, 1991).

Further in-depth discussion of this issue can be found in the writings of Birrell, Carrington and Maguire (cited above).
A review of 1970s and 1980s literature can be found in Parry (cited above).

8 Drug Abuse in Sport

INTRODUCTION

> Unless something is done soon international sport will be a competition between circus freaks manipulated by international chemists. (Lawson, cited in Beashel and Taylor, 1986, p. 84)

This chapter initially provides background information about drugs and how they have been used in sport. A short description is then given of the evolution of doping control and the testing procedures which have been adopted by sporting authorities. The remainder of the chapter explores various issues that have arisen in relation to doping in sport. For example, the many pressures that are placed on élite performers are examined, along with arguments put forward to legalise drug taking in sport.

BACKGROUND INFORMATION ABOUT DRUG USE IN SPORT

Drug use in sport is not a modern phenomenon. The Ancient Greeks believed that different kinds of mushroom improved athletic abilities and some athletes[1] are thought to have eaten sheep's testicles in preparation for the Olympic Games. Knights during the Middle Ages drank wine liberally before jousting contests, and drug use was widespread in horse racing towards the end of the nineteenth century, when horses were doped to speed them up or slow them down. Drug abuse was first identified in cycling in 1879 during a six-day race, and in the early part of the twentieth century, marathon runners took to mixing a potent cocktail of strychnine with brandy.

> The use of artificial means [to improve performance] has long been considered wholly incompatible with the spirit of sport and has therefore been condemned. Nevertheless, we all know that this rule is continually being broken, and that sportive competitions are often more a matter of doping than training. (Riesser in Hoberman, 1993, p. 281)

---

[1] 'Athletes' refers to all sportsmen and sportswomen, not just track and field athletes. The term 'anabolic-androgenic steroids' is shortened to anabolic steroids for convenience in this chapter.

This statement might be expected to have come from the late twentieth century, but in fact it was part of a discussion about doping in Germany in the 1930s. Numerous athletes were rumoured to be benefiting from doping at this time and counter measures were adopted by many countries in order to keep up with the Germans.

The alleged use of drugs by an ice skater in the 1950s brought a new meaning to the term 'speed skater'. However, it was during the 1950s and 1960s that drug abuse in sport became a serious, well publicised problem. The availability of powerful agents with less toxic effects gave athletes the potential to enhance their performance artificially (Mottram, 1988). Dramatic improvements in Soviet weightlifting results during the 1950s suggest that reports of anabolic steroid use were correct. However, the health implications of drug use were brought to light when Knud Jensen, a member of the Danish cycling team, died in the 1960 Olympic Games in Rome. The official cause of death was heatstroke, but he was alleged to have been heavily doped. More widely publicised in Britain was the case of the British cyclist Tommy Simpson, whose death during the Tour de France, it is alleged, was drug related.

During the cold war there was constant speculation that eastern European athletes used drugs to boost their performances to attain world domination in many areas of sport. After the reunification of East and West Germany, there have indeed been revelations of the massive, covert state-sponsored doping programme which operated in East Germany (Hoberman, 1993). The legitimacy of their past achievements is now open to question and clean athletes who competed against them must feel very frustrated. Despite the apparent widespread use of drugs in sport, the academic world was for many years equivocal about the benefits of drugs in enhancing sporting performance. For example, it was not until 1984 that the American College of Sports Medicine accepted that anabolic steroids aided athletic performance.

Facts About Drugs

Drugs are substances which may affect an individual's body function, emotional state or behaviour. They can be divided into *therapeutic drugs, recreational drugs* and *performance-enhancing drugs*. The medical and nursing professions use the word 'drugs' to refer to medicines – substances that can cure or arrest disease, relieve symptoms, ease pain and provide other benefits. The medical use of the term would also include essential vitamins and minerals that may be given to correct deficiency diseases. Some addictive drugs like nicotine in cigarettes and heroin have no medical use and are sometimes called recreational drugs. They are generally used to relieve tension or seek gratification. The use of any prohibited substance or prohibited method in sport is known as *doping* and it may be undertaken to enhance performance, treat an injury or illness, improve the effectiveness of training or alter body shape. It is important to note that, in medical terms, drugs are designed to rectify problems induced by disease and injury, but not to affect body systems in healthy people.

Doping in sport can be defined as the administration of substances belonging to prohibited classes of pharmacological agents and/or the use of various prohibited methods. While a particular drug may improve performance in one sport, it can have a detrimental effect in another. Calming drugs would be counterproductive in sports needing highly aroused competitors, and stimulants would not help in a sport where a steady state is essential. The true effects of drugs on performance may never be known because drugs are used covertly, and therefore appropriately designed studies will probably never be conducted.

Drugs may be administered in the following ways:

- *stacking* – combining drugs to achieve a stronger effect
- *tapering* – gradually decreasing intake
- *plateauing* – drugs no longer effective at a particular level
- *shotgunning* – trying out different drugs
- *cycling* – taking drugs for a period, coming off for a period and then repeating the cycle.

Most, but not all, governing bodies of sport abide by the Medical Code of the International Olympic Committee. This includes the following.

Prohibited Classes of Substances
A. Stimulants
B. Narcotics
C. Anabolic agents
D. Diuretics
E. Peptide and glycoprotein hormones and analogues

Prohibited Methods
A. Blood doping
B. Pharmacological, chemical and physical manipulation

Classes of Drugs Subject to Certain Restrictions
A. Alcohol
B. Marijuana

C. Local anaesthetics
D. Corticosteroids
E. Beta-blockers

PROHIBITED CLASSES OF SUBSTANCES

Stimulants

Stimulants affect the central nervous system, increasing alertness, reducing fatigue, increasing aggressiveness and masking pain. Stimulants have been widely used in many sports because they can arouse a competitor to produce a highly motivated performance. In addition to 'psyching up' an athlete, stimulants may also have been used to enhance training. Adverse effects include raised blood pressure, heightened body temperature and possible heart problems. In addition to these physical problems, athletes suffer from behaviour changes such as becoming more hostile and liable to irrational behaviour. The addictive potential of a stimulant like *cocaine* is high and dangers include heat problems, convulsions and seizure.

Caffeine is thought to give an endurance boost for athletes, but usage is problematic since the amount needed to produce an effect almost certainly leads to stomach cramps and diarrhoea, brought about because it is a gastric irritant. However, athletes have been known to use suppositories, containing the equivalent of 25 cups of coffee, to bypass the stomach and avoid irritation problems.

Sympathomimetic amines increase heart rate and muscle blood flow to provide a stimulant effect for an athlete. However, some sympathomimetic amines like ephedrine are readily available in cough, cold and sinus medications. Athletes could therefore innocently take these remedies to reduce cough and cold symptoms and be tested positive for doping. Although declarations of genuine use can be made, possible complications mean that it is advisable for athletes to opt for alternative decongestants which are not banned.

Narcotic Analgesics

Narcotic analgesics have mainly been used by competitors to increase the pain threshold in training or competition. Thus, if an athlete suffers an injury prior to or during a major event, narcotics have been used to deaden the pain and help the competitor perform to a high level. There may, however, be long term adverse effects, since the body may suffer further damage during competition and never fully recover.

Anabolic Steroids

Anabolic steroids are popular because they are considered to be effective, and consequently they have been used in a variety of sports from swimming to team sports. They stimulate tissue growth while inhibiting tissue degeneration, thus allowing the athlete to train harder and recover more quickly. It is thought that they are most effective if used in conjunction with a weight training programme and a high protein, high calorie diet. Anabolic steroids are derivatives of the natural male hormone testosterone and, because they increase male characteristics, they have the potential to develop muscle mass. Unfortunately, they produce other male body changes such as baldness, infertility and impotence in men. Although the physical side effects are worrying, the psychological effects are also disturbing. Psychotic behaviour among athletes using anabolic steroids includes aggressiveness, hallucination, ignoring personal safety and infliction of pain on themselves and others.

Females using anabolic steroids are at even greater risk because the masculine growth substance is antagonistic to the female body. Side effects include the development of masculine traits, disruption of growth, acne and hirsutism (hair growth), which may be irreversible. While research concerned with the effects of drugs on men is limited, it is almost non-existent in relation to women.

Diuretics

Diuretics were added to the banned list of substances in 1986 after it became evident that athletes were using them to dilute their urine and confound the testing procedure. Another main application of diuretics is to achieve weight loss, a tactic employed immediately before a competition, in an attempt to compete in a lower weight class. However, the problem with rapid weight loss is that it leads to fatigue, muscle weakness and cramps, which could give rise to poor performance. More serious problems can also result from the use of diuretics, since they interfere with the regulation of body temperature, which may lead to exhaustion or heart failure.

Human Growth Hormone

Human growth hormone is naturally produced by the pituitary gland to regulate growth and development. Competitors believe that it can increase muscle size, enhance bone growth and strengthen connective tissues. The advantage for athletes is that growth hormone abuse cannot be detected by existing drug tests. It is consequently in great demand and there are growing numbers of abusers who try to stimulate the production of naturally occurring substances like *testosterone*.

Athletes believe that growth hormone has no adverse side effects, and yet there are many health risks associated with the abuse of growth hormone (Smith and Perry, 1992). The growth of all tissues in the body is stimulated by growth hormones and therefore enlargement of external features and internal organs is likely, while thyroid problems, menstrual disorders, impotence and the onset of diabetes are all possible outcomes – conditions which would not be reversible.

Epoetin is genetically engineered human recombinant erythropoietin (EPO), which stimulates red blood cell production and is difficult to detect in athletes. The ergogenic potential is similar to that of blood doping, although there is little reliable evidence of its effect on performance. Adverse effects could occur if the drug is used by healthy individuals, particularly in respect of increased blood viscosity which may cause high blood pressure.

Growth Retardants

The spectacular performances achieved in women's gymnastics are dependent on sylphlike figures, and the onset of puberty means that weight increase and changes in body proportion decrease performance potential among female gymnasts. Consequently, it is thought that, in the case of some female gymnasts, puberty has been retarded by the use of drugs like medroxyprogesterone acetate, and cyproterone acetate which interfere with the hormonal balance of the female. If maturation can be postponed, a girl may benefit from an extra season of competition with a pre-pubertal figure.

PROHIBITED METHODS

Blood Doping

Blood doping involves the injection of blood into the body to increase the number of blood cells. This develops endurance since the increased number of red blood cells are thought to transport oxygen to muscle cells more efficiently. Approximately two pints of an athlete's blood are removed and frozen two to three months before competition. The athlete increases intake of food to replenish the lost blood and then, a short time before competition, the red blood cells, which have been separated from the serum, are infused back into the body. This could be of benefit in running, cycling, skiing and other endurance events since it is estimated that a 15–30 per cent improvement in endurance is possible with blood doping. Risks from the transfusion of blood include: allergic reactions, hepatitis or AIDS, overload of circulatory system, blood clots and kidney damage. Other hazards include heart failure due to increased blood pressure and additional work load on the heart.

Pharmacological, Chemical and Physical Manipulation

This is the use of substances and methods which alter urine samples in doping control. Examples include catheterisation, urine substitution and/or tampering and inhibition of renal excretion, such as by probenecid.

CLASSES OF DRUGS SUBJECT TO CERTAIN RESTRICTIONS

Tests may be conducted for *ethanol (alcohol)* and *cannabinoids (marijuana, hashish)* and the results may lead to sanctions. Injectable *local anaesthetics* are permitted under certain conditions, while the use of *corticosteroids* is banned except for topical use, by inhalation and by intra-articular or local injection.

Beta-blockers are now mainly used to reduce nervous tension in sports where steadiness is paramount and where physical activity is of no or little importance. Thus, they are particularly helpful in sports such as shooting, archery and golf where a steady finger and firm hand are needed for accuracy. However, they may also help skaters and gymnasts where palpitations from nervousness can upset a precise, balance routine. Because beta-blockers slow the heart rate, there is the possibility of heart problems arising with healthy athletes, and reduced blood flow to muscles may make exertion more difficult, possibly causing breathlessness in asthmatics.

Nutritional Aids

Because of the increased sophistication of drug testing, the banning of diuretics and probenecid, the severity of penalties and the greater awareness of serious health risks, athletes have sought alternative non-pharmacologic (ergogenic) methods of performance enhancement. Recent research has explored the use of large doses of specific nutrients to act as drugs and, because most are legal, attention has been focused on their role in enhancing sports performance.

Williams (1994) considered that the benefits of nutritional aids were still unproven, but outlined some areas which showed promise. For example, it is thought that increased endurance can be achieved by enhanced carbohydrate intake, or *carbohydrate loading*, prior to competition. This nutritional approach increases glycogen levels and delays fatigue, thus aiding performance in endurance events such as the marathon. Recently, studies have shown the benefits to performance of dihydroxyacetone and pyruvate to give an effective increase of muscle glycogen stores without added bulk in the intestinal tract. Athletes requiring strength and power have regarded *protein* as an important nutrient to build up muscle mass. Although there is still doubt regarding their effect on protein, the supplementation of branched chain amino acids may lead to ergogenic potential by delaying fatigue in prolonged endurance events.

Creatine is made up of two naturally occurring amino acids, the majority of which is found in skeletal muscle. It is thought that ingestion of creatine supplement increases the amount of creatine phosphate available and delays depletion of phosphocreatin stores during maximal exercise. This would be of value to power athletes competing in explosive events, enabling them to continue exercise for longer. The adverse effects of creatine supplements are not known.

Vitamin supplements have generally been shown not to improve performance among athletes with a balanced diet. However, some positive experimental results have been found when megadoses of vitamin B have been taken to aid relaxation and vitamin E to reduce muscle tissue damage during training. *Mineral* supplements may offer some performance improvement although the research is equivocal, while *water* supplementation has been successful in improving performance capacity, especially in warm and hot conditions.

Table 8.1 describes the different types of drug used in sport, their possible benefits and potential adverse effects on a healthy person.

PREVALENCE OF DRUG ABUSE IN SPORT

The merciless rigor of modern competitive sports, especially at the international level, the glory of victory, and the growing social and economic rewards of sporting success increasingly forces athletes to

Table 8.1 Effects of use and potential harm of drugs in sport

Doping class	Example substances	Effects of use	Potential harm
Stimulants	Amphetamine Caffeine Cocaine Diethylpropion Ephedrine Phentermine Phenylpropanolamine Strychnine	Reduces tiredness. Increases alertness, competitiveness and aggression.	Rise in blood pressure and body temperature. Increased and irregular heart beat. Increased anxiety and aggressiveness. Loss of appetite. Addiction.
Narcotic analgesics	Dextropropoxyphene Methadone Morphine Pethidine	Deadens pain. Masks injuries. Increases pain limit.	Breathing problems. Nausea and vomiting. Loss of concentration, balance and co-ordination. Addiction.
Anabolic agents	Androgenic anabolic steroids: Boldenone Mesterolone Stanozolol Testosterone Beta2 agonists: Clenbuterol Salbutamol* Terbutaline* Salmeterol*	Increases muscle size. Increases aggression.	Risk of liver disease. Premature heart disease. *In males:* Acne; increased aggression, sometimes resulting in violent sexual behaviour; leading to impotence in the long term; kidney damage; development of breasts; premature baldness. *In females:* Development of male features; irregular periods; increased

(*continued on p. 138*)

Table 8.1 (continued)

Doping class	Example substances	Effects of use	Potential harm
			aggression; more hair growth on face and body; deepening of voice.
Diuretics	Bendrofluazide Frusemide Hydrochlorothiazide Triameterine Spironolactone	Quick loss of weight. Increases rate at which urine can be passed, in an attempt to make it more difficult to detect a banned substance.	Dehydration leading to: Faintness and dizziness. Muscle cramps. Headaches and nausea. Kidney and heart failure.
Peptide hormones and analogues	Chorionic gonadotrophin Corticotrophin Growth Hormone Erythropoietin	Stimulates production of naturally occurring steroids; builds up muscles; mends body tissue; improves body's ability to carry oxygen.	Muscle wasting. Abnormal growth of hands, feet, face and internal organs. Thickening of the blood, leading to risk of blood clotting and stroke.
Beta-blockers	Atenolol Oxprenolol Propranolol	Steadies nerves. Stops trembling. Calms and relaxes.	Low blood pressure. Slow heart rate. Tiredness.

* All permitted by inhalation.

Source: Adapted from Sports Council, 1995a.

improve their performance by any means possible. (International Olympic Committee, cited in Goldman and Klatz, 1992, p. 329)

Because of the covert nature of drug use in sport, it is difficult to establish accurate figures about prevalence. Many individuals and official reports (for example, Senate Standing Committee Report, Australia, 1989; Dubin Report, 1989) have claimed that large numbers of athletes have taken drugs, but these figures have not been proven. In fact, only ten competitors were disqualified for drug abuse from the Seoul Olympics in 1988, out of a total of 13 000 athletes. However, the relatively small number of doping convictions in sport does not necessarily reveal the true level of drug abuse. It is well known that only a minority of crimes in society result in convictions and it may be that only a minority of sporting drug abusers are convicted. Evasion techniques described later may explain this low rate of detection and conviction.

Weinhold (1991) asserted that, in America, $400–500 million was spent on steroids each year. However, the proportion used by sportsmen and sportswomen, compared with recreational bodybuilders, could not be established. Since then, stricter doping control procedures in sport may have dented a lucrative trade. Nevertheless, it was estimated that 50 000 people were taking anabolic steroids in America in the mid 1990s. Voy (1991) claimed that stimulants were so widespread among American basketball and football players that 'candy jars' filled with amphetamine tablets were common in training rooms. A recent investigation in Britain by Korkia and Stimson (1993) found that anabolic steroid use was prevalent in many gymnasia in different parts of the country. However, most users were bodybuilders and their investigation did not indicate level of use in sport.

In America, a publication called the *Underground Steroid Handbook* informed sports competitors how they could get access to banned substances and gave information on how to use them. The worrying feature about this was that tens of thousands of copies of the book were sold and repeat editions printed. Radford (1992) stated that drug abuse was a serious problem in sport, although a Sports Council survey in 1993–4 found that only 1 per cent of the 4000 tests on British competitors proved positive (Sports Council, 1995b). The wealth of evidence now available indicates that, prior to the 1990s, drug use was widespread among sportsmen and sportswomen. The recent adoption of a stricter doping control system may have led to a considerable reduction in drug usage. Nevertheless, it is probable that a small proportion of athletes who have access to sophisticated, scientific medical assistance are still experimenting with substances such as human growth hormone, which are difficult to detect.

DRUG-RELATED INCIDENTS IN DIFFERENT SPORTS

Doping appears to offer considerable benefits to competitors in a sport like athletics, while there would seem to be little advantage gained from drug use in some other sports. Table 8.2 illustrates significant drug-related incidents in a variety of sports.

DOPING CONTROL

Doping control has had a chequered history because of the difficulties of developing an effective system. In the early years of the twentieth century, athletes were simply asked to give their word that they were free of drugs, but the inadequacy of this method led to the development of tests to detect drugs in athletes. The first urine tests were carried out in Italy during the 1950s when soccer players and cyclists were tested by the Italian Medical Sports Federation (Yesalis, 1993). Although some experimental testing was performed earlier, the first official tests for anabolic steroids were performed at the 1976 Olympic Games in Montreal. The positive drug test of Ben Johnson during the 1988 Seoul Olympic Games was a significant point in doping control, since the general public became acutely aware of the issue of drugs in sport.

Doping control has encountered many complicated problems such as:

- getting consensus for a satisfactory definition of doping
- distinguishing doping from legitimate medical treatment
- establishing proof of a doping offence.

Proposals for testing have run foul of national laws and international agreements and there has sometimes been a lack of standardisation in procedures across the globe. Recently, Radford (1993) commented on the confusion in Britain about whether a national governing body, the Sports Council or an international organisation governs doping control for an athlete.

Council of Europe Anti-doping Convention

The Council of Europe Anti-doping Convention was established in 1990 and now has 28 countries giving full commitment to it. The main value of the Convention is that governments are obliged to implement minimum national standards for the organisation of doping control. The

Table 8.2 Different sports: different drugs

American football	Widespread use of anabolic steroids to increase strength and stimulants to heighten competitiveness and aggressiveness.
Athletics	Stimulants used to increase arousal and competitiveness. Anabolic steroids used to increase muscle mass; beneficial for throwing events and sprinting. Ben Johnson banned for using the steroid stanozolol. Athletes of both sexes in a variety of events have tested positive.
Basketball	'Speed' (amphetamine) has been popular in the USA to cope with demanding competition schedules.
Bobsledding	Three Americans were suspended for steroid use in 1989.
Boxing	Stimulants allegedly used to increase alertness and aggression. Diuretics have been used to reduce weight prior to fights. Lloyd Honeygan fined in 1989 for using lignocaine as painkiller for hand.
Cricket	Not an issue to date.
Cycling	First record of drug abuse in cycling was 1879, but deaths of two cyclists mid-twentieth century brought the issue to a head. Main drugs used were stimulants to increase endurance, but US cycling team alleged to have employed blood doping in 1984 Olympics.
Football	Players sent home from 1974 and 1978 World Cup Finals for stimulant use. Since 1979 only 4 positive tests out of 700. Some recent recreational drug use.
Gymnastics	It is alleged that growth-retarding drugs have been used.
Judo	Diuretics could be used to reach lower weight category. Olympic bronze medal taken from Kerrith Brown for using diuretics to reduce inflamed knee.
Rowing	Eastern European coach suspended when crew tested positive for steroids.
Rugby	Stimulants allegedly used for competitiveness and aggression in France, but no evidence.

(*continued on p. 142*)

Table 8.2 (continued)

Shooting	Beta-blockers would provide steadiness in finger and hand.
Snooker	Beta-blockers may reduce nervous tension and are banned.
Swimming	Dutch swimmers alleged to have taken 'dope' in 1865. Anecdotal evidence of eastern European swimmers forced into programme of steroids and cortisone.
Tennis	Occasional accusations but little evidence. Players competing in the 1988 Olympics were subject to International Olympic Committee testing.
Weightlifting	Obvious benefit of steroids for strength, but diuretics also used to reach lower weight class and possibly to conceal use of steroids. Soviet weightlifters in the 1950s were reported to have used anabolic steroids. More recently, a number of weightlifters have tested positive and been banned from competition.

Convention also has functions such as gathering 'data on the structure of national anti-doping organisations, financial arrangements, policies and legislation, programmes of testing, education, information and research' (Sports Council, 1996, p. 17).

Senate Standing Committee Report, Australia (1989)

The Black Inquiry was set up in 1988 by the Australian Senate Standing Committee of the Environment, Recreation and the Arts to investigate the use of performance-enhancing drugs by Australian sportsmen and women. Important issues to emerge from the inquiry were as follows:

- Drug-testing agencies needed to be independent of the sport being tested.
- International agreement and cooperation on doping control was necessary.
- There was a need to establish effective tests for substances used to stimulate the production of naturally occurring chemicals in the body.

Dubin Report (1989)

The Dubin Inquiry was also established in 1988 by the Privy Council of Canada to study the use of drugs and banned practices which increased athletic performance. According to Radford (1992), the impact of the report lay not so much in recommendations about the mechanics of doping control, but in the ethical pronouncements regarding sport. Its tone chastised those who had cheated and posed the question of whether there was too much emphasis by the public and media on the winning of an Olympic gold medal. Both the Black and Dubin inquiries accepted that drug taking among sportsmen and sportswomen was widespread.

A valuable international agreement was the Memorandum of Understanding set up in 1991 by Australia, Canada, Norway and the UK. It involved a five-year exchange of information and experience in relation to measures adopted to counter doping in sport. It has also enabled collaboration on testing in the four countries involved.

Evasion of Doping Control

Sportsmen and sportswomen have tried to avoid detection of drug abuse in several ways:

- *Manipulation of urine samples.* In order to confound the testing procedure, condoms filled with clean urine have been taken into the testing room, large amounts of water have been drunk prior to testing and toilet bowl water has been scooped up and added to the competitor's sample. These methods have been used when the collection procedure has been poorly supervised.
- *Catheterisation of the urinary bladder.* Catheters have been used by athletes to drain off contaminated urine.
- *Use of drugs such as diuretics and probenecid.* These drugs, although now banned, have been used in the past to confound test results and conceal the use of banned substances.
- *Coming off drugs prior to testing.* Lengthy warnings about being tested were a great weakness in the past because it was possible for athletes to stop using drugs and, consequently, for them not to show up in the test. This was especially the case when testing only occurred during competition.
- *Trial testing prior to competition.* It has been alleged that some countries chose to ignore drug abuse among their athletes. However, when testing became more accurate, it was clear that a positive result could provoke bad publicity for the country concerned. This led countries to organise their own testing programmes prior to major international events and to bar competitors from entering if positive results emerged.

Because of these evasion tactics, improper practices which conceal the use of proscribed drugs have been banned (for example, the use of diuretics). However, athletes and their medical advisers have tried to keep one step ahead of doping control agencies. For example, quicker-acting drugs have been used to avoid detection, but these are more toxic and, consequently, more dangerous. The trend has therefore shifted to drugs such as human growth hormones which are still difficult to detect.

International Olympic Committee Medical Code

The International Olympic Committee Medical Code provides the framework for global doping control, setting out principles and guidelines for eliminating the drugs problem in sport. The Medical Code covers areas such as:

- accredited laboratories
- prohibited classes of substances and prohibited methods
- standard operational procedures for doping control
- guidelines for sanctions and penalties
- appeals procedure.

Sports Council Doping Control Unit

The Sports Council Doping Control Unit has major responsibility for interpreting and applying international agreements in the United Kingdom and ensures that Britain has a comprehensive programme of education, research, testing and analysis. Each governing body of sport prescribes rules about doping control, but they will also have a working relationship with the Sports Council, whose officers administer the rules.

Testing Strategies

After-event testing is employed to detect prohibited substances taken immediately prior to the competition. This is not effective, however, in detecting drugs used during training and it has been possible for athletes to stop using anabolic steroids a few weeks before an event, and for the drug to clear out of the body by the time of competition. Although tests have been developed which can trace anabolic steroids taken up to three months previously, it was still possible for athletes to evade detection. The answer has thus been to adopt frequent, unannounced testing during training periods. Even the sophisticated medical support available to some athletes is foiled by random, out-of-competition testing conducted at short notice, and thus it becomes effective as a deterrent. However, this has led to experimentation with other forms of doping which are not so easy to detect.

The strict testing code which now exists has emerged from the deficiencies and fallibility of previous years. The procedures instituted at the Seoul Olympic Games of 1988 could trace the equivalent of a grain of sugar in a bucket of sand! In addition, testing laboratories around the world have to be accredited before they can contribute to the doping control system. Many countries are now involved in doping control, with international flying squads testing across national boundaries. Nevertheless, there are still considerable difficulties in operating an effective system throughout a world where devious politics and dishonest behaviour can jeopardise the integrity of the process.

The testing programme depends, for each sport, on the competition calendar, training patterns, type of activity and potential for drug misuse. It encompasses not only major competitions but also selection events and training sessions. Competition testing is undertaken to detect drugs which improve performance, such as stimulants, beta-blockers and diuretics. Selection of competitors for testing may be done by places achieved in a competition, or by disciplines in a sport, and may include team members who have not actually taken part. World, national and area records must be ratified by a negative doping result in athletics, weightlifting, swimming and cycling.

Training period testing aims to identify abuse from drugs such as androgenic steroids and other anabolic agents, peptide hormones and manipulation techniques. Selection is determined by sampling a register of competitors within an eligible category, agreed by the Sports Council and the relevant governing body. Competitors may be notified of their selection for testing at any time. The testing procedures are shown in Table 8.3.

Scandinavian researchers have found ways of detecting blood doping, but their methods are not as yet consistently accurate. Voy (1991) asserted that, if blood samples were taken in doping control, a more comprehensive analysis of chemicals in the body could be achieved and abnormal concentrations of growth hormone could be detected. This would also help to control blood doping because it might be possible to set a standard percentage of red blood cells which would be considered acceptable. As a result of work carried out at the University

Table 8.3 Doping control in sport: testing procedures

1. Notify athlete	After an event or during training, competitors are notified in writing by a Sports Council Independent Sampling Officer of their selection for a drug test. With out-of-competition testing, the competitor may be given short or no notice.
2. Reporting for testing	The Sampling Officer or a chaperone accompanies the competitor to the Doping Control Station waiting room. Competitors are entitled to have a representative (from his/her sport's national governing body) present.
3. Selecting a collection vessel	When the competitor is ready to provide a sample of urine, he/she selects a sample collection vessel.
4. Providing a sample under supervision	The competitor must remove sufficient clothing that the Sampling Officer can directly observe the competitor providing the urine sample, usually 100 ml. Only the competitor should handle the sample, unless he/she elects not to.
5. Selecting the sample containers	The competitor selects a pair of pre-sealed bottle containers.
6. Breaking security seals	The competitor breaks the security seals.
7. Dividing the sample	The competitor divides his/her sample between the A and B sample bottles, putting approximately two-thirds of the sample into the A bottle and a minimum of 30 ml into the B bottle.
8. Sealing the sample	The Sampling Officer ensures that the bottles have been tightly sealed. The competitor selects two numbered containers and seals the A and B bottles.
9. Recording the information	The Sampling Officer records the bottle code and seal numbers, which are checked by the competitor. The competitor declares any medications taken in the previous week.
10. Certifying the information	The competitor checks all the information on the Drug Control Collection Form and, if satisfied, signs the form. The Sampling Officer also checks and signs the form and gives the competitor a copy. The competitor is free to go.
11. Transferring samples to laboratory	The samples are sent to an accredited laboratory by a secure chain of custody for analysis. The competitor is not identified at this stage.
12. Reporting the result	Following laboratory analysis of the A sample, if no banned substances are found, a negative result is reported to the relevant governing body and the B sample is destroyed. If banned substances are found, the governing body is informed. The governing body then notifies the competitor.

Refusal to be tested is treated as if the urine sample gave a positive result.

Source: Adapted from Sports Council, 1994.

of Quebec in Canada, Olympic officials have recently introduced a test to detect erythropoietin. However, the contest between evasion and failsafe testing will continue. While more effective methods of detecting drugs will be designed, scientists will probably synthesise new anabolic steroids, which may initially escape detection by testing laboratories. At the same time, the extensive nature of drug-testing procedures means that the costs are escalating higher and higher.

Penalties

At present, according to International Olympic Committee rules, if a banned substance is detected, an athlete is banned from competition for two years for a first offence and then banned for life after a second offence. Each international sports federation is entitled to set its own penalties, and although most are consistent with the International Olympic Committee, there are exceptions.

THE DOPING DEBATE

This section discusses the main issues that have arisen in relation to drug use in sport.

Fair or Unfair?

When athletes believe they have fulfilled their potential but not achieved adequate success, they may turn to other ways of improving performance. There is sometimes a fine line between accepted medical practice and illegal doping. The following methods are legal:

- *Mechanical and biomechanical.* As long as mechanical and biomechanical developments in clothing and equipment fall within governing body rules, then it is acceptable for the athlete to avail of them.
- *Psychological.* A number of psychological ploys are allowed which aim to help competitors improve performance – for example, imagery, hypnosis and mental dissociation are used to optimise arousal or create a state of relaxation.
- *Physiological.* Physiological manipulation has been achieved through permissible methods, such as training at altitude.
- *Medical.* Grey areas in the drugs issue are exemplified in relation to treatment of pain. An élite performer may experience pain in training,

when reaching the limits of performance or in sustaining an injury. A local anaesthetic injection to mask the pain of an injury is legal and yet it might be considered an artificial, chemical method of aiding performance (Donald, 1983).

The question to be asked is whether these methods fall within the true spirit of sporting ethics or whether they give competitors an unfair advantage. The related question is whether the use of drugs differs from these methods.

The following practices are illegal:

- *Beta-blockers*. There has been a continual dilemma over the use of beta-blockers. In the 1980s commentators asked whether it was appropriate to ban shooting and archery competitors from using beta-blockers when their effect on performance was unproven (Collier, 1988). The situation is still unsatisfactory since competitors suffering from angina and arrhythmias could be given a better chance of taking part if they were able to use beta-blockers. However, proof of effect is not a fundamental element of the International Olympic Committee Medical Code.
- *Nutritional aids*. Abnormal quantities of nutritional supplements are needed to achieve a significant effect on training capacity or performance, and therefore the question must be asked as to whether nutritional aids contravene the International Olympic Committee doping rule, which bans any physiological substances taken in abnormal quantities. This issue illustrates the fine line between acceptable athlete preparation and illegal cheating. Are nutritional supplements contrary to sporting ethical principles? Since abnormal amounts of caffeine have been banned prior to competition, should other nutritional aids be subject to the same criteria?
- *Blood doping*. In a similar way, it could be asked whether blood doping, where athletes utilise their own blood, is cheating and should be put in the same category as anabolic steroids. Is blood doping any more unfair than availing of an expensive, but legal, piece of scientific equipment used in athlete preparation, which may not be available to poorer athletes? Voy (1991) commented that, even though athletes use their own blood, there is an abnormal quantity of a foreign substance entering the body and this contravenes the spirit of the International Olympic Committee doping rules.
- *Coughs and colds*. At the highest levels of sport, the demanding nature of an athlete's training and competition schedules renders them vulnerable to infections such as coughs and colds. Ironically, a cold

remedy such as pseudoephedrine, which could help the athlete to feel better and take part, is also a stimulant which, if taken in large quantities, could improve performance and is, consequently, a banned substance. This means that athletes have to make sure that they take cold remedies which contain no banned substances.

The problematic nature of this situation can be illustrated by the case of Solomon Wariso, a British sprinter, who tested positive for taking a banned stimulant. During a hectic competition schedule, Wariso took a pick-me-up called *Up Your Gas*, thinking that it contained no banned substances. Wariso even stated on the drug control form that he had taken the tablets, but he was pulled out of competition and given a short ban for testing positive. It does not matter whether the illegal substance is taken intentionally or unintentionally, it is still an offence.

> Why should I be allowed to drink coffee but not take amphetamines? To relax with a beer but not a barbiturate? Everybody else uses them, why shouldn't I? (Curry and Jiobu, 1984, p. 224)

Reasons for Drug Use in Sport

Goldman and Klatz (1992) suggested that some of the values of modern society provide a tempting environment for drug use in sport. For example, people are often obsessed with:

- *time* – wanting instantaneous results
- *performance* – winning becomes all important
- *indolence* – sloth leads to short cuts to success
- *pill culture* – thinking nothing of taking a pill for every ill.

When deciding whether to use drugs, an athlete could be influenced by:

- *perceived benefits* – for example, a belief that drugs will improve performance to reach a particular goal
- *ethical considerations* – for example, if an athlete perceives drug use as normal and acceptable behaviour, then it is understandable that he or she might as well do the same as others:

> Given the widespread use of all drugs in sport ... and the monetary reward structure ... the choice to use drugs is logical. (Figone, 1988, p. 31)

Drug use may result from pressures on the competitor. These may include:

- retaining sponsorship
- keeping place in team

- earning a living
- getting through long training and competition sessions
- attraction of fame
- worries about injuries
- dealing with the fear of a brutalising, contact sport.

Pressures to succeed come from many different sources including parents, coaches, peers and the media. Coaches, passionate about their sport, will have a strong desire for their charges to succeed and they may turn to cheating in order to vindicate their coaching methods or, perhaps, in the hope of sharing the monetary rewards of success.

Young competitors may need to adapt to a demanding lifestyle of training, travel, pressure and financial dependence. It may be tempting to seek relief through recreational drugs and to take a leap up the ladder of success via performance-enhancing drugs. Younger athletes may also copy the drug-taking behaviour of older athletes, especially if it appears to bring success. Information about types of drug and how to use them is known to be picked up from older athletes (Fuller and LaFountain, 1987). In the later stages of a career, performance deterioration due to ageing may persuade competitors to turn to drugs in the belief that they may gain a few extra years at the top. It would, therefore, seem prudent to identify when athletes are most vulnerable to drug initiation and try to design an intervention programme which aims to prevent drug abuse.

It is quite evident that drug abuse can lead to addiction, toxicity, illness and other dangerous side effects. It has been suggested by Staudohar (1987) that many sportsmen and sportswomen are arrogant and feel invulnerable, leading them to suppress thoughts of danger to their health. In addition, athletes accept the risks of drug abuse because of the high need to gain success and the potential fame and wealth which accompanies achievement in sport.

Views of Athletes

The Sports Council (1995b) undertook a survey of 468 élite sportsmen and sportswomen from 26 winter and summer Olympic sports to obtain views about the Doping Control Programme of the Sports Council's Doping Control Unit. Competitors were generally satisfied with the testing process, although many thought that testing should be more frequent and widespread. There was a strong desire for more information about drug-testing procedures and an education programme that

Figure 8.1 Sanctions for testing positive for anabolic steroids (first offence)

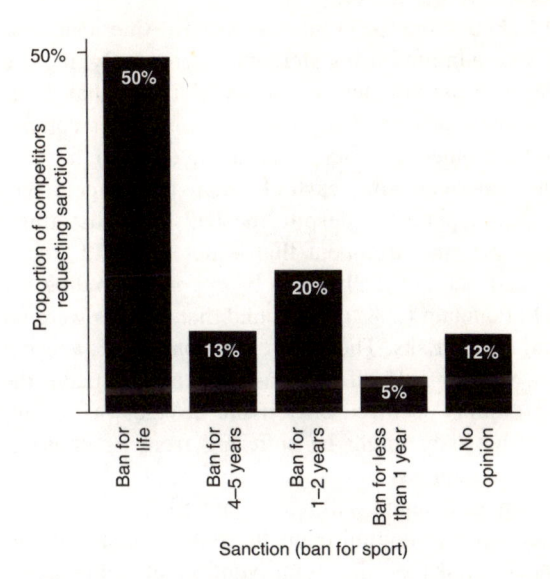

[Bar chart: Ban for life 50%; Ban for 4–5 years 13%; Ban for 1–2 years 20%; Ban for less than 1 year 5%; No opinion 12%. Y-axis: Proportion of competitors requesting sanction. X-axis: Sanction (ban for sport).]

Source: Sports Council, 1995b, p. 4.

included health and ethical issues. Interestingly, although competitors were naturally keen for individuals to be treated fairly, there was considerable support for tougher penalties for those found guilty of doping offences. For example, Figure 8.1 shows that half the sample thought that a life ban was appropriate if an individual tested positive for anabolic steroids, even though it might be a first offence.

In the late 1980s, Anshel (1991) conducted personal interviews with 126 American élite athletes, aged 18–23 years, competing in a range of sports from American football to golf. Although performance enhancement was the main reason for using drugs, athletes also mentioned other physical benefits such as pain reduction, injury rehabilitation, heightened energy and weight control (mainly females). Psychological advantages included intensifying competitive mood, overcoming fear of failure, boosting self-confidence and demonstrating their invincibility, while the main social reason centred upon the modelling of other competitors. Most athletes made rational decisions about taking drugs and believed (in the late 1980s) that getting caught and being prosecuted was unlikely. However, Anshel acknowledged that coaches could also have directly or indirectly encouraged the use of drugs, although it was not reported by the athletes.

Fuller and LaFountain (1987) interviewed 50 American athletes, aged 15–40 years, who admitted using steroids. Interestingly, the use of drugs was rationalised in the athletes' minds by claiming that the abuse was causing no harm to anyone. They believed that other competitors, especially those from other countries, were taking drugs to improve performance and that American athletes took them to compete on an equal footing. This belief persisted despite the fact that most athletes tested negative. Ironically, the argument that athletes should compete on an equal basis is the position usually taken by opponents to drug use in sport.

Fuller and LaFountain (1987) also found that athletes were not worried about potential health risks. The apparent inconclusive, anecdotal nature of the evidence about side effects was sufficient to make the athletes believe that problems occurred only if the dosage was too high. None acknowledged that they might be suffering from psychological mood changes, such as aggressiveness, despite complaints reported to the researchers from girlfriends. Athletes claimed that steroid use was a form of dedication and commitment to sport, which was on a higher plane than health risks or the contravention of some hazy ideal of fairness. They even condemned the critics of drug use in sport: 'Rules should not be made and enforced by people who don't know what they are talking about' (Fuller and LaFountain, 1987, p. 973).

One study, cited by Radford (1992), claimed that 50 per cent of international athletes would take a tablet which guaranteed them an Olympic gold medal – even if it killed them within one year! The extreme nature of this finding shows the determination of athletes to take risks, and because most drugs do not seem to have such fatal consequences, it is not surprising that some athletes are willing to use them. Despite emanating mainly from America during the 1980s, these studies are disturbing since they show that steroid use was not a last ditch attempt to gain a slight athletic advantage, but behaviour considered to be a normal part of serious commitment to sports competition, undertaken because other athletes were already taking drugs.

Corruption of Sport

Zakus (1992) pointed out that the drugs issue needs to be seen in a broad perspective since professionalism and commercialism had moved sport into the entertainment market place:

It is not only the athletes who stand to reap economic benefits from the sale of their performances, but also the capitalist enterprises promoting and sponsoring élite sport (especially the television industry) and, more directly, the International Olympic Committee and other world sport organisations. (Zakus, 1992, pp. 348–9)

Tension has increased in élite sport because athletes, coaches and officials are expected to uphold Pierre de Coubertin's moral stance of fairness, integrity and honesty whilst, at the same time, facing commercial pressures, financial incentives, the demands of nationalistic fervour and the ever greater emphasis put on winning by the general public. The temptation to cheat is immense and the 'glittering prizes' now on offer in sport mean that athletes might easily see winning as far more important than taking part. Shapiro (1991, p. 6) commented that 'drug taking corrupts the ideals of sport', but it could be argued that the sale of sport for sponsorship leads to worse corruption. Of course, sponsors do not want bad publicity caused by being associated with drugs, and Ben Johnson and Katrinna Krabbe are said to have lost millions of dollars in sponsorship deals because of their drug involvement.

It is strange that officials in sporting organisations have been aware of and even supported drug use among athletes and yet overtly expressed condemnation of it in major inquiries. While acknowledging that many other countries turned a blind eye to doping in sport, Hoberman (1993, p. 279) noted that the concealment of doping had been official state policy in the German Democratic Republic and 'the rule' in the Federal Republic of Germany since the 1970s. Voy (1991) claimed that there had also been cover-ups to protect organisations that administer sport, because the officials suffer if sport receives bad publicity. Apart from the shame and controversy caused by cheating, which is broadcast to the world during major events, there are also massive financial pressures. Sponsors do not want to be associated with controversy, attendances fall because spectators feel they are being duped and sport in general loses out. As a consequence, it has been alleged that officials engage in all kinds of prevarication and invoke technical irregularities to outmanoeuvre the doping control system.

Testing Issues

Doping control has experienced serious problems during its history. For many years the ineffectiveness of control arrangements led to controversy and disillusionment, while avoidance of detection was commonplace.

Critics in the 1980s intimated that sporting authorities had muddled sporting principles with medical and legal issues (Collier, 1988). There was clearly a need to improve doping control to ensure it was consistent, scientifically and medically justifiable and implemented during training as well as competition. Unlike some other countries, Britain does not have specific laws which control the use of drugs in sport. However, the British government has been actively involved in developing and ratifying international agreements on anti-doping in sport to move towards increased harmonisation on the issue.

Buti and Fridman (1994) pointed out that there were legal difficulties with mandatory drug testing in sport. For example, urinating in the presence of a drug testing officer could be seen as an invasion of privacy. Second, and perhaps of greater concern, the analysis of the urine sample may disclose personal medical information which is normally protected: that is, drugs which could in no way aid training or enhance performance may be identified and the information used to prosecute an individual. Although the public may be supportive of drug testing in sport, it is possible that they would not be in favour of the application of criminal law after a positive test result. Individuals are tested simply because they are competing, not because there is any evidence that they have committed a crime. This situation is potentially dangerous since any extension to it could threaten personal freedom.

Procedural problems in drug testing have invoked legal challenges, most notably in the case of the British athlete Diane Modahl, who tested positive, appealed against legal irregularities and won her case. The collection, security and scientific testing of samples all have potential for intended and unintended breaches of the system. Further challenges can occur in respect of the penalties imposed on athletes and, if there is no consistency, the system will be ridiculed. The suspension and banning penalties are open to challenge, and with the successful appeal of Diane Modahl, there is the problem of how she could ever be compensated for her loss of competition time.

This all illustrates the necessity of an independent, national testing agency to ensure a rigorous and uniform set of procedures. A doping control system that is demonstrably effective is necessary to identify drug-free athletes as much as to filter out cheats and, at present, the system demonstrates that the majority of competitors are drug free. Shapiro (1991) noted the pre-eminence of British drug testing and the enthusiasm with which Britain was pursuing doping control programmes. However, he cynically asked whether such zeal would have been shown if British sporting success had matched that of America and eastern Europe in recent years!

Despite the known effectiveness of the present doping control system, some athletes still test positive and this is possibly because the pressures are so great that they gamble on not being tested. The majority of drug tests are negative and the majority of sportsmen and sportswomen are honest, but this does not make exciting news and is mostly ignored by the media. The legacy of drug abuse means that any outstanding performance invites a suspicion that drugs have helped the competitor. Nevertheless, the sporting authorities have recently established a doping control system that has boosted the confidence of the general public, and drug abuse is perceived to have been greatly curtailed. The rules must be fair to all and the system will be flawed if some athletes gain an unfair advantage by using drugs which cannot be identified in the testing procedure.

Legalising Drug Taking in Sport

There have been suggestions that it would be fairer to allow athletes to take drugs:

> since our genes decide our body chemistry, why shouldn't we if we choose, modify that chemistry in order to increase our athletic performance? (Donald, cited in Buti and Fridman, 1994, p. 497)

The essence of true competition is that competitors start under the same conditions and yet drugs give an unfair and unnatural advantage. It has to be said, however, that competitors never start from the same point, since training facilities and coaching expertise vary throughout the globe. One suggestion has been to legalise the use of drugs in order to give all competitors an equal chance. However, as with training facilities, some athletes would have access to more refined drug applications than others.

Another argument put forward is that drug testing is undertaken to allow fair competition, but there is little empirical evidence to show that drugs improve performance and therefore the drugs issue is not straightforward. Many would counter this by saying that the evidence now shows that drugs can enhance performance. For example, although the findings regarding the effect of anabolic steroids have been mixed, more recent and sophisticated studies have led the American Medical Association to recognise that:

> 'certain benefits to athletic performance seem probable' with the use of anabolic steroids, including possibly a growth in 'lean muscle mass.' Strength may be increased in some persons if they are 'in a

continuing program of intensive exercise coupled with a high protein diet.' (Marshall, 1988, p. 184)

Some commentators have employed different arguments to expose inconsistencies regarding drug use in sport. For example, in other spheres of life, drugs are alleged to have stimulated great achievements:

> the poems of Baudelaire or Rimbaud are always included among the greatest masterpieces of the French language, when they were written under the influence of cannabis or alcohol and would doubtless not have the same qualities if they had been composed sober. (Oswald, 1993, p. 36)

At present there is a general belief that participation in sport embodies clean living and healthy behaviour and that drug use by sportsmen and sportswomen destroys that image. However, in the middle of the twentieth century, professionalism was seen as cheating and some athletes were punished if caught accepting money for sporting activities. In the future, social attitudes may change and drug use to improve sports performance may be viewed as exciting and acceptable.

Health Risks

The health risks of drug abuse in sport are wide ranging and, while everyone should be made aware of the health risks, particularly young athletes, it is a separate issue from that of cheating. Radford (1992) stated that the long term health and welfare of the competitor is an important consideration in doping control. However, an individual has the right to determine his or her own behaviour, provided it is within the law. Taking part in contact sports such as rugby or boxing may give the athlete as high a health risk as taking drugs. Athletes cannot be stopped from taking stimulants such as ephedrine because of the health risk, any more than an athlete can be prevented from smoking cigarettes.

One of the reasons that doctors give drugs to athletes is because they believe that the risks of harmful effects are low. In general, adverse reactions to drugs occur in only a small proportion of people and, since athletes are otherwise healthy, the chances of a performance-enhancing drug causing problems would also seem to be low. The evidence about health risks is growing, although the covert nature of drug taking in sport means that scientific proof is difficult to establish. Serious health problems and even death have been linked with drug abuse in sport, and yet there is still a lingering doubt about the relationship. Many athletes probably rationalise the health risks by referring to medical opinion which says that moderate doses of drugs like anabolic steroids seem to have minimal health risks in the short term. However, a more disturbing situation is that, as far as American athletes are concerned, a high percentage of anabolic steroid users would not give up, even if unequivocal evidence of serious health risk was confirmed (Yesalis, 1993).

Education

Staudohar (1987, p. 50) believed that educational approaches through anti-drug programmes could be effective if they led 'to peer pressure against rather than in favor of the drug culture'. Taking a different line, Lycholat (1993) suggested that doping control needed the coach to be an educator and to act as an ethical and moral role model. In contrast, Figone (1988) criticised the naiveté of an educational approach which relied on athletes and coaches to ameliorate the problem. He considered that, whatever knowledge was provided or commendable values advanced, competitors saw that the gains far outweighed the disadvantages and would decide to use drugs. Despite misgivings like these, the Sports Council Doping Control Unit is committed to expanding its educational programme since it is believed that this is the most effective approach in the long term.

CONCLUSION

It is apparent that drug abuse in sport is a difficult problem which will cause controversy for many years to come. There still exists a 'cat and mouse' situation where athletes and coaches try to stay one step ahead of doping control agencies. The drugs problem also raises the whole issue of fairness in sport. Can the use of medical, mechanical, psychological and physiological practices be justified, when they give some athletes a greater competitive advantage than drugs ever could?

REFERENCES

Anshel, M.H., 'A Survey of Elite Athletes on the Perceived Causes of Using Banned Drugs in Sport', *Journal of Sport Behaviour*, 14 (1991), pp. 283–307.

Beashel, P. and Taylor, J., *Sport Examined* (Basingstoke: Macmillan, 1986).

Buti, A. and Fridman, S., 'The Intersection of Law and Policy: Drug Testing in Sport', *Australian Journal of Public Administration*, 53 (1994), pp. 489–507.

Collier, J., 'Drugs in Sport: A Counsel of Perfection Thwarted by Reality', *British Medical Journal*, 296 (1988), p. 520.

Curry, T.J. and Jiobu, R.M., *Sports: A Social Perspective* (Englewood Cliffs: Prentice Hall, 1984).

Donald, K., *The Doping Game* (Spring Hill: Boolarong, 1983).

Dubin Report, *Commission of Inquiry into the Use of Drugs and Banned Practices Intended to Increase Athletic Performance* (Canada: Canadian Government Publishing Centre, 1989).

Figone, A.J., 'Drugs in Professional Sport: External Control of Individual Behaviour', *Arena Review*, 12 (1988), pp. 25–33.

Fuller, J.R, and LaFountain, M.J., 'Performance-enhancing Drugs in Sport: A Different Form of Drug Abuse', *Adolescence*, 22 (1987), pp. 969–76.

Goldman, R. and Klatz, R., *Death in the Locker Room 11: Drugs and Sports* (Chicago: Elite Sports Medicine Publications, 1992).

Hoberman. J., 'The Reunification of German Sports Medicine, 1989–1992', *Quest*, 45 (1993), pp. 277–85.

Korkia, P. and Stimson, G.V., *Anabolic Steroid Use in Great Britain* (London: Centre for Research on Drugs and Health Behaviour, 1993).

Lycholat, A., 'Who Says They Don't Work?' *Coaching Focus*, 23 (1993), pp. 9–10.

Marshall, E., 'The Drug of Champions', *Science*, 242 (1988), pp. 183–4.

Mottram, D.R. (ed.), *Drugs in Sport* (London: E and FN Spon, 1988).

Oswald, D., 'Doping: The Sports Movement Leads the Way', *Olympic Review*, 303/4 (1993), pp. 34–7.

Radford. P.F., 'The Fight against Doping in Sport: The Last Five Years', *Sport and Leisure*, May/June (1992), pp. 27–31.

Radford, P.F., 'Who Writes the Rules?' *Coaching Focus*, 23 (1993), pp. 19–20.

Senate Standing Committee Report, Australia, *An Interim Report of the Senate Standing Committee on Environment, Recreation and the Arts* (Canberra: Australian Government Publishing Service, 1989).

Shapiro, H., 'Running Scared: The Use of Drugs in Sport', *British Journal of Addiction*, 86 (1991), pp. 5–8.

Smith, D.A. and Perry, P.J., 'The Efficacy of Ergogenic Agents in Athletic Competition Part 11: Other Performance-enhancing Agents', *The Annals of Pharmacotherapy*, 26 (1992), pp. 653–9.

Sports Council, *Testing Procedures: A Guide for Competitors and Officials* (London: Sports Council, 1994).

Sports Council, *Doping in Sport* (London: Sports Council, 1995a).

Sports Council, *Doping Control in the UK: A Survey of the Experiences and Views of Elite Competitors 1995* (London: Sports Council, 1995b).

Sports Council, *Report on the Sports Council's Doping Control Service 1995–96* (London: Sports Council, 1996).
Staudohar, P.D., 'Drug Abuse Programs in Professional Sport: Lessons for Industry', *Personnel*, 64 (1987), pp. 44–50.
Voy, R., *Drugs, Sport, and Politics* (Champaign: Human Kinetics, 1991).
Weinhold, L.L., 'Steroid and Drug Use by Athletes'. In L. Diamant (ed.), *Psychology of Sports, Exercise and Fitness* (New York: Hemisphere, 1991).
Williams, M.H., 'The Use of Nutritional Ergogenic Aids in Sports', *International Journal of Sport Nutrition*, 4 (1994), pp. 120–31.
Yesalis, C.E., *Anabolic Steroids in Sport and Exercise* (Champaign: Human Kinetics, 1993).
Zakus, D.H., 'The International Olympic Committee: Tragedy, Farce and Hypocrisy', *Sociology of Sport Journal*, 9 (1992), pp. 340–53.

FURTHER READING

The Sports Council Doping Control Unit has a number of helpful publications. Apply to Walkden House, 3/10 Melton Street, London NW1 2EB.

Further information can be found in the work of Korkia and Stimson, Mottram, Voy and Yesalis (cited above).

9 Football Hooliganism

DEFINING THE SITUATION

Although crowd violence has occurred in many sports and in countries all over the world, this chapter focuses upon football hooliganism in Britain. This is because crowd behaviour is a complex issue and, although violence in other sports and other countries may have similar features, the topic is too wide ranging to cover here. Nevertheless, football hooliganism provides a valuable insight into issues surrounding crowd violence and sport spectating.

The chapter will be divided into three sections. First, consideration will be given to the nature and extent of football hooliganism in Britain, since the media have sometimes portrayed hooliganism as a nationwide phenomenon undermining the fabric of society. Second, there will be an examination of theories put forward which seek to explain football hooliganism; the extensive number of competing explanations illustrate the complexity of the issue. Finally, there will be a review of strategies employed by the football authorities and the police to prevent this kind of anti-social behaviour.

What is Hooliganism?

Hooliganism is difficult to define because people interpret behaviour in different ways and views change over time: for example, behaviour that was acceptable in the nineteenth century is now considered inappropriate. Verbal abuse that threatens physical injury may be frightening to an occasional spectator, but seen as merely part of the ritual banter by the hardened fan. In addition, crowd behaviour has cultural variations with sport: for instance, engendering a sense of carnival in countries like Brazil and Italy.

Although there are various forms of violence (for example, psychological violence), this chapter will mainly be concerned with physical violence associated with football matches in Britain, where malicious damage is caused to people or property. Sporting violence between players on the field will not be a major focus, although it may be a contributory factor to crowd violence. Violent acts may be pre-planned or occur 'on the spur of the moment', they may take place in the stadium, en route to and from matches, or erupt hours later after the game has long finished. They may be perpetrated by relatively small groups of hooligans or, more disturbingly, they may involve large crowds and result in widespread damage, injury and even death.

Historical Snapshot

Before the introduction of the organised, professional game in the second half of the nineteenth century, football had a brutal history with hundreds of people involved in large scale violent incidents. In effect, the disorder surrounding football games mirrored the unruly nature of society. As far as the modern professional game is concerned, it is a myth that football-related violence is a recent phenomenon, following a long period of football matches with well behaved spectators. Crowd disorder was prevalent in the late nineteenth century, with many instances of pitch invasion, clashes between rival supporters and fighting en route to matches. Twenty clubs were even closed by the Football Association between 1895 and 1898, as punishment for crowd misbehaviour.

An incident from a match between Burnley and Blackburn in 1890, reported by Dunning, Murphy and Williams (1988, p. 61), illustrates the precarious position of match officials during this period:

> the referee was mobbed at the close ... The official had to be protected by the committee and so demonstrative were the spectators that the police could not clear the field. [He] had to take refuge under the grandstand and, subsequently, in a neighbouring house. The police force was increased and eventually the referee was hurried into a cab and driven away followed by a howling, stone-throwing mob.

The inter-war years in the twentieth century brought larger, but more orderly crowds, and although incidents still occurred, they seem to have been on a more isolated basis and mainly non-vicious. For example, pitch invasions were more likely to be caused by lack of space rather than fighting between opposition fans. There seems to have been minimal public concern about football crowd behaviour, which meant that it was not defined as a significant social problem. However, it should be noted that the incidence of football hooliganism remained high in Scotland during the inter-war years.

In England regular crowd trouble re-emerged in the post-war years. Dunning, Murphy and Williams (1988, p. 133) reported substantial evidence of 'spectator disorderliness and misconduct at soccer matches' at this time. The more lethal nature of post-war incidents can be gauged from a match between Millwall and Brentford, neighbouring South London rivals, when a (dead) hand grenade was thrown on the pitch. In addition to sporadic, ad hoc violence, the 1970s and 1980s witnessed the emergence of what was thought to be planned and organised football hooliganism. Gangs of fans, like the Chelsea Head Hunters, identified grudge or revenge matches and distributed leaflets encouraging others to confront opposing fans. This led Dunning, Murphy and Williams (1988) to suggest that a spiral of control and punishment on the part of the police was countered by fans devising new ways to reach and fight opposing fans. Although there has been occasional involvement by the National Front organisation and a number of racist incidents, there is no evidence of widespread organisation of football fans by left-wing groups.

The current concern about hooliganism can be attributed to a number of factors. Firstly, Maguire (1986) observed that there has been a change in the definition of decent or acceptable behaviour that is tolerated in public, with a supposedly civilised late twentieth century being far more disapproving of loutish and violent behaviour. This civilising process has been extensively analysed in the figurational approach of Elias (1978). During the 1960s and 1970s attendances declined significantly and football authorities became ever more anxious about the negative image given to the game by crowd trouble. However, a small number of large scale incidents with numerous deaths and injuries, like the 1985 Heysel tragedy in Brussels, had a dramatic impact on the general public. The whole population was made aware of these events, since they were portrayed graphically by the media, with television images relaying the issue into people's homes. The media seem also to have exaggerated incidents and sensationalised events to an extent where the public have great fears about football hooliganism, exhibiting what might be called a 'moral panic'. There can be no doubt that ugly, violent incidents still break out in the 1990s, but they do not seem to be on the scale witnessed during the 1970s and 1980s.

Sporting Violence and Attendances

Does the excitement generated by aggressive behaviour increase or reduce attendances at football matches? Whether or not the football is of a high standard, a crowd undoubtedly gets more excited if a match contains incident and controversy, certainly when compared to a dull game with no goals. On the field a player with a volatile reputation attracts interest and has the capacity to draw spectators to a match. Although violent incidents off the field may excite some people, the majority perhaps fear getting caught in the violence and, consequently, stay away from matches. There are not many studies on this issue, but the evidence from America (Russell, 1986) does not seem to support the notion of violence increasing attendances at sporting events.

EXPLANATIONS OF FOOTBALL HOOLIGANISM

The complexity of football hooliganism can be gauged by the fact that, despite extensive efforts by many parties to eradicate it, the problem still exists. For example, England's match with the Republic of Ireland had to be abandoned in 1995 because of crowd trouble, and the police had to deal with serious disorder after England lost to Germany in the European Football Championships in 1996. This section briefly reviews the main sociological and psychological theories that endeavour to explain the reasons for hooliganism.

History and Sociology: Theories and Concepts

A Ritualistic Game
Based on the relatively small number of serious injuries suffered during spectator violence in the 1970s, Marsh, Rosser and Harre (1978) maintained that football hooliganism was a *ritualistic game* which had no seriousness about it. From observations of Oxford United's home games, they believed that football fans followed a set of social rules which formed a symbolic display aimed at getting rival fans to back down. Thus, the rules prescribed the commencement, structure and ending of the confrontation, and the main intention of the fans was to humiliate and gain supremacy over rival fans by taunts and threats, but not to injure them.

Violence tended to occur through unexpected confrontation: for example, if some fans were detached from the main crowd and got cornered. There was enough violence to make it exciting, but not so much as to spoil the game. Sometimes, however, serious violence was initiated by a minority of 'nutters' who broke the rules and, in more recent times, by infiltrators who did not belong to the original gangs. A breakdown in the ritualistic nature of the event could also be caused by police intervention, when the delicate balance of the rules was cast asunder and violence erupted, leading to an inevitable escalation. Although a ritualistic element seems to exist in football hooliganism, it has not always been restricted to a low level of violence. Incidents in recent years have shown that violent confrontation was a potential outcome of the ritual, whether or not it was intended. The planned violence of some hooligan episodes seems to have hijacked what might otherwise have turned out to be a relatively harmless affair.

Working Class Frustrations

Although violent episodes have occurred throughout the history of football, there are many who consider that the nature of violence has changed. Taylor (1982), for example, asserted that the more serious forms of spectator violence were instigated during the 1960s, as a result of changes in the way football was organised. Prior to this time, football was a working class game wherein working class supporters were involved in club activities relating to players and policies. When, in the 1960s, football became more bourgeois, with affluent officials, players and supporters, the working class saw the game going out of their control and they felt a loss of ownership. Taylor maintained that football hooliganism was a violent reaction to this process.

The pattern of football spectating certainly changed during the 1960s and 1970s. Whatever the reason for present day football hooliganism, it seems clear that earlier in the century, a friendly, light-hearted atmosphere existed at football matches. Dads and lads went along together, rival supporters were not segregated and there was no antagonistic chanting or gesturing. According to Dunning, Murphy and Waddington (1991), the rise in football crowd disorders in the 1960s was paralleled by warlike reporting in the press and an exaggeration of the scale and seriousness of violent incidents. This may have attracted more aggressive individuals to football matches, such as the skinheads, and may have been the catalyst for the ugly, violent incidents of recent decades.

Prior to the 1960s, working class youths had been controlled at matches by their dads. Later, working class boys went to games in groups of their own age, and the roughness of these youth groups meant that they were ostracised by other spectators and a hooligan fringe was born. Violence occurred, perhaps limited at first, but amplified by the media, and consequently the hooligans started to live up to their riotous reputation. As unemployment grew in the 1970s, Taylor (1982, p. 169) referred to the 'decomposition of the working class community', where more and more became unemployed and unemployable, developing into an underclass. As a result of material and psychological frustration with their unemployed circumstances, and resentment that the rest of society was reaping the rewards of affluence, the underclass sought ways of venting their frustration. Football hooliganism became an expression of the frustration and resentment that the underclass were experiencing.

Taylor's thesis rests on the supposition that hooliganism, as a serious social problem, has emerged since the 1960s. Historians have shown that violence has been associated with football through most of its history and the idea of the working class reacting to the loss of 'ownership' is not easy to assess. Prior to the 1960s, football may well have been perceived as a working class institution, but the hypothesis that its changes caused a violent reaction is difficult to accept.

The Insider's View
Hobbs and Robins (1991) have argued that pre-war football-related disorder was as different from contemporary soccer violence as 'shoplifting is from armed robbery' (p. 565). They maintained that crowd trouble in the early years of the century was directly related to football, while, in recent times, crowd violence has emanated from more complicated sources. Based on the views of hooligans themselves, Hobbs and Robins identified the 'casuals' who, despite coming predominantly from the working class, were not class conscious, but were aware of differences between themselves and other fans, mainly based on dress and speech. A major concern, for example, became the need to obtain and display the latest expensive sportswear.

Hobbs and Robins (1991, pp. 568–9) offered a slightly different view of violence itself, declaring that hooligans had a 'willingness to fight' and even a 'love of fighting' which was described as 'a hyped up sensation'. The behaviour of the hard core was existential, lacking any rational reasoning, and although they were small in number, their impact was dramatic. They attracted a larger following of more calculating types who espoused a 'hard' reputation, but who avoided the extremes of behaviour exhibited by the hard core. In addition, it was noticed that modern hooligans were concerned about how the media constructed and sensationalised their activities, often claiming that it was another example of how the working class were misrepresented by the press. Hobbs and Robins believed that a better understanding of football violence could be achieved if further ethnographic studies were undertaken.

Figurational Approach
The figurational approach of Dunning, Murphy and Williams (1988) offered a complex theory of football hooliganism which involved

interaction between historical, psychological and sociological influences. Central to their thesis was the importance given to the:

> structural features of lower working-class communities which lead to the recurrent generation within them of male adolescent gangs, an aggressive masculine style and relatively narrow bonds of identification. (Dunning, Murphy and Williams, 1988, p. 212)

Their ideas involve consideration of the developments of the working class after the Second World War. Increased prosperity, greater working class assertiveness and a decline in working class deference to those higher on the social scale coincided with a rise in the affluence and power of youth and the emergence of a nationwide youth image, notoriously encapsulated in the 1950s by the teddy boy gangs.

Concern shifted over the years from the unruly behaviour of teddy boy gangs to the seaside clashes of the mods and rockers. The skinheads emerged in the 1960s with their boots, braces and prison crop hairstyles to give expression to working class 'hard' masculinity, which had been lacking in the mods, rockers and hippie groups. As mentioned earlier, working class youth started going to matches in gangs and created 'football ends' where young home fans staked out a particular home end as their territory. The tension, abuse and conflict caused by this territorial practice was a notable feature of violent incidents through the 1960s and 1970s.

The social composition of football crowds contained many 'respectable' working class individuals and a not unsizeable number of lower middle class men. Despite media attention given to affluent, employed middle class men, apparently involved in hooliganism, Dunning, Murphy and Williams (1988) claimed that the majority of convicted hooligans came from the lower working class, as shown in Table 9.1.

Hooligans have social standards at variance with most of society and these standards emanate from the social characteristics and social circumstances of certain groups. Dunning, Murphy and Williams (1988) pointed out that, although there will be exceptions, it is the *rougher sections of the working class* who are the main protagonists in football hooliganism. They are very low in the social hierarchy and aggressive confrontations are a normal part of their lives. The rough working class have very strong feelings about kinship and territory, with a certain degree of hostility to outsiders. This helps to explain how a close bond can be developed within a gang of young males, who have a staunch identity with the locality where the football club is located, and who have an in-built hostility to those from other areas who support rival

Table 9.1 Social class membership of football hooligans (Registrar General's classification)

Classification	Nos.	%
1 Professional, etc.	2	0.4
2 Intermediate	13	2.5
3 Skilled non-manual	29	5.6
Skilled manual	98	18.9
4 Partly skilled	132	25.4
5 Unskilled	245	47.2
Total	519	100

Source: Dunning, Murphy and Williams, 1988, p. 190.

football teams. Since the rougher sections of the working class value masculinity and respect 'macho' behaviour such as gambling, drinking and fighting, it is not surprising that they get involved in hooligan incidents. The theory of Dunning, Murphy and Williams could be viewed as a class-biased explanation that blames the working class for the problem and also treats the working class as a homogeneous group.

Disparateness
The empirical work of Armstrong and Harris (1991), based on two years' participant observation in Sheffield, provides evidence which contradicts the ideas of Dunning, Murphy and Williams (1988), and also gives no support to recent assertions that hooligans are organised by affluent men in middle class occupations. They found that football violence was not limited to 'rough' men, but was enjoyed by a variety of ordinary, working class men. None of the fans studied in Sheffield emanated from 'rough' estates and the only organisation that occurred resulted from incidental pub gossip just before matches.

In accordance with Marsh, Rosser and Harre (1978), Armstrong and Harris (1991) also noted that the core group of fans wanted to confront the core group of opposition fans to 'chase rather than injure them' (p. 437). Fighting could break out, but this was not the primary objective – the goal was to humiliate the opposition by getting them to run away (that is, mastery seeking). The lack of organisation, indifference to violence, transitory nature of fan groups and haphazard violent incidents may have been peculiar to the Sheffield supporters, but it nevertheless throws doubt on some of the other theories.

The occupational background of hooligans is unclear (Hobbs and Robins, 1991) and the emergence of some hooligans who are not unemployed or from the rough working class weakens sociological theories which lay emphasis on the socio-economic background of the perpetrators. However, it may be that the older, employed and more affluent hooligans of the 1980s originated from the working classes. It has been found that these people have a long history of violent behaviour and exhibit muscular, aggressive characteristics associated with the rough working class described by Dunning, Murphy and Williams (1988).

Theories with a sociological underpinning are, nevertheless, strengthened by the fact that, in Britain, violent incidents occurring at sports other than football are rare. Both rugby league and rugby union matches can attract large crowds with sets of opposing fans totally dedicated to their own club. The matches can be exciting and tense, and can arouse emotions to the highest level, and yet crowd disorder, although not unknown, is unusual. This underlines the need to study the types of people involved in hooliganism and the nature of its location, the football match.

Psychological Theories

Deprivation Theory

Deprivation theory assumes that everyone needs to gain satisfactions and pleasures out of life, and for most people this happens in socially acceptable ways at work or in leisure. Roadburg (1980) suggested that young people who were educationally, culturally and materially deprived sought ways of alleviating their frustrations. If they experienced no satisfaction at school or work, this was countered by the football match, which provided them with a highlight in their week. Roadburg described how excitement grew throughout the build-up to the match, from midweek talk about the game, through travel to the stadium and as a result of the highly charged atmosphere created by the chanting and taunting of fans.

Football hooliganism became a means of countering boredom: individuals who generally led a dull existence, perhaps because unemployed or engaged in mundane jobs, sought to escape boredom by seeking sensation and adventure through dangerous and risky behaviour. This cathartic process can be criticised since many deprived people do not exhibit violent behaviour and some advantaged individuals commit violent acts. Nevertheless, it is possible to see how this theory links with the working class frustrations described earlier and offers a mechanism for some of the hooliganism that occurs.

Negativism

A proposition which is closely linked to deprivation theory is that of negativism, where enjoyment and pleasure are derived by some people in being destructive (Kerr, 1994). Negativistic behaviour can be rebellious, hedonistic and gratuitous, purely for the thrill and excitement gained. Any concern that it is anti-social and may cause damage or injury is overwhelmed by the emotional craving for rebellious behaviour. Negativism may be hard to understand by those in society who have the resources to gain satisfaction from work or lawful leisure pursuits. If individuals are deprived of these outlets, they may look to negative forms of behaviour to gain pleasure and satisfaction. Some forms of negativistic behaviour may also occur as a result of provocation or in an attempt to gain revenge. For example, fans may react negatively to taunts and insults from rival fans or to aggressive acts by the police.

Mastery Seeking

Psychologists have put forward the idea that behaviour is often motivated by a need for competence: people gain satisfaction from mastering a skill or achieving a goal. In a footballing context, fans seek mastery of their situation by feelings of toughness and strength, perceiving that they are involved in a struggle or competition of some kind. Thus, fans strive to demonstrate dominance and hegemonic masculinity by bravado and hardness against rival fans and the police, attempting to gain an advantage in the struggle for superiority. Kerr (1994) proposed that the interplay between the countering of deprivations, negativistic behaviour and mastery seeking led to highly aroused emotional states that could provoke anger and possibly trigger serious violent behaviour.

Hooliganism Addicts

The idea of people being addicted to hooliganism seems far-fetched and yet it does provide a feasible explanation in relation to older hooligans. When studying addictive behaviour in general, Brown (1991) identified a number of stages of development for addictive behaviour. For football hooligans these stages involve an escalating cycle of violent behaviour where the violence becomes increasingly more salient, very often producing a heightened arousal level which is lacking in everyday routines. Emotional rewards are gained from thinking about, planning and preparing violent incidents, while in the aftermath, the hooligan can bask in the memory of the event, perhaps glorified by reports in the media.

Convergence

The people in any crowd will have something which links them together. The event, whether it be a film, a political rally or a sporting contest, will draw together people with similar interests and, in many cases, people with similar backgrounds. Thus, although different groups will be represented in the stadium, there will be a *convergence* of young males from working class backgrounds at football matches, many of whom will congregate at the 'ends' behind the goals. These individuals will have a local identity, with similar backgrounds, values, attitudes, norms of behaviour, intentions and goals. They will be amenable to influence from crowd leaders and perhaps even organised to engage in violent action.

Emergent Norms

Among the crowd there will also be individuals who would not normally engage in anti-social behaviour. In identifying with the crowd, the individual quickly accepts some crowd norms – for example, chanting and gesturing – and, over time, there may also be acceptance of new norms of behaviour, possibly prompting normally non-violent individuals to engage in violent acts. They could be influenced by crowd leaders whose behaviour incites others to copy them (that is, directing influences). It may well be, however, that newly acquired norms of behaviour are built on underlying, latent predispositions to act in a particular way.

Contagion

There is a driving force in crowd situations which incites people to do things they would not usually do as individuals. Anyone who has been in a crowd will have experienced feelings which are strangely different from when alone. There is a great difference between watching a football match on television and being in the middle of a crowd in a football stadium. The notion of *contagion* neatly describes the process and a number of factors can heighten the emotional arousal of the individual. Immersion in the highly charged atmosphere of the crowd, with its chanting, gesturing and volatile behaviour, will increase arousal levels, but it may be an incident during the match, such as a referee's decision, which provokes action. The flow of contagion allows a possible subordination of the individual's usual moral sanctions, possibly also dulled by alcohol, to the extent that irrational and uncharacteristic violent and criminal actions are enacted. The anonymity (deindividuation) afforded by the crowd further encourages the hooligan to behave in ways he may not accept or indulge in normally.

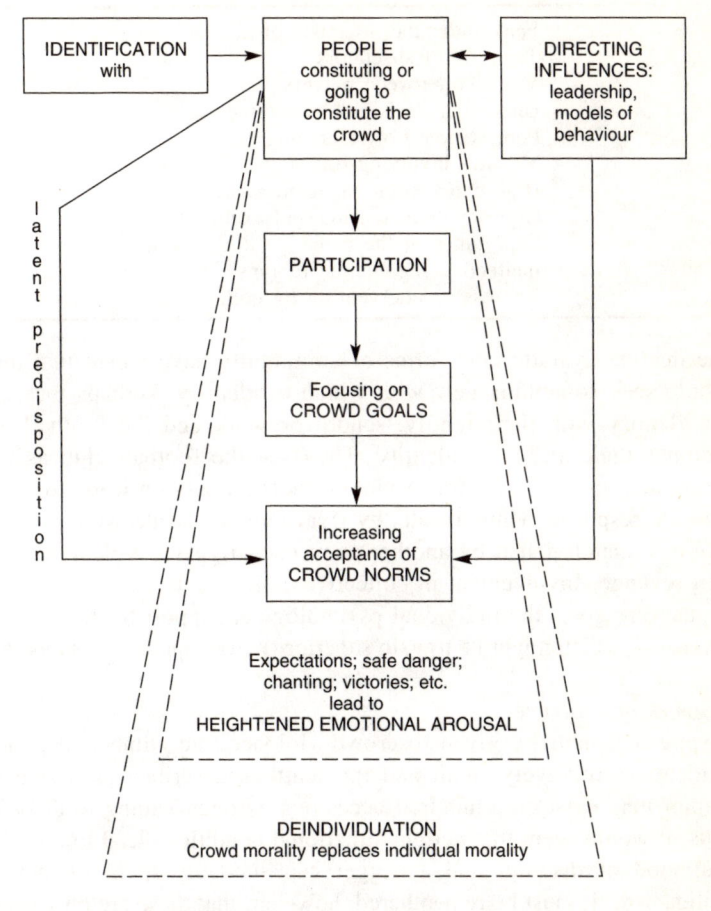

Figure 9.1 Psychological model of crowd behaviour

[Diagram: A flowchart showing IDENTIFICATION with → PEOPLE constituting or going to constitute the crowd ↔ DIRECTING INFLUENCES: leadership, models of behaviour. The central box leads down through PARTICIPATION → Focusing on CROWD GOALS → Increasing acceptance of CROWD NORMS. A "latent predisposition" label runs down the left side. The lower dashed boxes read: "Expectations; safe danger; chanting; victories; etc. lead to HEIGHTENED EMOTIONAL AROUSAL" and "DEINDIVIDUATION — Crowd morality replaces individual morality".]

Source: Brindley, 1982, p. 36.

Psychological Model of Crowd Behaviour
Figure 9.1 shows a psychological model of crowd behaviour proposed by Brindley (1982), which draws together many of the elements described in this section, to provide a framework for understanding the possible psychological sequence of events leading to football hooliganism.

Identification refers to the extent to which an individual perceives him or herself as similar to other members of a group; the greater the identification, the more likely the involvement in a group's behaviour.

Table 9.2 Situational conditions and triggers most likely to provoke football hooliganism

---
Fans under the influence of alcohol
Taunting of spectators
Violence between players
Unpopular decisions by referees
Poor standard of refereeing
Matches involving traditional rivalries
High expectations of team success
High levels of tension and excitement
Importance of the game
Ineffective segregation of fans
Aggressive intervention by police

The decline in traditional forms of community have meant that many people seek something new with which to identify. Perhaps they cannot identify with their family, school or work and the football club becomes their means of identity. They see the football club as their possession and any attempt to violate their possession leads to an aggressive response. Thus, insults by rival fans, a bad decision by a referee or a match defeat by another team may trigger a violent action to gain revenge. Involvement in collective action such as shouting abuse or chanting gives the individual psychological support for the goals of the crowd, which might be to gain superiority over opposition supporters.

Triggers of Violence
Despite the publicity given to crowd violence, the number of serious incidents is relatively small and the features described earlier in the chapter may exist on a hundred occasions without leading to disorder. Thus, it would seem that certain situational conditions lead to a greater likelihood of disorder and a trigger can suddenly spark off acts of hooliganism. It must be remembered, however, that these are only superficial, precipitating factors and not underlying causes. Table 9.2 shows the conditions and triggers most likely to provoke football hooliganism.

The Influence of the Mass Media

A fascinating conundrum is whether media coverage of sport has an influence on the level and type of football hooliganism. Editors explain that it is their duty to report violent incidents in sport, bringing them to the public's notice. It is also clear that such incidents provide exciting news and no doubt help to sell newspapers or increase viewing figures on television. It is not unknown for newspaper coverage of crowd violence to be exaggerated, as with one report which indicated that 200 fans had been arrested, when the actual number was seven! Presentation of incidents is also often highly dramatic with graphic headlines such as:

FANS GO MAD

and these are accompanied by vivid photographs of violent action. Descriptive accounts of the incidents have often contained warlike images, with phrases such as 'military showdown' prevalent. Television coverage of sporting violence can be ambivalent. Occasionally, an editor will avoid showing particular scenes, while at other times, incidents are shown in slow motion and repeated endlessly.

The intriguing question is whether people copy or model violent behaviour seen in the newspapers or on television. There is no doubt that, in experimental situations, if shown violent behaviour, some people engage in similar violent behaviour (Geen, 1983). After studying a variety of crowd disorder situations (although not specifically football crowds), Pitcher, Hamblin and Miller (1978) proposed that groups of people modelled their aggressive, violent behaviour on similar violence seen in the media. This idea is appealing since the media tend to dramatise events and, if hooligan behaviour appears exciting and rewarding, it could well attract potentially violent groups of people to act out what has been seen on television or in the newspapers. The theory is also strengthened by the fact that, when acts of hooliganism have been shown in the media, copycat incidents have often occurred.

A related explanation is that of *deviance amplification*. The sensationalism engineered by the media establishes football hooliganism as a serious social problem, creating a public anathema to the hooligans, who become labelled as the deviants of society. Whanel (1979, p. 331) highlighted the phenomenon whereby newspaper vocabulary labelled the hooligans in many dramatic ways:

> the thugs, the rowdies, rowdy mob, mindless moronic maniacs, brainless wonders, bird-brained maniacs ... soccer louts, the hysterical fans, soccer savages.

Seeing themselves as vilified but notorious public enemies, hooligans rejoice in the attention given to them and try to thwart the efforts of the authorities to confine their violent behaviour. Accordingly, violence escalates and hooliganism becomes a worse problem. Some of the most violent hooligans have made scrapbooks detailing their own exploits alongside press cuttings of football hooligan incidents. In this way, publicity of hooliganism seems to attract a wider group of disaffected youth, while reinforcing the behaviour of those already involved.

Despite the appealing logic of the above ideas, the true effect of the media on football hooliganism is not known. Modelling experiments tend to be based on short term effects and it may be that emotionally charged newspaper pictures of football violence are forgotten some days later when the next match takes place. It may also be the case that factors other than the media lead 'deviants' to engage in hooligan behaviour. Nevertheless, it seems more than a coincidence that the militaristic style of football reporting has paralleled the brutal hooliganism of recent decades.

Value-Oriented Approach

While it is possible to see how the above theories could explain violent behaviour at football matches, there are a great many games where there is no trouble of any significance. Male working class youths will have converged on a stadium and been affected by the contagious atmosphere created by an exciting game. Some will have sung and made gestures that they might not have done as individuals, but no violence occurs. Thus, it seems that all factors need to be taken into account, and these were usefully drawn together many years ago in Smelser's value-oriented approach (Smelser, 1962), an adaptation of which is shown diagrammatically in Figure 9.2.

Structural conduciveness refers to the existence of groups of people with social differences such as ethnic or class backgrounds or, in this case, allegiance with different football clubs. Structural strain involves real or perceived conflicts, deprivations or differences between different groups, while the close attachment of fans to the local club and their antagonism to other clubs produces an underlying tension widely identified by sociologists. There may be a generalised belief among the fans of one club that there is a need to teach opposition fans a lesson, perhaps emanating from a previous fixture.

The rivalry could be exaggerated by the media, leading to anticipation among fans of an explosive outcome. Tension may exist between two sets of fans, but nothing may happen unless there are facilitators such as crowd leaders who incite action, perhaps after a controversial event, such as a disputed penalty decision (a trigger of violence). Not all violent incidents fit perfectly into the Value Added Theory but, nevertheless, it offers a useful framework within which football hooliganism can be understood.

Figure 9.2 Value-oriented approach to football hooliganism

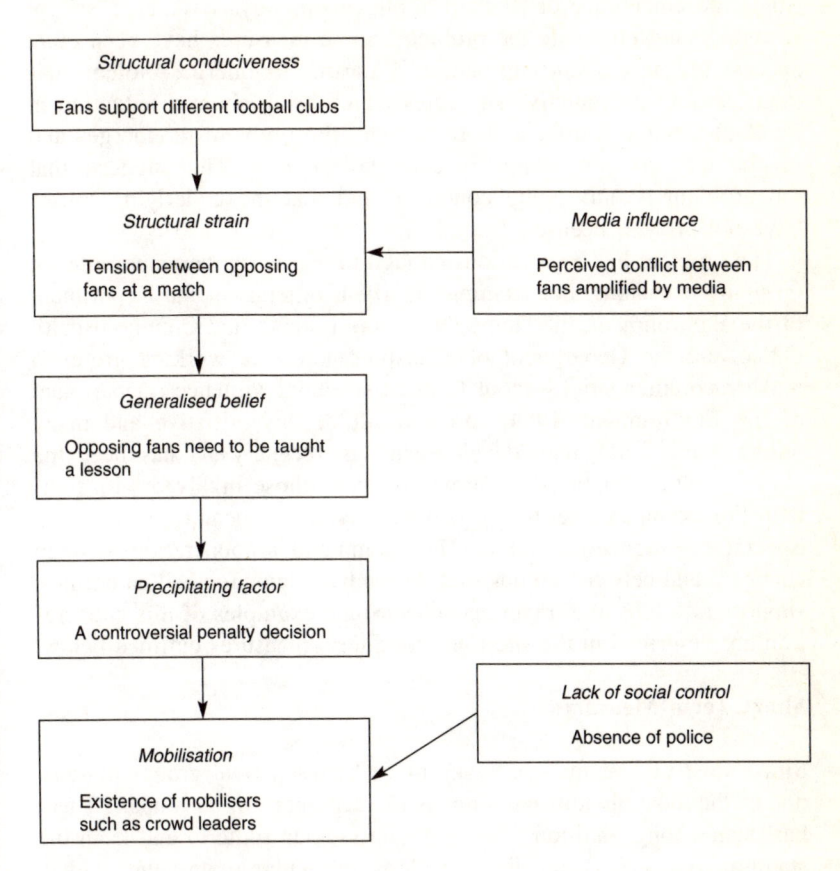

```
┌─────────────────────────────────┐
│ Structural conduciveness        │
│ Fans support different football │
│ clubs                           │
└─────────────────────────────────┘
                │
                ▼
┌─────────────────────────────────┐      ┌─────────────────────────────────┐
│ Structural strain               │◄─────│ Media influence                 │
│ Tension between opposing        │      │ Perceived conflict between      │
│ fans at a match                 │      │ fans amplified by media         │
└─────────────────────────────────┘      └─────────────────────────────────┘
                │
                ▼
┌─────────────────────────────────┐
│ Generalised belief              │
│ Opposing fans need to be taught │
│ a lesson                        │
└─────────────────────────────────┘
                │
                ▼
┌─────────────────────────────────┐
│ Precipitating factor            │
│ A controversial penalty decision│
└─────────────────────────────────┘
                │                          ┌─────────────────────────────────┐
                │                          │ Lack of social control          │
                │                          │ Absence of police               │
                ▼                          └─────────────────────────────────┘
┌─────────────────────────────────┐                    │
│ Mobilisation                    │◄───────────────────┘
│ Existence of mobilisers         │
│ such as crowd leaders           │
└─────────────────────────────────┘
```

Source: Adapted from Smelser, 1962.

Our understanding of the complexities of football hooliganism can be enhanced by integrating different approaches and theories. On its own a theory may not give an adequate explanation of violence: a football crowd may contain large numbers of people of a particular social origin and no violence takes place; a record crowd may reach a highly emotional state in a tense match and the authorities are not troubled at all; on another occasion there may be damage, injuries and even deaths among the spectators. These varying scenarios are not easily explained.

LOOKING FOR A SOLUTION

Since the emergence of football hooliganism, ways have been sought to reduce and eliminate the problem. Some measures have been quite successful, but a disturbing pattern is starting to emerge. Violent incidents lead to preventative strategies which bring about a reduction in incidents, and yet, after a short interval, the problem re-emerges and further measures are sought to curb the violence. This suggests that the problem is only being contained and that the underlying causes have not, as yet, been eradicated.

The problem has been serious enough to warrant government interest on many occasions. For example, in 1984, officials of the Department of the Environment, the Home Office, the Foreign and Commonwealth Office and the Department of Transport met as a working group to make recommendations about football spectator violence (Department of the Environment, 1984). As a result of this initiative and many others, one of the main developments in recent years has been the closer working relationship formed between those involved with football. For example, after the Heysel tragedy, a European Convention on Spectator Violence (Taylor, 1987) recommended cooperation between countries and between groups such as football clubs, football authorities, supporters' clubs and travel agencies. Some examples of this cooperation are described in the short and long term measures outlined below.

Short Term Measures

Since most violent incidents take place between rival groups of fans, one of the most obvious measures is to keep opposing fans apart. There has been a long tradition of segregating fans en route to and from the stadium. Away fans are directed along particular routes and, with a police escort, are kept away from home fans as much as possible. When home fans started to take over their 'home end' in football grounds, a target of away fans was to 'steal' the home end. The inevitable conflict which ensued quickly led clubs to allocate different parts of the ground to home and away fans, with barriers to segregate them. In some cases the barriers were not strong enough and they collapsed under crowd pressure, leading to violent confrontation between fans and tragedy, as in the Heysel stadium in Brussels when 39 spectators died and many others were injured. Perimeter fencing was also erected around pitches to prevent fans spilling on to the pitch and causing damage or fighting.

Despite these attempts at segregation, hooliganism continued and further strategies were employed. After the Hillsborough tragedy in 1989, when 95 supporters were crushed on the barriers, the Taylor Report (Taylor, 1990) recommended the abolition of terracing and advocated the principle of all-seater stadia to prevent mass movement around grounds. All major football clubs are now required to implement this recommendation and it will be interesting to see if architecture can civilise the hooligans. In effect, the seating idea corresponds with the wider principle of generally improving facilities in football grounds to attract a richer clientele (Miller, 1988). It coincides with significant commercial growth in football and the emergence of football clubs as major business concerns. The increased affluence of the big clubs has started to squeeze out the poorer, rougher groups of spectators from the grounds. Another development has been the greater publicity given to family sections, where parents can bring young children without fear of getting embroiled in dangerous incidents. This idea is favoured by many clubs since they envisage that, by making football a family entertainment, they will at least reduce the prominence of young, working class males who are most likely to cause trouble. It also links with the educational programmes and community involvement described in the long term measures below.

There are now much tighter controls regarding entry to matches. Many matches are all-ticket, which means that segregation of fans can be more easily achieved and entry to the ground can be faster, avoiding potential flashpoints as crowds mill around entrance gates. Two extreme entry measures are worthy of note. Luton Town football club excluded rival supporters of opposing teams by experimenting with a membership scheme limited to people living near Luton. Although there was a substantial reduction in arrests and policing costs, attendances were considered to be too low to make the scheme viable. Another idea, as yet untried, is that of a National Membership Scheme to control entry to football matches. Despite receiving support from government ministers, this scheme has not been introduced because of the difficulty and cost of successfully implementing it.

A number of measures have been introduced in an attempt to improve behaviour at football matches. For example, a lot of violent behaviour was considered to be alcohol related and therefore alcohol cannot now be taken into football grounds. It is probable that this step has reduced violent behaviour in stadia, but it is still possible to drink before and after matches, and therefore the problem may only have shifted to another location. It is also the case that different people behave in different ways after drinking alcohol. For example, it has been found that people inclined to violence tend to behave violently after consuming alcohol, while those with passive natures tend not to get aggressive (Buikhuisen, 1986).

Deterrents
One reaction to football spectator violence has been to mete out harsh sentences to offenders. This has been done partly to appease public anger about hooliganism and partly to act as a deterrent to would-be transgressors. However, there are a number of problems with this approach. If hooligan behaviour is spontaneous, as in the majority of cases, deterrents lose a lot of their pertinence. Even if violent activities are premeditated, as has been speculated in recent years, the anonymity afforded by the crowd gives the hooligan the confidence to be violent without fear of being caught. It is also questionable whether the harsh treatment given to hooligans is effective in preventing re-offending.

Police Strategies
Since there has been no specific offence of football hooliganism, the police have had to deal with incidents in relation to the Public Order Act and the Designated Sports Ground Act, which can apply to football stadia. Over the years, police tactics have become more and more sophisticated in an attempt to stay ahead of the hooligans. Where they once saw their role as marshalling and segregating rival sets of fans, the police have now adopted a scientific approach which ranges from pre-match intelligence gathering to closed circuit television surveillance.

A national intelligence network has been set up, involving cooperation between police forces in different parts of the country (and abroad), which can circulate information about known hooligans (information is held on more than 6000 potential troublemakers) and disseminate experiences regarding football crowd control. It was also used to make a pre-emptive move on known hooligans in advance of the 1996 European Championships held in Britain. While police continue to marshal fans to and from stadia, they also now deploy plain clothes officers, called 'spotters', within the crowd to act as 'tension indicators' (Sloan, 1989, p. 21), monitoring the crowd and nipping trouble in the bud. Police officers have even infiltrated hooligan gangs to obtain information leading to the arrest and conviction of hooligans.

One of the most successful strategies has been the use of closed circuit television for surveillance of football crowds. While this can be used to observe crowd behaviour for safety reasons, it can also be a valuable tool in spotting early signs of trouble and identifying the culprits of acts of hooliganism. The involvement and influence of club stewards has also increased in order that the police can maintain a low profile and not provoke trouble. Nevertheless, an appropriate police presence is maintained and there are fast reaction squads which can move rapidly to a trouble spot if necessary.

Encouragement has been given from many sources for the police to have close liaison with the football authorities. One result of this has been that football clubs, and match fixtures, have been rated according to the potential risk of trouble. In this way, intelligence can be gathered and efforts made to anticipate and avert serious problems. Police officers have even been trained to prevent or respond to football match incidents by an intricate, computerised crowd control simulation (Hilton, 1992). With sound, pictures, two-way radio link, telephone and a variety of realistic simulations, police officers can be alerted to incidents and trained to respond appropriately.

Long Term Measures

While most short term efforts aim to contain football hooliganism, long term measures attempt to eradicate the root cause of the problem. The main thrust of long term measures is therefore to change the behaviour of football fans. Numerous schemes have emerged and they can be roughly divided into three groups:

- the linking of club and community
- promoting better behaviour
- offering alternative activities.

Players and coaches from clubs visit schools and often run football sessions for pupils, while tours of the ground are often organised. These efforts to bring the club and community together have a double value. Not only can the football club encourage responsible behaviour among future generations of football fans, but it can also foster support among young people for the club. Some schemes, like the 'Football in the Community Campaign', target working class youth, organising jobs for the unemployed, such as coaching football.

Another strategy has been to try to improve the behaviour of fans. For example, a major theme, promoted at the European Convention on Spectator Violence (Taylor, 1987), has been to promote the 'sporting ideal' – as, for example, in upholding the notion of fair play. This is clearly a challenging task, but it is being attempted in all Football Association coaching programmes, through managers' notes in match programmes, and in other related schemes such as the 'Kick Racism out of Football' campaign (AGARI, 1995).

Kerr (1994, p. 113) referred to the role of alternative activities:

> The key factor in intervention treatment ... is to replace hooligan behaviour with some alternative form of rewarding activity or activities, which can provide the same levels of excitement and pleasure and intensity of experience but which are not antisocial.

While attractive in theory, this approach is hard to implement because of the cost of alternative activities, organisational problems and the difficulty of luring hooligans away from football, their central life interest. The effectiveness of long term measures is hard to evaluate and they may not alleviate the social problems identified earlier in the chapter. If sociological theories are accurate, violent behaviour is an issue for society, and football-related initiatives will deal with only a part of the problem.

CONCLUDING REMARKS

Although crowd disorder is not a new phenomenon, it has been seen as a modern social problem, often amplified by dramatic words and pictures in the media. Within the complex array of factors associated with football hooliganism, a key feature seems to be the hegemonic masculinity exhibited by young men, vividly depicted by Burford (1991). If a trigger for violent incidents occurs, such as apparent police provocation, it can release the muscular, aggressive behaviour that seethes below the surface of a hard core of fans. This belligerent attitude has been a recurring theme in the many theories put forward to explain hooliganism.

A recent Premier League survey (Sir Norman Chester Centre for Football Research, 1996) found that the vast majority of fans thought hooliganism had declined in the previous five years. The apparent lower levels of hooliganism – for example, a fall of around 40 per cent in arrests over the last decade – can perhaps be related to a change in the nature of football spectating. Increased entrance charges, passive seating arrangements, camera surveillance and sophisticated police operations have provided a different setting from that which existed in the 1970s and 1980s. However, it is possible that hooliganism has simply moved away from football grounds, out of sight of the television cameras. Time will tell whether the angry young men have been outmanoeuvred or whether this is just a lull before the storm, with hooliganism re-emerging as it has done a number of times before.

REFERENCES

AGARI, *Let's Kick Racism Newsletter* (London: Commission for Racial Equality, 1995).
Armstrong, G. and Harris, R., 'Football Hooligans: Theory and Evidence', *Sociological Review*, 39 (1991), pp. 427–58.
Brindley, J.M., 'Disruptive Crowd Behaviour: A Psychological Perspective', *Police Journal*, 55 (1982), pp. 28–38.
Brown, R.I.F., 'Gaming, Gambling and Other Addictive Play'. In J.H. Kerr and M.J. Apter (eds), *Adult Play* (Amsterdam: Swets and Zeitlinger, 1991), pp. 101–18.
Buikhuisen, W., 'Alcohol and Soccer Hooliganism', *International Journal of Offender Therapy and Comparative Criminology*, 30 (1986), pp. ix–xi.
Burford, B., *Among the Thugs* (London: Secker and Warburg, 1991).
Department of the Environment, *Football Spectator Violence* (London: HMSO, 1984).
Dunning, E., Murphy, P. and Waddington, I., 'Anthropological versus Sociological Approaches to the Study of Soccer Hooliganism: Some Critical Notes', *Sociological Review*, 39 (1991), pp. 459–78.
Dunning, E., Murphy, P. and Williams, J., *The Roots of Football Hooliganism* (London: Routledge, 1988).
Elias, N., *The Civilising Process* (Oxford: Blackwell, 1978).
Geen, R.G., 'Aggression and Television Violence'. In R.G. Geen and E.I. Donnerstein (eds), *Aggression: Vol. 2. Theoretical and Empirical Reviews* (New York: Academic Press, 1983).
Hilton, P., 'A Match for the Crowd', *Personnel Management*, 24 (1992), pp. 57–8.
Hobbs, R. and Robins, D., 'The Boy Done Good: Football Violence, Changes and Continuities', *Sociological Review*, 39 (1991), pp. 551–79.
Kerr, J.H., *Understanding Soccer Hooliganism* (Buckingham: Open University Press, 1994).
Maguire, J., 'The Emergence of Football Spectating as a Social Problem 1880–1985: A Figurational and Developmental Perspective', *Sociology of Sport Journal*, 3 (1986), pp. 217–44.
Marsh, P., Rosser, E. and Harre, R., *The Rules of Disorder* (London: Routledge, 1978).
Miller, R., 'Messages in the Battle', *Youth in Society*, no. 143 (1988), pp. 12–14.
Pitcher, B.L., Hamblin, R.L. and Miller, J.L.L., 'The Diffusion of Collective Violence', *American Sociological Review*, 43 (1978), pp. 23–35.

Roadburg, A., 'Factors Precipitating Fan Violence: A Comparison of Professional Soccer in Britain and North America', *British Journal of Sociology*, 31 (1980), pp. 265–76.

Russell, G.W., 'Does Sports Violence Increase Box Office Receipts?' *International Journal of Sport Psychology*, 17 (1986), pp. 173–82.

Sir Norman Chester Centre for Football Research, *FA Premier League Fan Surveys 1995/96* (Leicester: University of Leicester, 1996).

Sloan, A.K., 'Ver Heyden de Lancey Medico-Legal Lectures 1988–89: Soccer Hooliganism', *Medicine, Science and the Law*, 29 (1989), pp. 14–25.

Smelser, N.J., *Theory of Collective Behaviour* (London: Routledge and Kegan Paul, 1962).

Taylor, I., 'On the Sports Violence Question: Soccer Hooliganism Revisited'. In J. Hargreaves (ed.), *Sport, Culture and Ideology* (London: Routledge, 1982) pp. 152–96.

Taylor, J.C., 'The War on Soccer Hooliganism: The European Convention on Spectator Violence and "Misbehaviour" at Sports Events', *Virginia Journal of International Law*, 27 (1987), pp. 603–53.

Taylor, P., *The Taylor Report*, Cm. 962 (London: HMSO, 1990).

Whannel, G., 'Football, Crowd Behaviour and the Press', *Media, Culture and Society*, 1 (1979), pp. 327–42.

FURTHER READING

See Dunning, Murphy and Williams (cited above), Kerr (cited above) and a number of articles in volume 39 of *Sociological Review* (cited above).

10 Commercialism and Sport

INTRODUCTION

This chapter explores the relationship between commercialism and sport. In order to set the scene, the growth of commercialism in sport is traced and consideration is given to the ways in which sport has become a billion pound industry, including the part played by television in the process. This is followed by an analysis of how sportsmen and sportswomen have been affected by the financial and organisational changes that have occurred in sport. A major element of the sports industry nowadays is commercial sponsorship and therefore a wide range of issues are explored, including the controversial aspect of tobacco sponsorship of sport. Finally, the question is posed as to whether commercialism has had a positive or negative influence on sport.

THE GROWTH OF COMMERCIALISM IN SPORT

The link between commercialism and sport has a long history. In Ancient Greece the athletes who competed in the Games were essentially professionals, since they received patronage from cities, won cash and goods prizes in competition and even earned pensions for life (Finley and Pleket, 1976). Although the Olympic Games is reputed never to have given cash prizes, it is clear that other sacred Games awarded money, to the equivalent of £200 000 at today's prices, and even induced champions to compete for appearance fees. Moving forward to the end of the nineteenth century, industrialisation reached a point where workers had money left over after buying necessities, and a reduction in working hours for many people was brought about by political pressures. Mass culture emerged and many commercialised activities were offered to the public, since alert entrepreneurs saw the potential of sport as a means of entertaining the masses and becoming a part of the modern culture industry (Goldlust, 1987).

In recent times the growth of commercialism in sport has been a contentious issue in Britain because of the strength of the amateur ethos. Following the Greek classical ideal where sports participation contributed to the personal betterment of the individual, nineteenth century sport in Britain was championed for the love of taking part and not for monetary reward or an obsessive concern for victory. Sport, as conceived by the bourgeois founders of modern sport, contained a set of values and norms based on civilised behaviour. Qualities espoused were self-discipline, respect for opponents and the rules of the game, adherence to the spirit of fair play and competing well regardless of outcome (Mason, 1993). This legacy produced great resistance to commercial interference in sport.

By the twentieth century, sport was flourishing in many countries and after the Second World War:

> the major imperial powers jostled for position in an international capitalist system [and] the drama of their struggles became symbolically interwoven with the performances of individual athletes and national teams. (Gruneau, 1984, p. 6)

Furthermore, each nation which hosted the Olympic Games attempted to demonstrate its credentials as a main player in world commerce and trade. Thus, Rome, Tokyo and Mexico ploughed extensive sums of money into the Games, while many social services in these cities were left without funds.

However, until the 1960s, sport was still run in Britain by amateur, paternalist, voluntary administrators. The amateur ethos was ingrained so strongly that any intrusion of professionalism was, for a long time, seen as an undesirable threat to the ethics of sport. Many sports retained their amateur status during the twentieth century, not allowing anything other than expenses to be paid to athletes. For example, Dwight Stones, an international high jumper in the 1970s, was temporarily banned from athletics for receiving money after appearing in the television show *Superstars*, which had no link with the high jump event. As the commercial side of sport expanded, the circumvention of amateur rules escalated, with players allegedly receiving undercover payments. In the end, the strength of commercial forces led to the gradual erosion of amateurism at the élite level of performance. Hence, Whannel (1992, p. 68) commented that:

> the contradiction between the amateur and the entrepreneurial has been heightened dramatically as outside entrepreneurial forces have challenged the hegemony of the traditional authorities.

'Shamateurism', as it was known, gave way to sports becoming 'open', as tennis did in 1968, and it became possible for competitors to earn a living from their sport. Some sports, like athletics and rugby, set up trust funds where earnings could be held until the athlete retired from competition. Sports that are still amateur in nature are, for the most part, those that have little interest for the general public and therefore cannot attract large numbers of spectators and have limited commercial interest. Wilson (1988) has suggested that the true commercialisation of sport originated in the 1970s when large corporations first became involved in sponsoring international sporting events. It did not take them long to realise the value of sporting spectacles in terms of communication, advertising and public relations, and with deals involving millions of pounds, it is alleged that not all the money reached the sport for which it was intended.

Basketball is a good example of a sport that has been transformed in Britain in recent years. Utilising a figurational perspective, Maguire (1988) submitted that élite basketball had been affected by a number of interweaving factors. First, entrepreneurs, seeing the commercial potential of the game, wrested a degree of control of the sport from the governing body. In addition, basketball has been subject to Americanisation, with American players and coaches gradually infiltrating the game and creating a spectacle with a distinctive American style. To complete its commercial transformation, rule changes have been introduced 'to enhance its appeal' and there has been a 'growing ascendancy of values governing the conduct of play which emphasise display, "glitz" and entertainment' (Maguire, 1988, p. 308).

The Sports Industry

The sports industry consists of élite sportsmen and sportswomen, the thousands who take part in sport as a recreation and the millions who are entertained by the élite performers. The twentieth century has seen sport change from a largely amateur pastime to a multibillion pound industry. In Britain more is spent on sport than on motor vehicles, and more people are employed in sport-related jobs than in agriculture or the chemical industry.

A number of factors have led to this transformation:

- *Increased free time.* The majority of the population in Britain now has time free from employed work and domestic tasks, and, consequently, many choose to take part in sport for enjoyment, health, social and other reasons. Increased free time has also enabled people to spectate at sports events, whether as regular fans or on an occasional outing.

- *Increased affluence.* Whereas in the past most people had to spend their income on necessities, the twentieth century has seen a substantial increase in the amount of disposable income that can be spent on recreation. Thus, many people elect to spend money on sports membership fees, sports equipment and spectating at sports events. Trainers and sport-related clothing have become fashion leaders and everyday clothing for millions.
- *Television.* Sport is transmitted to almost everyone's living room by television. This has meant that the sports that are televised can attract large sums of money for the rights to cover matches and tournaments. The other major outcome of television coverage of sport is that it has raised awareness among the general public of a wide range of sports and stimulated recreational participation in them.
- *Business potential.* The expansion of sports participation and sports spectating has opened up a multitude of business opportunities. Sport sponsorship can help to sell goods, sports events can generate substantial income, while sports equipment and clothing can produce a massive turnover.

The Economic Significance of Sport

Sport has become 'a consumer commodity competing in a market against similar products' (Goldlust, 1987, p. 69), and its economic significance can be gauged by the substantial spending on sport and sport-related goods nowadays. It is estimated that well in excess of £5 billion is spent on sport every year (Key Note Market Review, 1994), with the main areas being participation costs, gambling, sports clothing, footwear and equipment. In addition, there is considerable carry-over from sport to other industries such as travel, media and tourism. The European Football Championships, which were held in Britain in 1996, attracted thousands of fans from competing European nations, who travelled around the country staying in hotels and spending a great deal of money. The financial, travel, retail and media potential of the Olympic Games has grown to gargantuan proportions in line with the worldwide popularity of the Games. When around 2,000 million people watch the Olympic Games on television it is perhaps not surprising that major corporations will pay out millions of pounds to be associated with them.

Advertising, Promotion and Entertainment
While sports devotees will probably attend sporting events without much prompting, it is the advent of the sports promoter that has helped to

push sport into the commercial world. Promoters arrange events and publicise them to attract the largest possible audience. In the early part of the twentieth century, George 'Tex' Rickard organised elaborate publicity stunts in America to draw audiences of over 100 000 to boxing prize fights (Cashmore, 1990). The enormous television audiences for sport nowadays are a great attraction for companies to advertise during sporting events. This is curtailed to a certain extent in Britain because the BBC does not allow advertisements and yet holds the rights to show many major events like Wimbledon, the Grand National and international cricket matches.

Each sport now vies with other sports and other leisure pursuits to attract consumers. However, Evans, James and Tomes (1996) found that British sports associations did not have a strong marketing orientation and made little attempt, for example, to acquire knowledge of consumer needs or to consider external forces affecting the sporting market place. It appears that, while some elements of the sports industry have fully embraced commercialism, many British sports associations retain an amateurish approach to the marketing side of their affairs.

Advertising on players' clothing and on hoardings at sports events is another important commercial element of sport. This kind of advertising can be seen by many spectators attending the event, but of course most impact is made if the occasion is televised. There is therefore a pricing scale which is determined by the likely number of people who will see the advertisement. The value of sports advertising can be gauged by the fact that advertising stickers on Grand Prix racing cars are costed by the size and position of the sticker on the car; a few centimetres one way or another can change the cost considerably.

Sporting Goods
The growth in sport has led to massive expansion in the sale of sport-related items. The sporting goods industry is worth many billions of pounds worldwide and is still growing. It is important for international trade, especially since developing countries export considerable amounts of sporting goods to industrialised countries. Numerous companies supply sports equipment for sports centres, schools, sports clubs and fitness studios, while every high street in Britain has a store selling sports goods like badminton rackets and tracksuits. Some shops are entirely devoted to the sale of trainers and yet it is estimated that approximately 70 per cent of buyers of trainers do not take part in sport, but have them for casual wear!

Table 10.1 Factors influencing attendance at sporting events

Weather	Degree of rivalry in
Team performance	competition
Population size	Popularity of star players
Composition of community	Convenience of fixture date
Amount of violence on and off the pitch	(e.g. weekend)
Cost of tickets	Competing alternatives
Accessibility of stadium	(e.g. other fixtures)
Degree of promotion	

Source: Adapted from McPherson, Curtis and Loy, 1989, p. 121.

Gate Receipts
Attendance at a sporting event is a crucial factor in the business side of sport. In the past, most sports depended on gate receipts for a significant proportion of their income, but nowadays a higher percentage is generated by television rights and related business such as merchandising. Nevertheless, gate receipts remain important for most sports since they provide people to buy the merchandise, generate income and establish the platform for attracting television coverage. A televised event is not usually successful if the stadium is almost empty.

Sports such as football, rugby, cricket and horse racing attract large audiences at various times in different locations. McPherson, Curtis and Loy (1989) identified factors that explained variation in attendance at sporting events, as shown in Table 10.1.

Television Rights
The money generated from television rights has rocketed in recent years. Contracts worth millions of pounds are now negotiated for sports like football, rugby, cricket, tennis and major sporting championships. This is due to the great demand by the public to see sporting events on television, and the intense rivalry between television companies, both terrestrial and satellite. Television rights are negotiated by sport's organising bodies, like the Football League, or by event organisers. Where an organising body of sport is involved, it is usual for a proportion of the income to be spread among different clubs and invested in the development of the sport.

Related Business Income
The commercial influence in sport has led to a concomitant expansion in related business. Major sporting events can generate substantial business

for the local community, whether it is in terms of hotel rooms or hotdogs. Visitors to the event are like tourists, stimulating the local economy through their spending, which, in turn, increases spending among the local population. Sports clubs now offer almost unlimited goods and services, ranging from T-shirts to toilet seats and keyrings to hotdog stands, and even have supermarkets on-site at stadia. Perhaps the most successful example, however, has been Manchester United football club which, availing of its immense national and international popularity, extending far from the environs of Manchester, has generated millions of pounds from merchandising and other related goods.

Lottery Fund
All kinds of community sporting facilities have been built in the second half of the twentieth century, and opportunities for further expansion have been stimulated by the availability of grants from the National Lottery Sports Fund. Millions of pounds have been allocated to schemes for the building and improvement of sports facilities, and more recently, money has also been distributed to talented individuals and teams to help them develop in their sport.

The Commercial Value of Sport

Occasionally, the hosting of major international championships leads to the construction of stadia and other large scale sporting facilities. In 1976 Montreal hosted the Olympic Games and, while costs were estimated at $1.4 billion, revenue was at best only $400 million. It is sobering to note that the difference of $1 billion could have provided 400 community facilities or free transportation for ten years in Montreal. However, the business potential of the Olympic Games was realised by the time of the Los Angeles Games in 1984. With private sector funding and management, costs were limited to $469 million while revenue rose to $619 million and Los Angeles ended up in profit. The turnaround in the financial fortunes of the Olympic Games is due to high profile international companies sponsoring the Games to produce the mammoth spectacle that now exists. The positive side of this is that facilities are of a high standard, sporting performances have improved, athletes are relatively well financed and much of the world's population can be entertained by televised Olympic events.

Thus, sports have a commercial value if they can attract a large spectatorship at events and can also secure media coverage, especially television. The commercial world seeks to increase sales either directly at a sporting event or, indirectly, through raising awareness of a company and/or a product at sporting events. In Britain sports like netball and field hockey do not have widespread public interest and therefore commercial investment in them is substantially less than in a sport like football which commands massive public interest. Ticket prices at sporting events depend upon what promoters believe they can charge and still sell tickets – a case of supply and demand. The Wimbledon Tennis Championships can set high prices and continue to fill the grounds, whereas a lowly rugby club might reduce entrance charges and yet not attract a larger audience.

There is at present little commercial potential in the provision of facilities for non-élite sports participation. Widespread public provision of playing fields, sports halls and swimming pools has meant that there is no commercial incentive to move into this area. In effect, the public subsidy to many indoor and outdoor sports has led to the public paying relatively little for recreational sport, and therefore there is strong resistance to paying the high prices that need to be charged for a sports facility to be a profitable commercial concern.

Even where there is little or no public subsidy, commercial activity is often not viable because costs are kept low by sports clubs operating on a non-profit basis. Hence, sports like tennis, golf, bowls and badminton are mainly run by volunteers and any excess of income over expenditure is used to develop club facilities. Thus, economic theory is inappropriate in the pricing of sport (Berret, Slack and Whitson, 1993) and commercial operations are limited to facilities such as ten-pin bowling alleys, fitness clubs and indoor tennis centres, where there has been no tradition of public subsidy and people are willing to pay enough to give profitability to a company.

A similar situation exists in respect of spectator facilities for sports events, since it is not usually viable for a commercial concern to own sports stadia. This is because they lie empty most of the time and maintenance costs are high. There are a few exceptions, like Wembley stadium and a number of football stadia, but there may be others in the future if companies believe they can expand usage of a stadium across sports and other entertainments to attract good sized audiences.

Television and Sport

A tennis match at Wimbledon in June 1937 was the first televised sporting event and few realised that this inauspicious event was the forerunner of an association that was to shape the development of sport.

During the first half of the twentieth century, sport expanded gradually and commercial opportunities grew slowly. It was television that provided 'market penetration' with the broadcasting of sport to massive audiences (Goldlust, 1987, p. 143). During the 1960s communication satellites enabled live television coverage of sporting events around the globe, and over the years, technological advances in video editing, slow motion photography and high quality colour reproduction have made sport a marvellous spectacle on television. The amount of televised sport has continually increased, rising to over 3000 hours per year in the 1990s. Television needs sport to increase its viewing figures and sport needs television for the massive income it generates.

Sports like snooker have benefited immensely from being televised:

> [Snooker] is the archetypal television-promoted sport whose players twenty years ago were languishing unpaid and unrecognised in obscure clubs throughout the country. (Barnett, 1990, p. 49)

Television can recruit new spectators to a sport by creating interest, enabling people to learn the rules and patterns of play and helping them to form an identity with individual athletes and with sports teams. An example was the television coverage of the American basketball 'dream' team which played in the 1992 Olympic Games. This high profile event gave a boost to basketball around the world, generating more interest, players and spectators. This, in turn, meant that companies were more interested in sponsoring basketball and that more basketball-related goods were sold.

> Television can therefore act as a marriage-broker: bringing an apparently unlikely sport to a sponsor's attention by providing the incentives of televised credits, and leaving the newly-weds to a (reasonably) happy reciprocal relationship. (Barnett, 1990, p. 113)

While television sports coverage has generally been successful, there have been a few sports that have fallen by the wayside. Wrestling, squash and greyhound racing are examples of sports which have faded from the public eye or moved to satellite channels. Squash has tried many rule changes to make it more attractive to a television audience, but it has not yet succeeded.

Whether a sport will gain financial and publicity benefits from television depends not only on its capacity to achieve a large viewing audience, but also on the type of audience it attracts. Young, urban, affluent audiences are most responsive to advertising, and therefore sports like motor racing, golf and rugby have greater bargaining power because they appeal to this kind of audience. The lack of visibility on television of women's sport, especially netball, suggests that it cannot attract large audiences or people at whom advertisers are aiming. In recent years, sports have recognised that they are competing with one another for participants, spectators, television coverage and financial support. They are in the business market place like any other business product or service, and since television is an essential ingredient for success, each sport vies with other sports to present an attractive spectacle for television audiences.

A much higher proportion of a sport's income now comes from television. Despite the huge amounts paid for television rights, Whannel (1992) considered that, at somewhere between £40 000 and £60 000 per hour, sport was still a relatively inexpensive form of television. Goldlust (1987) made the point that commercial television companies need to make profits to remain operational, and therefore, despite the enormous sums of money paid for television rights to show sporting events, companies would not keep returning to televise sport if it was not financially viable for them.

The commercial link between sport and television has not been without problems and criticisms. The multimillion pound investment in athletics by ITV during the 1980s led to accusations of overcommercialisation in a supposedly amateur sport. Satellite television channels are still in their infancy and their impact on sport is awaited. While numbers subscribing to satellite channels are relatively small, they are increasing, and multimillion pound deals have been negotiated to gain exclusive rights to many sporting events. The government has protected some major British sporting events like Wimbledon, but competition between terrestrial and satellite channels will undoubtedly influence sporting developments in the next millennium.

PROFESSIONAL SPORTSMEN AND SPORTSWOMEN

As mentioned at the start of the chapter, athletes participating in the Ancient Games were professionals in the sense that they earned at least part of their living as sportsmen. There are known to have been professional bullfighters in Spain around 1700 and some jockeys earned a living from horse racing in the late nineteenth century. In the first half of the twentieth century, a number of cricketers, tennis players and footballers also made their living as professional sportsmen. However, the numbers were very small compared to the thousands now engaged in professional sport, some of whom earn millions of pounds a year.

Prior to the 1960s when sport started being televised regularly, few sporting professionals made large amounts of money from sport. Although a great many 'behind the scenes', undercover payments in cash and kind were made to players, they were small when compared to today's standards. Television's injection of money and publicity transformed the earning potential of top competitors and they now have an entourage of personal managers, professional advisers and agents to look after their commercial interests.

There are three main ways in which professional athletes can earn a living:

- having a contract with a club and receiving a basic salary which can be supplemented by bonuses for winning matches
- receiving earnings from tournament winnings
- receiving fees for competing in an event (that is, appearance fees).

The 'personalisation' of television presentation has turned élite sportsmen and sportswomen into public, and even cult, figures. Their instant recognition and high status make them ideal for the endorsement of products: football boots worn by Ryan Giggs will be chosen by thousands of aspiring and admiring youngsters. Thus, a relatively small number of élite sportsmen and sportswomen can add substantially to their earnings by endorsing products. A small logo on a tennis player's shoulder can cost a company and earn a player (and his or her agent) a large amount of money. It is estimated that, for a player such as Boris Becker, only one tenth of his total income was made directly by his play on the tennis court. While a few top level international competitors with high media profiles earn more than MPs and heart surgeons, there are thousands at lower levels who earn much less and may hardly cover the expenses of competing. Although there are schemes to provide financial aid for the development of sporting talent among young people, monetary rewards are mostly restricted to élite performers.

There is a constant interplay between money and achievement for athletes. Nearly all athletes are motivated by both sporting achievement and monetary return, while the degree of importance attached to each depends upon ever changing circumstances. The young, improving athlete may see financial reward as a major drive, and may even consider cheating to achieve success, while a financially secure élite performer may, on the other hand, mainly have achievement goals.

It is difficult to look at the increasingly desperate lengths to which competitors are prepared to go in the pursuit of victory, and avoid the feeling that somehow the virtue of athletic endeavour, of striving for athletic and competitive achievement, has been irrevocably tarnished by the arrival of large sums of money. (Barnett, 1990, p. 152)

Elite sportsmen and sportswomen have now become entertainers and are subject to the demands of their audiences. For example:

- Every performance is important – spectators do not appreciate lack of effort.
- Competition schedules can be demanding, with extensive travel and a high number of performances.
- There is high profile publicity, promotion and marketing, with press conferences and other media events.

In line with performers in other spheres of entertainment, athletes tend to be managed by agents or agencies. These people negotiate contracts for participation in certain events, arrange sponsorship deals and manage related business interests. While the agent can gain increased commercial benefit for the athlete, the agent will also receive a proportion of the income achieved by the athlete.

The Worklike Characteristics of Sport

Sport now has all the characteristics and practices of worklike situations which exist in other sectors of industry (McPherson, Curtis and Loy, 1989). Table 10.2 provides examples of work practices in sport.

There is, however, one subtle difference between sport and other business sectors. While the economic viability of a professional sports club usually depends on success on the field, it does not want to see other clubs go out of business since it needs opposition for future matches. In this respect, it is important for a sport's governing body to help less successful clubs, possibly by distributing money received from television rights to all clubs.

SPONSORSHIP OF SPORT

Commercial sponsorship of sport has expanded significantly in the second half of the twentieth century and it clearly plays a significant role in the funding of sport in Britain. The value of sponsorship rose from

Table 10.2 Work practices in sport

Characteristics of industry	Example in sport
Exchange of goods	Transfer of players
Division of labour	Managers, players, ground staff
Job satisfaction	Professional enjoying playing
Unions	Professional players' associations
Strikes	US footballers striking in the 1990s
Depreciation	Depreciation of value of player with age
Tax concessions	Companies using sponsorship for tax relief
Operating revenues	Operating revenue of a football club
Bonuses	Bonuses for winning matches
Marketing	Marketing of companies through sponsorship

about £2.5 million in 1971, to £100 million by 1983, and is now estimated to be over £300 million. By the 1980s the situation had become so complex that a committee of inquiry was set up by the Central Council of Physical Recreation, under the chairmanship of Denis Howell, to investigate the sponsorship of sport by commercial companies. The Howell Report (Central Council of Physical Recreation, 1983, p. 7) defined sponsorship as 'the support of a sport, sports event, sports organisation or competitor by an outside body or person for the mutual benefit of both parties'. It produced 73 conclusions and recommendations and has had widespread influence on the development of sport sponsorship.

Sponsorship of sport is not usually part of a company's main commercial operation, but will involve a contribution in cash or kind for which the company expects a return in terms of positive publicity. Companies generally spend less than 5 per cent of their advertising budget on sponsorship, although expenditure is difficult to assess because of the unwillingness of sponsors to reveal their full financial commitment and the problem of assessing the value of contributions in kind. Although televised sponsorship has a high profile, it is probable that local and regional sponsorship accounts for about a quarter of the total sponsorship of sport.

Whannel (1992) considered that there were two main factors that led to the dramatic growth of sport sponsorship in recent times. First, the televising of sport in the 1950s and 1960s brought sport into the homes of millions, and second, the banning of cigarette advertising on television had an important influence. Companies that sponsor sport come from many different sectors of industry and yet the tobacco industry has, for a long time, been a major sponsor of sport and also spends the highest proportion of its total advertising budget on sponsorship. A major reason for this is that, since 1965, the tobacco industry has been banned from direct advertising on television and sport sponsorship provides a subtle way around this. (However, British television will not now show tobacco-sponsored sports events.) Other industries significantly involved in sports sponsorship have been alcoholic drinks, soft drinks, oil companies, banks, insurance and leisure-related industries.

In the business world, the aim of advertising a product is obviously to stimulate sales. Gratton and Taylor (1985) pointed out that the effect on company sales of sport sponsorship is extremely difficult to evaluate. Sponsorship does not generally involve the advertising of specific products and therefore an immediate rise in sales will probably not occur. Sport sponsorship often aims to raise awareness of the company name and develop goodwill over a period of time. An insurance company, for example, will hope that people buy its services because the name of the company is recognised and because it is associated with a positive, healthy aspect of life such as sport.

Additional surveys are often conducted to evaluate the degree of awareness and goodwill achieved from a particular sponsorship. Also, in recent years, there has been a developing trend for companies to use their product name in sport sponsorship. In this way they can raise awareness, develop goodwill and, possibly, increase sales all at the same time; the 'Snickers' chocolate bar has, for example, been prominent in the sponsorship of international sporting events.

Types of Sport Sponsorship

There are a number of ways in which the sport sponsorship business works:

- *Event.* When a company or consortium of companies sponsor a particular sporting event, publicity may be achieved through the title of the event, through advertising during the event and through related business, such as merchandising. There is a great demand from companies to use the prestigious five ring Olympic Games symbol, because it has global recognition and is associated with a very positive aspect of society. The licence to use the symbol is held by many of the countries competing in the Games, and for the 1988 Games in Seoul, 150 countries sold their licence to 44 commercial companies anxious to put the rings on their products.

Table 10.3 Publicity achieved through sponsorship of motor sport

---
- Press conference announcing sponsorship agreement between company and racing team
- Preliminary promotion and advertising of motor sport event
- Advertisements on cars and hoardings around track
- Company name mentioned during race commentary
- Post-race press conference with drivers
- Media coverage of results of race, often including repeated highlights on television
- Company name on merchandising linked to motor racing
- Car advertisements with reports of motor racing successes

- *Individual.* Elite sporting performers may be sponsored to endorse a company or a product of the company.
- *Team.* In a team sport, the team might be sponsored by a company and all the players advertise the company on their clothing or equipment.
- *Coaching.* Companies may feel that they can reach different markets through giving financial support to a sports coaching programme. While media publicity may not be high in this form of sponsorship, it can associate the company with a good cause and provide valuable promotion among young people.
- *Award schemes.* Another way of targeting young people is through support given to sporting award schemes. These schemes are very popular among children and thus the large numbers involved can mean that the company gets widespread recognition.

Reasons for Sponsorship

There are many reasons why companies enter into sport sponsorship agreements.

1. Publicity
The widespread popularity of sport among the general population means that any advertising linked to sport is automatically going to reach a sizeable audience. Table 10.3 illustrates the extent of publicity available through the sponsorship of motor sport.

However, negative developments in sport mean that companies have to consider whether advertising and goodwill are negated by unsavoury publicity. For example, the scourge of hooliganism has sometimes dented the attractiveness of football as a sponsorship opportunity in England. Surveys have also found that awareness can be raised by sponsorship, but not always in the way envisaged by companies. For example, the public associated Gillette with sport after its sponsorship of cricket, but did not necessarily connect the company with the safety razor. Continued sponsorship does not seem to reach ever more consumers, since awareness levels plateau and this is one of the reasons for limited period sponsorship on the part of many companies.

2. Marketing and Promotion
Sport sponsorship has become a popular means of promoting companies and their products. An illustration of the influence of star individual performers can be shown by Boris Becker's endorsement of tennis rackets. In 1984 Puma sold 15 000 tennis rackets, but in 1985, when Becker promoted the rackets, sales jumped to 70 000 and by 1986 this had grown to 300 000. In a more general link with sport, a company can suggest, through advertisements, that an exciting feature of youth culture can be gained by eating a chocolate bar or wearing an item of sports clothing.

3. Building a Corporate Image
The publicity afforded through sport can contribute towards building a positive public image for a company. Sport portrays an image of health, strength, competitiveness, will to win and élite performance, and if associated with these positive attributes, a company is likely to benefit. Gruneau (1984, p. 1) considered that, by sponsoring sport, a company was seen to be doing good public work and 'establishing a set of deeply rooted symbolic connections with a target audience'.

4. Entry to New Markets
Companies seeking to establish themselves in a new market, which may be in a new country, avail of sport sponsorship. For example, drinks companies have established new markets in countries where they have gained a high profile by sponsoring major international events like the Olympic Games and the World Athletics Championships.

5. Entertainment and Trade Relations
The purchase of entertainment facilities at prestigious sporting events has a dual value. On the one hand, entrance and seats at a major event such as the Wimbledon Tennis Championships provide an attractive 'perk' for company employees while, at the same time, offering an advantageous setting to entertain business customers and associates.

6. *Public Relations and Contact with Local Community*
Small firms can benefit from local sponsorship of junior and senior sports teams. The limited amount of publicity emanating from this form of sponsorship is boosted by the community goodwill developed, which sometimes has a political benefit in the locality.

Sponsorship Agencies

In the early years of commercial sponsorship, decisions were often made according to the whim of top executives, perhaps depending on their liking for a particular sport. Because of the complexity of sponsorship nowadays and the specialised skills needed, many companies employ sponsorship agencies to deal with issues such as:

- matching the company to appropriate sports sponsorship opportunities
- drawing up sponsorship agreements
- administering sponsorship arrangements
- handling the media and general public relations issues
- organising sales promotion and advertising.

The fees paid to sponsorship agencies can be high and therefore the company spends more and sport receives less. However, sport sponsorship would probably not be as professionally organised and beneficial to both parties if agencies were not involved.

Mark McCormack emerged in the 1960s to represent sportsmen and sportswomen. His company, International Management Group, has acted as agents for sports stars such as Chris Evert, Muhammed Ali and Jean-Claude Killy (and also other personalities such as Michael Parkinson and even the Pope!). His organisation has also developed new sporting events like tennis tournaments and 'made-for-TV' events such as the World Triathlon Championships. A few of the larger governing bodies of sport are beginning to employ agencies themselves, since successful sponsorship cannot be administered by enthusiastic amateurs. Sports compete with one another to gain public support, and agencies can help to improve their profile and image, as well as finding suitable sponsors.

Benefits to Sport

The financial benefits to sport are obvious. An additional value is the increased publicity and promotion that may be achieved by the marketing resources of the sponsoring company. Gratton and Taylor

(1985, p. 64) saw sponsorship in terms of a 'circle of expanding demand for both product and sport': sponsorship enables sporting events to occur, television covers the event, interest is generated among the public, there is increased demand for the sport, increased events, more sponsorship and so on.

Costs to Sport

The negative side to sponsorship includes the following:

- *Loss of control over sporting events.* Sponsors may insist on control over sporting events in return for their investment. Changes might be needed to satisfy the commercial needs of the company and it becomes a controversial issue when rule changes are proposed to accommodate the sponsors. However, this does not seem to have been a serious problem to date in Britain.
- *High profile sponsorship.* Large commercial companies see most benefit in sponsoring high profile, major international athletes and sporting events, while smaller firms support local individuals and teams. Companies see little advantage in sponsoring the plethora of sportsmen and sportswomen and sporting events falling between the two. Nevertheless, the maintenance of a strong sporting base depends on this middle section.
- *Conflict of interest.* Conflict of interest can occur in relation to individual sports. Sponsorship deals for individual competitors, often arranged through agents, will involve no income for the governing body of the sport, even though it may have organised the event in which the athlete competes. This means that the governing body will find it difficult to invest in its junior programmes and other levels of competition which do not attract sponsorship.
- *Lack of continuity.* Companies rarely stay with one event or sport for long periods because it is felt that, after two or three years, they tend not to reach new consumers. Also, the costs of sponsorship are so high now that companies cannot afford to maintain a high level of investment for an insecure return.
- *Pressures to cheat.* Sport can suffer due to the pressures surrounding large sums of sponsorship money involved. It is very tempting for sportsmen and sportswomen to cheat, perhaps by taking drugs, when a performance could lead to financial security for life.

Table 10.4 Tobacco-sponsored sport on BBC TV

Sport	Year	Sponsor	Total exposure (Secs/hr)	Advertising value (30-second tobacco advert equivalents)
Bowls	1989	Embassy	186	6
Cricket	1991	Benson and Hedges	188	6
British Grand Prix	1991	Camel Marlboro	498	17
Rugby	1987	Silk Cut	484	16
Snooker	1989	Embassy	176	6

Source: Adapted from Health Education Authority, 1992, pp. 8–9.

Tobacco Sponsorship

In 1965 direct advertising of cigarettes was banned from British television and yet an indirect route on to television emerged through the sponsorship of sport. One of the great success stories of tobacco sponsorship has been the support of the World Professional Snooker Championships by Embassy. In 1984, 81 hours of television coverage was given to the championships with audiences of up to 10 million. The close-up camera work in snooker gave extensive exposure of the Embassy name and logo, with constant verbal repetition of the title 'Embassy World Snooker Championships'. The normal television commercial rate for this amount of advertising would have been about £68 million, while Embassy is believed to have spent less than £200 000.

The Health Education Authority (1992) claimed that the exposure of tobacco images on television had increased during the 1980s, despite voluntary agreements between the government and the tobacco trade. Table 10.4 gives examples of the amount of exposure possible for tobacco companies when they sponsor sport.

The debate about whether tobacco sponsorship of sport should be allowed has rumbled on for 30 years. The following reasons have been put forward against tobacco sponsorship:

- Smoking causes lung cancer, heart disease, chronic obstructive lung disease and risks to unborn babies. Sport is considered to be a healthy pursuit and therefore it is hypocritical for it to be funded by an industry which damages health.
- All tobacco advertisements are required by law to have health warnings, but television companies do not ensure that legible health warnings are shown during tobacco sponsored sports events.

- The law states that tobacco advertisements are not allowed to be glamorous, to be associated with success in business or to be connected with sport. The sponsorship of sport clearly contravenes all three.
- Tobacco-sponsored sport is seen on television by millions of young people who could be strongly influenced by the association between sport and smoking. This might negate health education and health promotional work conducted with young people.

However, counter arguments have also been put forward:

- Alcohol can lead to many health-related problems. Should the alcohol industry and other industries with health-threatening products be banned from sponsoring sports which are shown on television?
- There is little evidence to show that the sponsorship of sport by tobacco companies has caused people to start smoking.
- Sport would lose millions of pounds if tobacco companies were prevented from acting as sponsors.

Ironically, cigarette consumption increased after the television ban on tobacco advertising. This may have been unrelated to the television ban or it may have been caused by the wider publicity achieved through indirect advertising at sports events. In any case there have been many calls (for example, Health Education Authority, 1992; Madden and Grube, 1994) for a re-examination of tobacco advertising on television through sport.

HAS COMMERCIALISM CHANGED SPORT?

Cashmore posed the question of whether commercialism had corrupted sport or simply taken it in a new direction (Cashmore, 1990). It is sometimes suggested that commercial influences have forced undesirable changes on sport to accommodate commercial interests. However, Coakley (1994) believed that the basic structure of most sports had not changed as a result of commercialisation. Indeed, where changes have occurred, they could be said to have improved the attractiveness of a sport. The changes can be divided into four main types:

- *Changes which speed up action to prevent boredom.* A notable example is the introduction of the limited-over game to cricket. Realising that most people were not interested or able to watch long, midweek county matches, the cricket authorities introduced exciting one-day knockout and league competitions. This has enticed television viewers and sponsors, while generally increasing levels of public interest, because of the faster action and greater excitement generated in a cricket match which can be concluded in a day. As Goldlust (1987, p. 163) has commented, the changes have turned cricket into 'a twentieth century gladiatorial sport, rather than a leisurely nineteenth century rural pastime'.

- *Changes in scoring to create excitement.* Tennis now has tiebreaks to avoid overlong matches, golf has total stroke counts instead of matchplay so that star players are not eliminated early, and football has penalty shootouts to prevent further replays of drawn matches. For many years the rules of rugby union led to relatively unattractive, low scoring matches, and yet when rule changes occurred the game became faster, more open and higher scoring, and it now attracts millions of spectators worldwide. Was this brought about by commercial pressures or by imaginative administrators attempting to improve the game of rugby?
- *Creating equal competition and uncertain outcomes.* All sports have a system which brings together teams of approximately equal standing. The move towards super leagues with a relatively small number of top teams is an illustration of this. However, there is also a desire to retain occasional competition between teams of unequal standing, such as in knockout cup competitions, where there is great attraction because of the possibility of an upset, with the outsider beating the favourite.
- *Providing breaks in play to advertise products.* Sport has been disrupted very little in Britain, because the BBC does not have commercial breaks and commercial television companies have resisted pressure to interfere with play, delaying their advertisements until a natural break occurs, such as half time.

Thus, it does not seem as if commercialism has fundamentally altered sports and, where rule changes have been made, many sports have become more exciting and attractive. It remains to be seen whether large scale organisational changes, such as super leagues in rugby, brought about by commercial intervention, will have a damaging effect on sport. Despite the improvements outlined above, commercialisation has led to the ironic situation where increased professionalisation has fashioned robotic, individual performers and highly trained, efficient teams who are effective and therefore successful. In contrast, the public like to see creative, emotional, entertaining players who combine talent with the unusual. Because of this, characters like Andre Agassi and Paul Gascoigne are jewels in their sports because not only are they high level performers, but they provide immense entertainment as well.

Who Has Control of Sport?

It could be said that commercial sponsorship is necessary in a country where government public spending on sport is relatively small and where a non-commercial, public company (the BBC) plays a major role in televising sport. However, commercialisation has led to changes in the way sport is controlled. For most of the twentieth century, governing bodies of sport were run by voluntary, enthusiastic helpers, but as sport has gained greater funding, some governing bodies have employed paid administrators and this has no doubt given many advantages. However, the impact of commercialisation has also seen the growing influence of club owners, corporate sponsors, media personnel and professional management agencies. This has recently been evident in rugby where media organisations have influenced the nature of competitions, with rugby league developing a super league which is played in summer rather than winter.

> organizational decisions generally reflect the combined economic interests of many people having no direct personal connection with a sport or with the athletes involved. (Coakley, 1994, p. 311)

Increased involvement of commercial sponsorship means that British sport is more and more dictated by the commercial sector rather than by government or the people themselves. Business determines which sports flourish and which become minority activities – and this depends on their television potential. Nevertheless, people who invest in sport are not always simply interested in making money or they could have chosen other forms of business investment. In Britain, they are often personally involved with a club or team and willing to take the risk of financial loss.

A more critical view is offered by Simson and Jennings, since they saw Olympic sport 'as a marketing tool of the world's multi-national companies' (1992, p. ix), with secrecy about financial matters and officials 'who manipulate sport for their own ends' (p. x). With sport being auctioned to the highest bidders, they claimed 'sport to be hi-jacked and then raped by commercial interests' (p. 272). There is also concern that sportsmen and sportswomen are left out of the decision-making process and may suffer as a result of decisions made by those controlling sport. For example, competitors may be required to play too many matches and tournaments, which leads to injuries and staleness. However, players' organisations like the Professional Tennis Players' Association, have managed to exert influence to promote the players' points of view and, in general, commercialisation has brought significant benefits to competitors.

CONCLUSION

Throughout history sport has attracted spectators and, as such, has been a form of entertainment. It could be argued, therefore, that it is quite legitimate for sport to have commercial interests. Capitalism aims to exploit markets to the full, and sport in contemporary society clearly has a substantial market. Thus, in an age of abundant leisure, sport will be utilised for business purposes and, if the commercial world transforms sport in a negative way, the general public will lose interest and the market will be lost. It is, consequently, very much in the interests of business to ensure that it retains the principles of sport which appeal to the public.

REFERENCES

Barnett, S., *Games and Sets: The Changing Face of Sport on Television* (London: British Film Institute, 1990).

Berrett, T., Slack, T. and Whitson, D., 'Economics and the Pricing of Sport and Leisure', *Journal of Sport Management*, 7 (1993), pp. 199–215.

Cashmore, E., *Making Sense of Sport* (London: Routledge, 1990).

Central Council of Physical Recreation, *Committee of Enquiry into Sport Sponsorship: The Howell Report* (London: Central Council of Physical Recreation, 1983).

Coakley, J.J., *Sport in Society* (St Louis: Mosby, 1994).

Evans, A., James, T. and Tomes, A., 'Marketing in UK Sport Associations', *Service Industries Journal*, 16 (1996), pp. 207–22.

Finley, M.I. and Pleket, H.W., *The Olympic Games: The First Thousand Years* (London: Chatto and Windus, 1976).

Goldlust, J., *Playing for Keeps: Sport, Media and Society* (Melbourne: Longman Cheshire, 1987).

Gratton, C. and Taylor, P., 'The Economics of Sport Sponsorship', *National Westminster Bank Quarterly Review*, August (1985), pp. 53–68.

Gruneau, R., 'Commercialism and the Modern Olympics'. In A. Tomlinson and G. Whannel (eds), *Five-ring Circus* (London: Pluto Press, 1984), pp. 1–15.

Health Education Authority, *Tobacco and the BBC* (London: Health Education Authority, 1992).

Key Note Market Review, *Industry Trends and Forecasts: UK Sports Market*, (London: Key Note Market Review, 1994).

McPherson, B.D., Curtis, J.E. and Loy, J.W., *The Social Significance of Sport* (Champaign: Human Kinetics, 1989).

Madden, P.A. and Grube, J.W., 'The Frequency and Nature of Alcohol and Tobacco Advertising in Televised Sports, 1990 through 1992', *American Journal of Public Health*, 84 (1994), pp. 297–9.

Maguire, J., 'The Commercialization of English Elite Basketball 1972–1988: A Figurational Perspective', *International Review for the Sociology of Sport*, 23 (1988), pp. 305–23.

Mason, T., *Only a Game?* (Cambridge: Cambridge University Press, 1993).

Simson, V. and Jennings, A., *The Lords of the Rings* (London: Simon and Schuster, 1992).

Whannel, G., *Fields in Vision* (London: Routledge, 1992).

Wilson, N., *The Sports Business* (London: Piatkus, 1988).

FURTHER READING

Although American, further information can be found in Coakley and McPherson, Curtis and Loy (cited above).

Media issues are in Goldlust and Whannel (cited above).

Updating of sports business information is in *Industry Trends and Markets*, published by the Key Note Market Review, and *A Digest of Sports Statistics*, published by the Sports Council.

Author Index

AGARI, 126, 180
Alexander, S., 81–2
Allison, M.T., 75
Anderson, D.F., 100
Armstrong, G., 167
Armstrong, N., 20, 60
Ajzen, I., 32–3
Allen, L.R., 28
Anshel, M.H., 151–2
Atsalakis, M., 32

Bandura, A., 29
Barnett, M.S., 29
Barnett, S., 191, 194
Barrett, T.C., 28
Bayliss, T., 111, 113, 116
Beashel, P., 129
Berrett, T., 190
Biddle, S., 44
Birrell, S., 80, 109
Boothby, J., 31
Bourdieu, P., 91
Boyle, R.H., 12
Brandenburg, J., 34
Brindley, J.M., 171
Brodie, D.A., 25–6, 30–1, 51–3, 97, 100
Brohm, J.-M., 2
Brown, B.A., 73
Brown, R.I.F., 169
Buikhuisen, W., 178
Burford, B., 180
Burkhead, D.L., 29
Butcher, J., 37–8
Buti, A., 154–5
Butler, N., 44

Carrington, B., 76–7, 115, 121–2
Carroll, R., 109–10, 116
Cashmore, E., 109, 116, 119, 121, 123, 187, 202
Caspersen, C., 39, 45
Central Council of Physical Recreation, 195
Chappell, R., 103
Charlton, V., 39, 100, 104
Chatterjee, S., 68–9
Chisti, M., 125
Chu, D., 123
Clarke, A., 10

Clarke, J., 10
Coakley, J.J., 2, 77, 113, 118, 202, 204
Colley, A., 73
Collier, J., 148, 154
Corbin, C.J., 74
Council of Europe, 2, 13
Cox, B.D., 24, 52–3, 63, 65
Curry, T.J., 2, 149
Curtis, J.E., 30, 111–12, 123, 188, 194

Daley, D., 115
David, C., 110, 118, 125
Debusk, R.F., 46
de Coubertin, P., 12
Department of Education and Science, 84, 95, 124
Department of National Heritage, 18, 104
Department of the Environment, 176
Dobbs, B., 70
Dodds, P., 95
Dolan, J., 121
Donald, K., 148
Donnelly, P., 126
Driver, B.L., 32
Dubin Report, 139, 142
Duda, J.L., 39
Duffy, P., 101
Duncan, M.C., 80, 83
Dunning, E., 161–2, 164–8

Eccles, J.S., 35–6
Education, Science and Arts Committee, 18
Elias, N., 1, 162
Engel, A., 74
Evans, A., 183

Fennell, M.P., 73
Fentem, P., 39, 45
Figone, A.J., 149, 157
Figueroa, P., 124
Finley, M.I., 69, 183
Fleming, S., 114–15, 117
Foster, J., 72
Frankel, B.G., 73
French, K.E., 67
Fridman, S., 154–5
Fuller, J.R., 150, 152

Gallop, D., 121
Geen, R.G., 173
Giddens, A., 104
Glenn, S.D., 33
Godbey, G., 65
Goldbaum, G.M., 57
Goldlust, J., 4, 14, 183, 186, 191–2, 203
Goldman, R., 138, 149
Gratton, C., 21, 49–51, 196, 199
Griffey, D., 123
Grube, J.W., 202
Gruneau, R., 91, 184, 198

Hamblin, R. L., 173
Hanks, P., 3
Hargreaves, Jenny., 14, 70, 79–80, 83
Hargreaves, John., 93–4
Harold, R.D., 35–6
Harre, R., 163, 167
Harris, R., 167
Harter, S., 29
Hartmann, D., 120–1
Health Education Authority, 44, 46, 56, 201–2
Henderson, K.A., 78
Hendry, L.B., 38, 95
Hill, D., 111, 117
Hills, C., 40
Hilton, P., 179
Hobbs, R., 165, 167
Hoberman, J., 129–30, 153
Hollinshead, G., 110, 116
Holt, R., 93
Huizinga, J., 9
Hyde, R.T., 48–9

ILEA, 85
International Scientific Consensus Conference, 43

Jackson, E.L., 78
Jackson, G., 38, 101
James, T., 183
Jennings, A., 204
Jiobu, R.M., 2, 149
Johns, D.P., 37–8
Jones, S.G., 94

Kane, M.J., 82
Kass, R.A., 28
Kay, T., 38, 101
Kelly, J.R., 29
Kenyon, G., 11

Kerr, J.H., 169, 180
Key Note Market Review, 186
Killoran, A.J., 39, 45
Klatz, R., 138, 149
Klein, M.-L., 80
Koplan, J.P., 57
Korkia, P., 139

LaFountain, M.J., 150, 152
Lamb, K., 51–3, 97, 100
Lashley, H., 117
Laudato, M., 68–9
Leaman, O., 76–7, 115, 122
Lindner, K.J., 37–8
Lovell, T., 117, 119–20
Loy, J.W., 11, 30, 111–2, 123, 188, 194
Lumpkin, A., 80
Lycholat, A., 157

McCrone, K., 71
McIntosh, P., 39, 100, 104
McKay, J., 80
McPherson, B.D., 11, 30, 111–12, 123, 188, 194
Madden, P.A., 202
Maguire, J., 108, 119, 122, 162, 185
Marcus, B.H., 40
Marsh, P., 163, 167
Marshall, E., 156
Mason, T., 184
Matheson, J., 22, 31
Mees, A., 68
Metheny, E., 73
Miller, J.L.L., 173
Miller, R., 177
Montoye, H.J., 43, 48, 51
Mottram, D.R., 130
Murphy, P., 161–2, 164–8

National Curriculum Council, 75

Office of Population, Censuses and Surveys, 20–3, 61–2, 90, 96–7, 99
Oswald, D., 156
Ouseley, H., 107

Paffenbarger, R.S., 48–9
Pannick, D., 79
Parry, J., 109
Pate, R.R., 47
Perry, P.J., 134
Pitcher, B.L., 173
Pleket, H.W., 69, 183
Prochaska, J.O., 40

Author Index

Radford, P.F., 139–40, 143, 152, 156
Riddoch, C., 20
Riess, S.A., 92–3, 103
Rintala, J., 80
Roadburg, A., 168
Roberts, K., 25–6, 30–1, 51–3, 97, 100
Robins, D., 165, 167
Robinson, J.P., 65
Rosser, E., 163, 167
Rowe, D., 80
Russell, G.W., 163

Saunders, C., 95
Scraton, S., 75–6
Searle, C., 123–4
Senate Standing Committee Report, 138–9, 142
Shapiro, H., 153–4
Shilling, C., 102
Simson, V., 204
Singer, R.N., 3
Sir Norman Chester Centre for Football Research, 109, 180
Siscovick, D.S., 57
Slack, T., 190
Sleap, M., 18, 32, 101
Sloan, A.K., 178
Smelser, N.J., 174–5
Smith, D., 70
Smith, D.A., 134
Snyder, E.E., 104
Sports Council, 18–19, 39, 59–61, 80, 85–7, 124–5, 138–9, 142, 146, 150–1
Sports Council and Health Education Authority, 23–5, 30, 38, 46–7, 56, 63–4
Spreitzer, E., 104
Staudohar, P.D., 150, 157
Steptoe, A., 44
Stewart, M.J., 74

Stimson, G.V., 139
Stone, G.P., 100
Suits, B., 7

Taylor, I., 164
Taylor, J., 129
Taylor, J.C., 176, 179
Taylor, P., 177
Taylor, P., 196, 199
Thomas, J.R., 67
Tice, A., 21, 49–51
Tinsley, H.E.A., 28
Tomes, A., 183

Veblen, T., 90
Voy, R., 139, 145, 148, 153

Waddington, I., 164
Walsh, M., 109, 126
Wankel, L.M., 40, 56
Warburton, P., 18
Weinhold, L.L., 139
Weiss, M.R., 33
Wells, C.L., 66–7
Wertz, S.K., 3–4
Whannel, G., 173, 184, 192, 195
White, A., 77
Whitson, D., 190
Williams, A., 20
Williams, J., 161–2, 165–8
Williams, L.D., 80
Williams, M.H., 136
Williams, N., 1
Wilson, N., 185
Wing, A.L., 48–9
Women's Sports Foundation, 86
Wright, P., 29

Yesalis, C.E., 140, 157
Young, I., 80
Yoesting, D.R., 29

Zakus, D.H., 152–3

Subject Index

Acculteration, 126
Action Sport, 124
Advisory Group Against Racism and Intimidation (AGARI), 126
Aesthetics, 6
Afro-Carribean,
  pupils, 114–15
  women, 120
Agassi, Andre, 204
Ali, Muhammed, 199
Allied Dunbar National Fitness Survey, 23, 25, 30, 38, 46, 62–3
Amateur ethos, 184
Amateurs, 92
American College of Sports Medicine, 130
American Medical Association, 155
Ancient Greeks, 129
Appropriate sports, 73–4
Ashe, Arthur, 103
Asian
  pupils, 114–15
  women, 119, 125
Assimilation, 109, 114, 123

Barnes, John, 111, 117
Becker, Boris, 193,198
Best, Clyde, 109
Birmingham Pakistan Sports Forum, 125
Black professional footballers, 108–9
Blood doping, 131, 134, 145, 148
Bodybuilders, 139
Brighton Declaration of Women and Sport, 85–6
Bruno, Frank, 122
Burnout theory, 38

Capitalism, 11
Carbohydrate loading, 136
Carlos, John, 120
Casuals, 165
Character building, 1
Chelsea Head Hunters, 162,
Christie, Linford, 81–2, 111, 122
Civilising process, 162
Class polarisation, 94
Commercialisation of female body, 82–4
Commercialism and sport, 183–206

Commercial sponsorship, 183
Competence motivation model, 29
Competition, 6
Conflict perspective, 14
Conspicuous consumption, 90–1
Consumers, 10–11
Contact hypothesis, 123
Conteh, John, 122
Corporate image, 198
Council of Europe Anti-doping Convention, 140, 142
Crowd norms, 171
Crowd violence, 160–82
Culture, 10

Davies, Sharron, 82
de Coubertin, Pierre, 153
Developmental theories, 38
Deviance amplification, 173
Dimensions of health, 43–5
Discrimination, 109
  covert, 118
Doping control, 129, 134–5, 139–40, 142–7, 153–5
  evasion of, 143–4
  testing programme, 145–6
  testing strategies, 144–7
Doping in sport, 129–159
Dose-response relationship, 47
Drugs,
  alcohol, 131
  amphetamine, 137, 141
  anabolic steroids, 131, 133, 137, 139, 141–2, 144, 151–2, 155
  anaesthetics, 132, 135, 148
  analogues, 131, 138
  beta-blockers, 132, 135, 138, 142, 145, 148
  caffeine, 132, 137
  cannabinoids, 135
  cocaine, 132, 137
  corticosteroids, 132, 135
  creatine, 136
  diuretics, 131, 133, 138, 141–3, 145
  ephedrine, 132, 149, 156
  epoetin, 134
  erythropoietin, 134, 138, 147
  ethanol, 135
  growth retardants, 134, 141

Subject Index

human growth hormones, 131, 133, 138–9, 144–5
marijuana, 131
minerals, 136
narcotics, 131
narcotic analgesics, 132, 137
nutritional aids, 135–6, 148
protein, 136
stimulants, 131–2, 137, 139, 141, 145, 149, 156
sympathomimetic amines, 132
testosterone, 133–4, 137
vitamins, 136
water, 136
Drug abuse in sport, 129–59
education, 157
health risks, 156–7
manipulation techniques, 131, 135, 145
pressures to succeed, 149–50
sanctions, 151
urine samples, 143, 146
views of athletes, 150–2
Dubin Report, 139, 142–3

East Germany, 130, 153
Economic theory, 190
Edwards, Tracy, 82
Embassy, 201
Energy expenditure, 47
Equality in school PE and sport, 95
Equal opportunities, 124, 126
Ethnicity, 107, 110
Ethnic minorities, 110–26
European Convention on Spectator Violence, 176, 179
European Football Championships, 126, 163, 178, 186
Evert, Chris, 199
Exercise, 5
promotion of, 39
Explanations of sporting behaviour, 28–42
Expectancy value model, 35–6
Extra-curricular sport, 18

Federal Republic of Germany, 153
Female adolescent culture, 77
Female sports coaches, 79
Feminist approach, 14
Figurational perspective, 162, 165–7, 185
Football Association, 161
Football hooligans, social class of, 167
Football hooliganism, 160–82, 197
and attendance, 162–3
and mass media, 172–4
explanations of, 163–75: contagion, 170, 174; convergence, 170, 174; deprivation theory, 168; disparateness, 167–8; emergent norms, 170; figurational approach, 162, 165–7; hooliganism addicts, 169; insider's view, 165; mastery seeking, 169; negativism, 169; psychological model of crowd behaviour, 171; ritualistic game, 163–4; triggers of violence, 172, 174; value-oriented approach, 174–5; working class frustrations, 164–5
history of, 161–2
inter-war years, 161
meaning of, 160–1
measures to curb, 176–80: all-seater stadia, 177; all-ticket matches, 177; alternative activities, 179; banning of alcohol, 177; better behaviour, 179; closed-circuit television, 178; club and community links, 179; deterrents, 178; family sections, 177; police strategies, 178–9; segregation of fans, 176; simulations, 179
post-war years, 161–2
Football in the Community Campaign, 179
Football League, 188
Football Offences Act, 125
Functionalist perspective, 13

Gascoigne, Paul, 204
Gate receipts, 188
Gender stereotypes, 73, 76
General Household Survey, 20–2, 25, 31, 49, 61–2, 96–7
Giggs, Ryan, 193
Gillette, 198
Goal orientation, 7
Goal perspective theory, 39
Graham, Herol, 118
Grand Prix cars, 187
Gulli danda, 125
Gunnell, Sally, 81–2

Hanley, Ellery, 119
Harvard University, 48–9
Health
absence from work, 50
coronary risk, 52–3

Health *continued*
  health-related fitness assessment, 51–2
  health scores, 53
  perceived health, 53
  psycho-social, 44
  rating of, 50
  socio-psychological components of, 44
Health and sport, 43–58
Health and Lifestyle Survey, 24–5, 49, 52–3, 63–4
Health benefits, 43–5, 47
Health Education Authority, 43, 46, 56
Hegemonic masculinity, 180
Heysel tragedy, 162, 176
Hillsborough tragedy, 177
Howell, Denis, 195
Honeygan, Lloyd, 141

Images of femininity, 75–8
Interactional model, 33–4
International Olympic Committee, 131, 138, 142, 147–8, 153
Italian Medical Sports Federation, 140

Jensen, Knud, 130
Johnson, Ben, 140–1, 153
Joyner, Florence Griffith, 120

Kabbadi, 125
Kick Racism out of Football Campaign, 126, 180
Killy, Jean-Claude, 199
Krabbe, Katrinna, 153

Laban, Rudolf, 72
Leisure constraints, 38, 101
Lenglen, Suzanne, 71
Liverpool study, 25–6, 31, 51–5
Lottery Fund, 79, 189
Luton Town Football Club, 177

McCormack, Mark, 199
Manchester United, 189
Memorandum of Understanding, 143
Mexico Olympic Games, 120
Middle class and sport, 92
Minority group socialisation, 111
Modahl, Diane, 154
Morphological differences, 66
Multidimensional approaches, 32–7
Muslim girls, 108

National Clarion Cycling Club, 94
National Curriculum for PE, 75, 84, 124

National Front, 117, 162
National Intelligence Network, 178
National Junior Sports Programme, 39
National Membership Scheme, 177

Obogu, Victor, 119
Olympic Games, 1, 183–4, 186, 189, 191–2, 196, 198, 204
Olympic Project for Human Rights, 120
Organisational positions, 117

Pakistani cricketers, 123
Participation Demonstration Project, 124–5
Perceived ability theories, 37
Performance-enhancing drugs, 130–50, 155–6
Performance potential, 65–8
Pheidippides, 56
Photographic images, 83
Physical activity, 5
  levels of, 45–7
  recommendations for, 45
Physical prowess, 4
Physical recreation, 5
Physiological differences, 67
Play, 4, 8, 10
Podd, Ces, 109
Popular sports, 21, 25
Power situations in sport, 78–9, 117–18
Premier League Survey, 109, 180
Producers, 10–11
Professional Tennis Players' Association, 205
Professionals, 92, 192–4
Psychological approaches, 28
Puma, 198

Race,
  and gender, 119–20
  and physical ability, 118–19
  and protest, 120–1
  and social mobility, 122
  and sport, 107–28
  meaning of, 107
Race and sport in schools, 113–16
Racial,
  abuse, 109, 116–17
  discrimination, 110, 116–18, 125
  equality, 125
  integration, 108
  issues, 109–28
Recreational activity adoption process, 34–5

Subject Index

Recreational drugs, 130–1, 141, 150
Religious traditions, 114–16
Rickard, George 'Tex', 187
Role conflict, 75
Rough working class, 166–8

Sabatini, Gabriela, 82
Sanderson, Tessa, 120
Satellite television, 191–2
Scientific racism, 112
Senate Standing Committee Report, 138–9, 142
Seoul Olympics, 139–40, 145
Sex Discrimination Act, 79
Sex typing, 72–3
Shamateurism, 184
Simpson, Tommie, 130
Smith, Tommie, 120
Snickers, 196
Social class,
  and sport, 90–106
  and sports participation, 96–100
  differences, 100
  meaning of, 90
Social:
  deprivation, 110
  expectations, 73–4
  integration, 122–4
Social mobility through sport, 102–4
Socio-demographic variables, 30–2
Sport,
  and commercialism, 183–206:
    advertising, 186–7; attendance, 188; business income, 188; business potential, 186, 192; commercial value, 189–90; control of sport, 204–5; economic significance, 186–9; entertainment, 186–7, 194; merchandising, 189, 196; product endorsement, 193; public relations, 199; television rights, 188; work practices, 194–5
  and crowd violence, 160–82
  and doping, 129–59
  and drug abuse, 129–59
  and football hooliganism, 160–82
  and health, 43–58
  and race, 107–28
  and social class, 90–106
  and television, 190–2
  and women, 59–89
  as a form of work, 9
  careers, 53

changes to, 202–4
characteristics of, 4
definitions of, 2
equal opportunities in, 124, 126
harmful effects of, 56–7
injuries in, 55
levels of, 12,
marketing of, 40, 191, 198
meaning of, 1
nature of, 12
organisation of, 2
participation patterns in, 16–27
pressures to succeed in, 149–50
promoting of, 39
socialisation into, 29–30
sociological study of, 13
structure of, 7
unpredictability of, 7
values of, 11
withdrawal from, 37
women and, 59–89
Sport for all, 13, 17
Sporting,
  goods, 187
  improvement, 69
  misconceptions, 111
Sporting behaviour,
  explanations of, 28–42
Sporting opportunities for women, 84–7
Sports associations, 187
Sports centre usage, 97, 100
Sport sponsorship, 194–202
  benefits to sport, 199
  cost to sport, 200
  publicity, 197
  reasons for, 197–9
  sponsorship agencies, 199
  tobacco sponsorship, 195–6, 201–2
  types of, 196–7
Sports Council, 18–19, 39, 59–61, 80, 85–87, 124–5, 138–9, 142, 146, 150–1
  Into the 90s, 124
  The Next Ten Years, 39, 124
Sports Council Doping Control Unit, 144–7, 150, 157
Sports industry, 185
Sports participation, 16–27
  of girls, 59–60
  of women, 61–65
Stacking, 119
Stages of change, 40
Stereotyping, 111, 125
Stones, Dwight, 184

Subcultural influences, 38
Superstars, 184

Television and sport, 190–2
Theory of planned behaviour, 32
Therapeutic drugs, 130
Transtheoretical model, 40

Underground Steroid Handbook, 139
Upper class sport, 90–2

Veblen, Thorsten, 90–1

Wariso, Soloman, 149
Wembley, 190
Willis, Bob, 123
Wimbledon, 190, 192, 198
Women's sport, 59–89
    contextual influences on, 78
    cycling and, 70
    historical influences on, 68–72
    media influences on, 80, 83
    newspaper coverage of, 81
    religious and cultural influences on, 78
    soccer and, 85
    television coverage of, 81–2
Women's Sports Foundation, 86
Working class sport, 92–4
World Athletic Championships, 81–2, 198
World Professional Snooker Championships, 201
World Triathlon Championships, 199

Young people, 18–19